the Story of the World
HISTORY FOR THE CLASSICAL CHILD

Volume 1: Ancient Times
From the Earliest Nomad to the Last Roman Emperor

Curriculum Guide and Activity Book

Edited by **Susan Wise Bauer**

Turn The Story of the World into a multi-level history program!
Comprehension questions, sample narrations,
recommended readings, maps, coloring pages and activities to accompany
The Story of the World: History for the Classical Child, by Susan Wise Bauer.

With activities and drawings by:
Joyce Crandell, Sheila Graves, Terri Johnson, Lisa Logue, Karla Middleton,
Tiffany Moore, Matthew & Katie Moore, Kimberly Shaw, Sharon Wilson

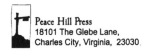
Peace Hill Press
18101 The Glebe Lane,
Charles City, Virginia, 23030.

Printed in the U.S.A.

ISBN: 0-9714129-5-2

LCCN: 2002108474

Table of Contents

How to Use *Activity Book One*.......................3
Pronunciation Guide for Reading Aloud.................6

Introduction..8
Chapter 1: *The Earliest People*.....................10
Chapter 2: *Egyptians Lived on the Nile River*...........13
Chapter 3: *The First Writing*.......................16
Review Cards, Introduction-Chapter 3.............SP 11

Chapter 4: *The Old Kingdom of Egypt*...................19
Chapter 5: *The First Sumerian Dictator*...............23
Chapter 6: *The Jewish People*.......................25
Chapter 7: *Hammurabi and the Babylonians*...............27
Review Cards, Chapters 4-7........................SP 24

Chapter 8: *The Assyrians*...........................29
Chapter 9: *The First Cities of India*...............31
Chapter 10: *The Far East: Ancient China*...............33
Chapter 11: *Ancient Africa*.........................36
Review Cards, Chapters 8-11......................SP 33

Chapter 12: *The Middle Kingdom of Egypt*...........42
Chapter 13: *The New Kingdom of Egypt*...............45
Chapter 14: *The Israelites Leave Egypt*..................48
Chapter 15: *The Phoenicians*.......................52
Review Cards, Chapters 12-15......................SP 45

Chapter 16: *The Return of Assyria*...................55
Chapter 17: *Babylon Takes Over Again!*...............57
Chapter 18: *Life in Early Crete*....................59
Chapter 19: *The Early Greeks*......................63
Review Cards, Chapters 16-19......................SP 55

Chapter 20: *Greece Gets Civilized Again*...................67
Chapter 21: *The Medes and the Persians*.................73
Chapter 22: *Sparta and Athens*......................76
Chapter 23: *The Greek Gods*........................81
Review Cards, Chapters 21-23......................SP 72

Chapter 24: *The Wars of the Greeks*....................84
Chapter 25: *Alexander the Great*......................88
Chapter 26: *The People of the Americas*................92
Chapter 27: *The Rise of Rome*......................96
Review Cards, Chapters 24-27......................SP 86

Chapter 28: *The Roman Empire*......................100
Chapter 29: *Rome's War with Carthage*.................104
Chapter 30: *The Aryans of India*...................108
Chapter 31: *The Mauryan Empire of India*...........111
Review Cards, Chapters 28-31......................SP 97

Chapter 32: *China: Writing and the Qin*..............113

Chapter 33: *Confucius*...............................117
Chapter 34: *The Rise of Julius Caesar*.................119
Chapter 35: *Caesar the Hero*.......................122
Review Cards, Chapters 32-35.................SP 107

Chapter 36: *The First Roman Prince*.................126
Chapter 37: *The Beginning of Christianity*...........128
Chapter 38: *The End of the Ancient Jewish Nation*...132
Chapter 39: *Rome and the Christians*...................135
Review Cards, Chapters 36-39......................SP 117

Chapter 40: *Rome Begins to Weaken*...................139
Chapter 41: *The Attacking Barbarians*...............143
Chapter 42: *The End of Rome*......................145
Review Cards, *Chapters 40-42*......................SP 123
Contributors.......................................148

SP=Student Pages, located at the back of the book

How to Use
The Story of the World:
Activity Book One

History is the most absorbing and enthralling story you can tell a young child, because it's true. A good history narrative is as strange and wondrous as a good fairy tale. Kings, queens, mummies, wooden horses, knights and castles can be as fascinating as giants and elves – but they *really existed!*

In classical education, history lies at the center of the curriculum. The chronological study of history allows even small children to learn about the past in an orderly way; after all, the "best way to tell a story," as the King tells Alice in *Alice in Wonderland,* "is to begin at the beginning and go on to the end." When the study of literature is linked to history, children have an opportunity to hear the stories of each country as they learn more about that country's past and its people. History teaches comprehension; young students learn to listen carefully, to pick out and remember the central facts in each story. History even becomes the training ground for beginning writers. When you ask an elementary-aged student to "narrate," to tell back to you the information he's just heard in his own words, you are giving him invaluable practice in the first and most difficult step of writing: putting an idea into words.

How do you study history classically? Find a central text, or "spine," that tells the story of history chronologically. This activity guide is designed to go along Volume 1 of Susan Wise Bauer's *The Story of the World: History for the Classical Child.* Think of each section in *The Story of the World* as a "springboard" into the study of world history. This book provides you with a simple, chronological overview of the progression of history. It isn't intended to be complete, but when you do history with elementary-grade students, you're not aiming for a "complete" grasp of what happened in ancient times. Instead, you want to give the child an enthusiasm for history, a basic understanding of major cultures, and an idea of the chronological order of historical events.

Using this guide at home

For each section in *The Story of the World*, follow this pattern:

1) Read the child one section from *The Story of the World.* Longer chapters are divided into several sections, each section appropriate for one session of history. Good readers can read the section to you instead.

2) For each section, ask the child the Review Questions provided. Answers given are approximate; accept any reasonable answer. You can also make up your own questions. Always allow the child to look back over the text when answering questions, especially if proper names are part of the answer. This is training in reading comprehension (and it will help you evaluate whether the child is listening with attention, or whether he's really understanding what he's reading).

3) Have the child tell you in two to five sentences what the history lesson was about. You can prompt the child with the Review Questions. Encourage the child to include the major facts from the history reading, but not EVERY fact. We have supplied sample narrations simply to give some idea of acceptable answers, not to imply that your child's narration should match word for word!

4) Write down the child's narration if the child is not writing independently. Good writers can be asked to write the narration down themselves. To help with this process, listen carefully to the child's narration and repeat it back to her while she writes; this will help with "writer's block." For any given section, you can instead ask the child to draw a picture of her favorite part of the history lesson and then describe the picture to you. Write the description at the bottom of the picture. Put the narration or

picture in a History Notebook – a looseleaf notebook that will serve as the child's record of her history study.

5) When you have finished all the sections of a chapter, stop and do additional reading and activities on the topic covered by that chapter. This Activity Guide provides titles of books that you can find at your library for additional reading, along with maps, coloring pages, crafts, and hands-on activities. Some topics (ancient Egypt or Greece, for example) have many more resources available to elementary-grade children than others (ancient Akkadia).

When you reach a topic that has a wealth of interesting books and activities connected to it, stop and enjoy yourself and don't feel undue pressure to move on ("We've got to get through Akkadia by Christmas!"). Check your local library for titles before buying. The recommended titles range in difficulty from first grade read-alones to advanced fourth grade. When appropriate, ask the child to draw pictures or narrate about the additional reading as well. Put these pictures and narrations in the History Notebook, which should begin to resemble the child's own one-volume World History. Don't ask the child to narrate every book, or she'll grow frustrated; use this as occasional reinforcement for a topic she finds particularly interesting.

We have provided cross-reference numbers to the appropriate pages in *The Kingfisher Illustrated History of the World, The Kingfisher History Encyclopedia, The Usborne Book of World History*, and *The Usborne Internet-Linked Encyclopedia of World History*. Use these books for additional supplemental reading, especially for those topics (Hammurabi, Assyria, the Phoenicians) that don't have extensive lists of age-appropriate library books to go with them.

6) Choose appropriate titles from the recommended literature lists and read these with your child. Most elementary students should also be doing a phonics and/or a phonics-based spelling program; this reading should supplement those programs. Classical philosophy discourages the use of "reading textbooks" which contain little snippets of a number of different works. These textbooks tend to turn reading into a chore, an assignment that has to be finished rather than a wonderful way to learn more about the world. Instead of following a "reading program," consider using the "real books" from these literature lists. **(RA = read aloud, IR = independent read, for children reading on a 1-2 grade level)**

7) Optional: You can administer written tests (available separately from Peace Hill Press) if you desire a more formal evaluation or wish to develop your child's test-taking ability.

Multilevel teaching

The Story of the World is intended for children in grades 1-4. However, the maps and many of the activities in this book are also appropriate for children in grades 5-8. Each chapter of the activity guide also contains cross-reference page numbers for the *Kingfisher History Encyclopedia* and the earlier edition of this work, *The Kingfisher Illustrated History of the World*. Both are good middle-grade world history reference works. To use *The Story of the World* as the center of a multi-level history program, have your older child read *The Story of the World* independently, follow this with the appropriate pages from the *Kingfisher History Encyclopedia*, place all important dates on a timeline, and do additional reading on his or her own level. For book lists and more detailed directions on classical education methods for both elementary and middle-grade students, see *The Well-Trained Mind: A Guide to Classical Education at Home,* by Jessie Wise and Susan Wise Bauer (W. W. Norton, 1999), available from Peace Hill Press (www.peacehillpress.com) or anywhere books are sold.

For parents

Families differ in their attitudes towards teaching myth, in their willingness to view partially-clothed people in ancient art, and in their sensitivity towards the (inevitable) violence of ancient times. We suggest that you skim through the activities in this Guide, glance through the literature that we recommend, and skip anything which might be inappropriate for your own family. In addition, both the *Kingfisher History Encyclopedia* and the *Usborne Internet-Linked Encyclopedia of World History* contain a number of pages on prehistoric peoples which may not agree with your family's convictions about humankind's beginnings. If this might pose a problem for you, preview these books before purchasing.

Using this book in the classroom

Although this Activity Guide was initially designed to be used by home-schooling families, it adapts well to the classroom. Here is a sample of how a chapter may be taught:

1) The teacher reads aloud a chapter section while the students follow along in their own books. When you reach the end of a section, ask the review questions provided in this book to selected students. Depending upon the length of a chapter, you may read the entire chapter in one day or break it up over two days. The children should write their summaries (narration exercises) in their history notebooks and then share them aloud.

2) Using the review questions and chapter tests* as a guide, type up a list of facts that the students should memorize, perhaps employing a fill-in-the-blank format. Give one to each student to help them prepare for the upcoming test.

3) Have the students do the maps and coloring pages in the Student Pages. To purchase a license to photocopy the reproducible pages for student use, contact Peace Hill Press.

4) You may want to do occasional chapter projects. Classroom and Co-op-friendly projects are marked by this symbol: C

5) Each day there should be an oral or written review. You can make it fun by playing oral quizzing games such as "Around the World" or "Last One Standing."

6) On the last day before the test, have the students color their chapter review card.

7) Test the students.

8) You will want to periodically review the past review cards so that the students remember ancient history chronologically.

*If you would like to adminster formal tests, you may purchase them separately from Peace Hill Press.

Pronunciation Guide for Reading Aloud

Abraham - AY bruh ham
Acropolis - uh KROP uh lihs
Aegeus - EE joos - EE juice
Ahmose - AH mohs - AH mose
Akkad - AK ad - AH kahd
Akkadia - uh KAY dee uh
Amen-em-het - ahh men EM tot
Amenhotep - ahh men HO tep
Amun - AH muhn
Amytis - AH mee tis
Anansi - ah Nahn see
Anu - AY noo - AH noo
Aphrodite - af ro DYE tee
Appian - AP ee uhn
Aqueducts - AK wuh duhktz
Archaeology - ahr kee AHL uh jee
Ariadne - air ee AD nee
Aryan - AYR ee un
Ashurbanipal - ah shoor BAH nee pahl
Asoka - uh SO kuh
Assur - AH sir
Assyria - uh SIHR ee uh
Astyges - As TI gees
Athens - ATH ihnz - ATH uhnz
Attila - AT uh luh - uh TIHL uh
Augustus - aw GUHS tuhs - uh GUHS tuhs

Babylon - BAB uh Luhn - BAB ih luhn
Barbarian - bar BEAR ee un
Bethlehem - BETH luh hem - BETH leh hehm
Bhagiratha - Bag ear RATH uh
Boadicea - boh ad ih SEE uh
Brahmin - BRA mihn
Bucephalas - bew SEF a lus - bew SEF uh lus
Bucephela - bew SEF a lah - bew SEF uh luh
Byzantine - BIZ un teen - BIZ uhn teen

Canaan - KAY nuhn
Canopic - kuh NOE pik - ka NO pick
Carnarvon - kar NAR vun
Carthage - KAHR thihj - CAR thij
Cassius - KASH ih uhs
Caste - kast
Caesar - SEE zuhr - SEE zur - SEE zer
Celts - kelts
Centaur - sen TAUR
Ceres - SIHR eez - SIR eez
Cheops - also known as Khufu - KOO foo
Chin - jhin - gin
Cincinnatus -sihn suh NAH tuhs
Citadel - SIT uh dul

Civilization - sihv uh luh ZAY shun
Claudius - KLAW dee oos
Cleopatra - klee oh PAT ruh - klee oh PAY truh
Confucius - kun FOO shus
Constantine - KAHN stuhn teen - KAHN stuhn tyn
Constantinople - kahn stan tuh NOH pul
Crete - kreet
Croesus - KREE suhs
Cuneiform - kyoo NEE uh fawrm - kyoo NEE uh form
Cyclops - SY klahps - sigh KLOE pees
Cyrus - SY ruhs - SAI ruhs

Delta - DEL tuh
Democracy - dih MOK ruh see - dih MOCK ruh see
Dido - DIE doe
Diocletian - dy uh KLEE shuhn - di uh KLEE shun
Dorians - DAWR ee uhnz

Enkidu - EN kee doo - IN kid oo
Eris - EAR ihs
Etruscans - ih TRUHS kuhnz
Euphrates - yoo FRAY teez

Fasces - FAS eez - fas EZ
Frieze - freeze

Gallic - GAL lik - GAL ick
Ganga - GUNG guh - GUNG ga
Ganges - GAN jeez
Gaul - GAWL
Gilgamesh - GIHL guh mesh - GIL gah mesh
Giza - GEE zuh
Gladiator - GLAD ee ay tuhr
Gordian - GOR dee un - GOR dee uhn

Hades - HAY deez
Halberd - HAL bird
Hammurabi - hah mu RAH bee - hah moo RAH bee -
HAM uh rah bee
Hannibal - HAN uh bull
Haran - HAY ruhn
Harpagus - Har PAEG us
Hatshepsut - hat SHEP soot - hot SHEP sut
Hera - hir uh - HAIR uh
Hieroglyphics - hy uhr uh GLIHF ihks - hi roy GLIF ix
Hindus - HIHN doo
Homer - HOE mur
Honoria - Hon OR ee a
Horus - HOR us
Huang Di - hwang dee
Hyksos - HIHK sahs - HICK soes

Indus - IN duhs - IN duss - INN duss
Iliad - ILL ee ad - ILL ee ud
Ishtar - CESH tar
Isis - EYE sis

Jakata - Jah KAH tah
Janus - JAN us
Jericho - JEHR uh koh - DZHEHR ih ko - JER ih koh
Julius - JOOL yus
Juno - JOO no

Kish - kihsh
Knossos - NAHS uhs - k NOH sos - NOSS suhs

Labyrinth - LAB er rinth
Empress Lei Zu - Leh Zoo
Lyre - lie er

Macedonia - mas ih DAHN nee uh - mas eh DO nih uh
Mauryan - MOW ree uhn - MORE yuhn
Maximian - mack sim ee un
Mahayana Tripitaka - mah huh YAH nuh tri PIH tah kah
Marathon - MAIR uh thahn
Marduk - MAR dook
Mari - Mahr REE
Mastaba - MAS tuh buh
Media - MEE dee uh
Menelaus - men ah LAY us - men uh LAY uhs
Mesopotamia - mehs uh puh TAY mee uh
Milvian - MILL vee an
Min Lai - mihn lie - mihn lye
Minoans - min OH ans - mih NO uhns
Minos - MY nuhs
Minotaur - MIN oh tor - MIN uh tor
Miriam - MIHR ih uhm
Mohenjo-Daro - moe hen joe DAHR oh
Momyllus - MOM ill us
Monarchy - MAWN are key
Mongols - MAWNG gul - MAHN gul
Monotheism - MAH no THEE ih zum
Moses - MOW zis
Mycenae - my SEE nee
Mycenaeans - my suh NEE uhns

King Narmer - NAR mur
Nazareth - NAZ ur uth - NAZ uh rehth
Nazca - NAHZ kuh
Nebuchadnezzar - nehb uh kahd NEHZ uhr
OR NAB oo kuhd nez uhr
Nero - NEER oh
Nineveh - NIHN uh vuh - NIHN eh veh
Noman - NO man - KNOW mun
Nubia - NOO bee uh
Numitor - NOO mi tor

Octavian - ahk TAY vee uhn
Odysseus - oh DIS ee uh - oh DIS ee uhs
Olmec - OHL mek - OHL meck
Orestes - ohr ES teez - o RES tez
Osiris - oh SI ris - oh SIGH ris

Palestine - PAL uh styn
Papyrus - puh PY ruhs - puh PY rus
Paris (prince of Troy) - PAR is - PAR uhs
Parthenon - PAHR thun nahn
Patricians - puh TRISH unz
Peloponnesian - peh luh puh NEE shuhn
Pharaoh - FIAR oh - FAY roh - FAY row -
FEHR o
Pharos - FAH ros
Philistines - fih LIHS tihnz
Phoenician - fih NIHSN uhn - fih NEE shun -
Plato - PLAY toh
Polytheism - PAH lee THEE ih zum
Pompey - PAHM pee - PAHM pay
Poseidon - puh SY duhn - poh SIGH don - po
SIGH dun
Potiphar - POT uh fur
Ptolemy - TAHL uh mee - TALL uh mee
Pumice - PUM ihs
Punic - PYOO nihk
Purusha - POOH ruh shuh

Qin - CHIN - CHIHN
Qin Zheng - Chin Zeng

Ra - rah
Remus - REE muhs
Romulus - RAHM yoo luhs
Rubicon - ROO buh kahn

Sakka - SAH kah
Salamis - sah lah MEES - SAH lah miss
Sarai - SAY raw - sah RYE
Sarcophagus - sar KOF a gus
Sargon - SAHR gahn - SAHR gone
Scepter - SEHP ter
Scipio - SIHP ee oh
Secutor - Seh CUTE or
Seleucid - suh LOO sihd - sih LOO sid
Seleucus - sih LOU kus - suh LOO kus
Senecca - SEN e kah - SEN eh kah
Set - Set
Shamshi-Adad -
Shang - SHAHNG
Shi Huangdi - shihr hwahng dee
Shiva - SHE vuh
Siddhartha - sih DAHR tuh - sih DAHR thuh
Sphinx - sfihngks
Stilicho - STILL ih koe - STILL ih ko
Suddhodana - SUD dough dah nah

7

Oasis - oh AY sis

Suetonius - swee TOE nee us
Sumer - SOO muhr - SOO mur
Syria - SEER ee uh

T'ang - tahng
Terah - TEE ruh
Thebes - theebz
Thera - THEER uh - THEAR uh - THER uh
Theseus - THEE see uhs
Thutmose - TUT mohs is - thoot MO suh
Tiber - TY buhr
Tigris - TY grihs - TIE gris
Queen Tiye - Queen Tie yee
Toga - TOE guh
Tutankhaten - TOOT an kam un - toot ahng KAH muhn
Tyre - tire

Ur - her - oor
Uruk - OO rook
Utnapishtim - cot nah PEESH teen

Vandal - VAN dul - VAN dle
Veda - VAH duh
Visigoths - VIZ ih gawths

Xi'an - shee ahn

Yangtze - yahng dzuh - yang zuh

Zeus - zoos
Ziggurat - ZIHG oo rat - ZIG uh rat

INTRODUCTION

Usborne Book of World History (UBWH), 2-3
Usborne Internet-Linked Encyclopedia of World History (UILE), 104-105
Kingfisher Illustrated History of the World (KIHW), 1-8
Kingfisher History Encyclopedia (KHE), viii-ix

Review Questions, What is History?

What do we call someone who reads letters, journals and monuments to find out about the past? *A historian.*

What do we call the story that historians write about the past? *History.*

Narration Exercise, What is History?

Ask the child to tell you in his own words about two ways that historians learn about the past. Acceptable narrations might include, "Historians read letters and look at monuments," or "People wrote letters and kings told people to write down stories. Historians can read them."

Review Questions, What is Archaeology?

What do *archaeologists* do? *Dig objects out of the ground and learn about them.*
What kinds of things did people leave behind them, in the story we read? *Dishes, tools, toys.*
Narration Exercise, What is Archaeology?
Ask the child to tell you in his own words about the kinds of things that archaeologists dig out of the ground. An acceptable narration might be, "Archaeologists dig things like dishes and toys out of the ground." You can prompt the child to add, "They find out about the past from these things."

Additional History Reading

Me and My Family Tree, by Joan Sweeney, illus. Annette Cable (Dragonfly, 2000). A picture-
     intensive book that explains a family tree in very simple terms. (RA [read-aloud])
Archaeologists Dig for Clues, by Kate Duke (HarperCollins, 1997). Explains archaeological
     work using a cartoon format. (RA)
The Magic School Bus Shows and Tells: A Book About Archaeology, by Jackie Posner
     (Scholastic, 1997). The Magic School Bus goes on a dig; also available in video. (RA)
I Can Be an Archaeologist, by Robert Pickering (Children's Press, 1987). Explains
     archaeology with simple text and real pictures. **Out of print; check your library.** (RA)
Writing Down the Days: 365 Creative Journaling Ideas for Young People, by Lorraine M.
     Dahlstrom (Free Spirit Publishing, 2000). For children who enjoy writing. (RA)

Projects

Writing/Craft Project: Make a *History of My Family* book: $\boxed{\text{C}}$
Materials List:
     History of My Family cover and Family History page (see Student Pages 1-2)
     Crayons, pencils and pens
     Photographs of family members
     Double stick tape or glue, hole punch, brass plated fasteners, tape recorder (optional)
1. Color the cover page for your *History of My Family* book and write your name where it says "taken by."
2. Make a copy of the Family History page for each member of your family.
3. Interview family members to answer the questions on each person's History page. Use a tape recorder if one is available. Paste or tape their picture on the page.
4. Punch holes and fasten book together with brass fasteners.

Writing/ Craft Project: Make a *This is My Life* Timeline
Materials List:
     Timeline (Student Page 3)
     Photographs
     Doule stick tape or glue

Use the timeline sheet to record the important dates in your history. Each number on the timeline represents a year in your life so this timeline will last until your tenth birthday. You can leave the timeline in one piece or cut it on the dotted line and cover it with contact paper for durability.

1. Start at zero and write in your birthday and paste your first picture close to the date. You can draw a line or glue a piece of string from the date to your picture.
2. Add as many dates and pictures as you can. You can even draw pictures and glue souvenirs like theater tickets on your timeline.

Some ideas for things to include on your timeline are when you got your first tooth, when you first sat up, crawled, or ate with a spoon, your birthdays, and when your brothers and sisters were born.

Activity: A Dirty Dig! (a simulation of an archaeological dig)
Materials:

> Items from your household that represent our civilization
> Place to bury the above items
> Small shovel or garden trowel
> Small brushes
> Bucket and containers
> Screen or sieve for sifting dirt
> Plastic bags, string, paper, pencil

Directions:

1. Assemble items to bury. Try to find things that would answer these kinds of questions: What did these people eat? What kind of transportation did they have? What kind of houses did they live in? What did they do for entertainment? Did they read and write? Think of some questions of your own.
2. Make a list of the things then bury them in a sandbox or some dirt. If you can, spray the site with water and let it sit for a few days.
3. You will pretend you are an archaeologist digging up the ruins of an ancient civilization.

   a. Use the string to mark off sections of the dig area (make a "grid" with the string across the surface of the ground). For elementary students, you should probably use only two strings to divide the ground into quarters:

   $$+$$

   Older children can use three or more pieces of string to divide the "dig" area into six or nine spaces.
   b. Excavate one section at a time using the small shovel. Work carefully so the artifacts don't get damaged.
   c. Use the small brushes to gently brush dirt from the artifacts.
   d. Sift the dirt you remove from the hole so the smaller artifacts aren't missed.
   e. As you remove the artifacts write down what you found and what square of the "grid" you found it in. Use plastic bags and containers to hold the artifacts.
   g. Tell what you learned about this ancient civilization.

CHAPTER ONE
The Earliest People

UBWH 4-7, *UILE* 108-109
KIHW 18-19, *KHE* 8

Review Questions, The First Nomads

What sort of food did nomads eat? *Plants such as grasses, leaves, grain, roots, berries; large animals such as elk, deer, reindeer, bison; other foods such as eggs, honey, lizards, snakes, and fish.* See if your child can remember one type of food from each of the three categories. Prompt her by asking, *"What kinds of growing things did they eat? What kinds of large animals did they hunt? What other kinds of food could they find?*

Where did nomads sleep? *In caves or tents*

Why did nomads move from place to place? *Because they hunted all the game and ate all the plants in one place, and had to move to another to find food*

What does "nomad" mean? *One who wanders or roams around*

Narration Exercise, The First Nomads

"Nomads moved around a lot. They lived in tents. They gathered grasses and berries and hunted animals for food. " OR

"Some people in olden times didn't have homes. They slept outside. They ate food that they picked and hunted, and they went from place to place."

Review Questions, The First Nomads Become Farmers

Why was the Fertile Crescent a good place to live? *Because there was water, good soil, and plenty of grass and plants*

Why was it called "fertile"? *Because lots of plants grew there*

What was it shaped like? *A crescent OR The new moon*

What did the first farmers grow? *Wheat and barley*

Did farmers move from place to place like nomads? *No.* Why? *Because they had to stay in one place long enough to tend their crops, water them, and harvest them*

How did farmers water their crops? *They dug canals from the river and built shadufs.*

Did the farmers still hunt wild animals? *They kept their own tame animals.*

What did the farmers build their houses out of? *Mud bricks and reeds*

How did they protect their villages? *They built stone walls around them.*

Narration Exercise, The First Nomads Become Farmers

" Some nomads settled down and grew crops. They watered the crops and built houses. They built walls around the houses. They lived in the Fertile Crescent" OR

"Some people in olden times didn't have homes. They slept outside. They ate food that they picked and hunted, and they went from place to place. Farmers grew wheat and barley. They dug canals to water their plants. They lived in villages."

Additional History Reading

It's Disgusting and We Ate It! True Food Facts from Around the World and Throughout History, by James Solheim, illus. Eric Brace (Simon & Schuster, 1998). Includes the foods that prehistoric peoples ate. (Possible IR [independent read])

Prehistoric World: Usborne World History (E.D.C. Publications, 2000). Assumes evolution of humans as fact. (RA)

How People First Lived, by William Jaspersohn, illus. Anthony Accardo (Franklin Watts, 1985). A basic account of nomadic life. (RA)

Corresponding Literature Suggestions

Mik's Mammoth, by Roy Gerrard (Sunburst, 1992). Left behind when the other cave dwellers move on, a small caveman rescues a mammoth. (RA)

One Small Blue Bead, by Byrd Baylor (Atheneum, 1992). A boy makes it possible for an old man in their primitive tribe to go in search of other men in far-off places. (RA)

The First Dog, by Jan Brett (Harcourt Brace, 1998). A cave boy makes friends with a wolf who saves him from danger. (RA)

Tonka, the Cave Boy, by Ross Hutchins (Rand McNally, 1973). The adventures of a boy living 8,000 years ago in an Alabama cave. (RA) **Out of print (check your local library).**

Map Work (Student Page 4)

1. On the black line map provided, locate and circle the first towns of Jericho and Catal Huyuk.
2. Trace the Tigris and Euphrates Rivers in blue; color the seas blue.
3. Use a green crayon or pencil to color in the area between the two rivers. This is Mesopotamia.

Coloring Page (Student Page 5)

Projects

Art Project: Make a Cave Painting

Materials:

> Brown paper grocery bag or other paper
> Acrylic paints in black, beige and reddish-brown
> Thick paintbrush

Directions:

1. Cut the paper bag open so that you have a large surface area to paint on. Next, crumple the paper, and then smooth it flat. This is to add irregularities to the painting surface to simulate painting on a cave wall.
2. To simulate the charcoal used by prehistoric man to draw pictures, use the black paint and draw a simple outline of an animal. Draw the animal's most obvious feature (e.g. tusks or antlers) in an exaggerated way. You can also add several stick figures carrying spears to depict a hunt.
3. After the animal outlines have dried, use the beige paint to fill in the design. Next use the reddish-brown paint to add highlights. This color resembles the red-ochre used by early man.
4. Let the entire piece dry completely, then hang it up to admire.

Craft Project: Make a Prehistoric Hunter's "Game Bag"

Materials:

> 18" x 22" animal print material
> 1 yard of thin rope or drawstring cord

Directions:

1. Fold right sides together so the piece measures 18" x 11". Sew a 5/8" seam along the bottom and side edges. Be sure to leave the top of the bag open for turning.
2. Turn the bag right side out. Fold down a 2" hem towards the inside of the bag and top stitch 1" down from the folded edge. This will make the casing for the drawstring.
3. Next, with a sharp pair of scissors snip a small opening on one side of the casing. Make sure that you only cut through the top layer.
4. Finally, use a bodkin or a safety pin to thread the rope or cord around the bag and out the same opening. Tie the ends together and push the fabric down the cord to gather the material and close the bag.

Activity Project: Build Your Own Hut

> After reading the chapter, go out in your backyard and try to construct a shelter from whatever materials are available in the yard. The hut can be for your favorite stuffed animal or if you are more adventuresome for yourself. Use sticks or branches to make the support structures then cover them using leaves, grass, fabric (an animal print would be nice) or an old blanket.

> If you built a hut large enough for yourself, why not spend the night in it with another family member? When you're done, make a "What We Did" narration page that talks about what you think it

was like for prehistoric man to live outside. What materials did he use to make his home? What did he have to worry about when he made it (i.e., weather, wild animals, other hostile people)? Was it an easy way to live? Be sure to include a drawing or picture of the hut you made, so that it can be added to your history notebook.

CHAPTER TWO
Egyptians Lived on the Nile River

UBWH 14-15, *UILE* 114-115
KIHW 26-27, *KHE* 10-11

Review Questions, Two Kingdoms Become One
Where is the Nile River? *In Africa*
What country did the Nile run through? *Egypt. You may have to explain the difference between a continent — a huge land mass — and a country — a certain group of people who live on the land mass.*
What did the Nile do every year? *It flooded.*
Why was this important? *Because it watered the land and brought silt up onto the riverbanks*
What were the two tribes who lived in Egypt called? *Upper Egyptians and Lower Egyptians*
Who ruled them? *The King with the Red Crown and the King with the White Crown*
Were they friends? *No, they fought constantly.*
Who won the battle between the White Crown and Red Crown Kings? *The White Crown King*
What kind of crown did the new king wear? *The Double Crown*

Narration Exercise, Two Kingdoms Become One
"The Nile is in Africa. Farmers liked for it to flood because it watered their land. The Egyptians fought each other until one king conquered the other and ruled the whole country. He wore both crowns."
OR
"The Upper Egyptians lived along the straight part of the Nile. The Lower Egyptians lived up in the delta. The Nile flooded every year. They grew crops in the soil."

Review Questions, Gods of Ancient Egypt
Did the Egyptians worship one god or many gods? *Many gods*
Can you name any of them? *Ra, Horus, Isis, Osiris, the pharaoh*
Do you remember the name of Osiris' evil brother? *Set*
How did Set get Osiris to lie down in the coffin? *He said that he would give it to whoever fitted it best.*
Did Osiris stay dead? *No, he came back to life again.*

Narration Exercise, Gods of Ancient Egypt
"The Egyptians believed in many different gods. Osiris was the king of the gods. His brother tried to kill him, but he came back to life." OR
"Set wanted to kill his brother. He got him to lie down in a coffin and then threw it into the river. But Osiris didn't stay dead. That's why the Nile fills up every year."

Additional History Reading
Journey Through History: Prehistory through Egypt, Gloria Verges, illus. Maria Rius (Barrons, 1998).
    Short and interesting (although unconnected) facts about ancient life. (RA)
The Nile River, by Alan Fowler (Children's Press, 1999). Pictures and descriptions of the
    land along the Nile. (RA)
Egyptian Gods and Goddesses, by Henry Barker (Grossett & Dunlap, 1999). Describes each

Egyptian god briefly, along with pictures. (RA)

The Ancient Egyptians (History Starts Here), by Jane Shuter (Steck Vaughn, 2000). Good
colorful illustrations of ancient Egyptian life. (RA)

Corresponding Literature Suggestions

Bill and Pete Go Down the Nile, by Tomie dePaola (Paperstar, 1996). Bill and Pete (a little
crocodile and his toothbrush) go on a class trip to the museum where they attempt to save the
Sacred Eye of Isis. Will they succeed? You'll have to read to find out! (Possible IR)

Croco'nile, by Roy Gerrard (Penguin Books, 1999). A young boy and his sister journey down
the Nile River where they find a baby crocodile. (Possible IR)

Cry of the Benu Bird, by C. Shana Gregor (Houghton Mifflin, 1996). An ancient Egyptian
story of creation. (Possible IR)

Egyptian Myths, by Jacqueline Morley (Peter Bedrick Books, 1999). Legends include tales of
creation, life after death, good and evil and the search for knowledge. (RA)

Map Work (Student Page 6)

1. On the map provided, locate the Nile River, and trace its course with a blue pencil or crayon.

2. Draw a blue triangle around the Nile delta, where the river breaks into several smaller rivers and empties into the Mediterranean Sea.

3. Draw a red crown in the area of Lower Egypt. Then, draw a white crown in the area of Upper Egypt. Remember, the Lower Egyptians lived in the area of the Nile delta, and the Upper Egyptians lived along the straight part of the river.

4. When King Narmer conquered the Red Crown King, he wore the red crown over his own white crown. He made Egypt into one country. To show this on your map, shade in the area of Egypt on your map, in one colour.

NOTE: The following map is reprinted from Terri Johnson's "Blackline Maps of Ancient History" set, with her kind permission. For a full set of blackline maps, coordinated to *The Story of the World*, visit Knowledge Quest Maps at http://www.knowledgequestmaps.com, or contact Knowledge Quest at 7722 SE 282nd Avenue, Gresham, OR 97080 (503/663-1210). You can also buy these maps from Peace Hill Press at http://www.peacehillpress.com.

Coloring Page (Student Page 7)

Using your coloured pencils, crayons or markers, colour the picture of Osiris in the coffin he won from Set. Everyone wouldn't look so happy, if they knew Set was going to throw Osiris into the Nile River!

Projects

Craft Project: Make a Model of the Nile
Materials:
  grass seed, potting soil, rocks and pebbles
  large waterproof pan (such as a disposable aluminium roasting pan), about 3" deep.
  tin foil
  water
Directions:
1. Fill the container 2/3 full with soil.

2. Push the soil away from the area of the Nile River to make the riverbed. Look at your map to see what shape the Nile should be. It should run through the centre of the container, just as the Nile River runs through the centre of ancient Egypt. Don't forget to make a triangle or Y shape at one end, where the delta will be located.

3. Using a double layer of aluminium foil, line the riverbed. Ensure the foil is long enough to reach over the top of the container at each end, otherwise your river might drain into the surrounding soil. To make the Y shape for the delta, just cut the foil into the same shape and mould into the riverbed you created in step 2.

4. Spread some pebbles into the river to weigh down the foil.

5. Sprinkle grass seed along the banks of the Nile.

6. Place some larger rocks along the right side of the container, to imitate the mountains in ancient Egypt.

7. Fill the river with water, letting it flood over the banks to water the seeds. This is the first method used for watering the crops.

8. Each week, water your model by flooding the Nile. Watch the grass flourish!

9. For added realism, make clay replicas of the pyramids and place them on your model of ancient Egypt, and float some grass boats (gather fresh or dry grass, and tie off each end, spread out grass in the centre to make a boat shape) in your river, just like the ancient Egyptians would have floated their reed boats.

Craft Project: Make the White Crown of Upper Egypt
Materials:
>   tape
>   paper (one sheet of 8 ½" x 11")
>   waxed paper (or a large sheet of white paper)

Directions:

1. Wrap the waxed paper around your head to make a cone shape. Tape the edges to hold the shape, then cut off any excess paper.

2. Scrunch the 8 ½" x 11" sheet of paper into an egg shape.

3. Push the ball of paper into the peak of the cone, and gently mould the waxed paper around it. This should result in a cone with a flattened top and an indent at the bottom of the egg-shaped top.

4. Cut the bottom edge of the cone so it fits nicely onto your head. Then, cut out the area around the ear.

5. Wear the White Crown on its own to be King of the Upper Egyptians.

Craft Project: Make the Shepherd's Crook of the Pharaohs
Materials:
>   masking tape (wider is better)
>   newspaper
>   paint and brushes
>   wrapping paper tube (or several paper towel or toilet paper tubes taped together)

Directions:

1. Twist the newspaper into a cylindrical shape, and bend to form a hook or C shape, leaving a straight tail at one end to insert into the tube. The hook should be about 5-6 inches from top to bottom, at most.

2. Insert the tail into the tube. Using masking tape, cover the hook, attaching it firmly to the tube. The entire hook should be covered with masking tape, to make painting possible (alternately, use your favourite paste and cover the hook with paper mache. Be sure it dries entirely before painting, if you do this).

3. Paint the tube to decorate as you think a pharaoh would see fit. Let it dry completely.

4. Wear your double crown, and carry your crook as the pharaohs did years ago. If you want to be even more like the ancient pharaohs, tie a swatch of yarn to one end of another tube, decorate, and you'll have your own switch, too.

CHAPTER THREE
The First Writing

UBWH 10-122, 15, UILE 110-111
KIHOW 28-29, KHE 9-10

Review Question, The First Writing

What two types of writing did we talk about? *Cuneiform and hieroglyphics*

What two countries wrote in cuneiform and hieroglyphics? *Egypt and Sumer*

What three things did the Egyptians and Sumerians write on? *Stone, clay, and paper (or papyrus)*

Which is easiest to write on? *Paper*

Which ones lasted the longest? *Stone and clay*

Which one fell apart? *Paper*

What does "Mesopotamia" mean? *Between the river.*

Do you remember what "hippopotamus" means? *River-horse!*

Narration Exercise, The First Writing

Have the child tell you in three to five sentences what the history lesson was about. You can prompt the child with the questions listed above. The child's narration should include something about both cuneiform and hieroglyphics; you should prompt him for these names. Acceptable narrations might include: "The Egyptians wrote on stone. These were called hieroglyphics. The Sumerians wrote on clay. These were called cuneiform." OR

"Writing on stone was called hieroglyphics. Writing on clay was called cuneiform. This writing lasted a long time. Writing on paper didn't."

Additional History Reading

Hieroglyphs from A to Z, by Peter Der Manuelian (Scholastic, 1991). Illustrations of a number of different Egyptian hieroglyphics. (RA)

Footsteps in Time: The Egyptians, by Ruth Thomson (Watts Books, 1995). An informative book with several fun activities which can be completed by the child, with minimal assistance from an adult or older sibling. (RA)

Corresponding Literature Suggestions

Seeker of Knowledge : The Man Who Deciphered Egyptian Hieroglyphs, by James Rumford (Houghton Mifflin 2000). The story of the quest to understand Egyptian writing. (RA)

The Everyday Life of An Egyptian Craftsman, by Giovanni Caselli (Macdonald & Co., 1986). Information about various crafters from ancient Egypt, told by a school-aged Egyptian boy whose father has just been promoted to be a scribe. **Out of print (check your local library).** (RA)

Map Work (Student Page 8)

Locate Egypt (remember, Egyptians lived along the Nile River and around the Nile delta) and Sumer (outlined on your map). These are the two countries where people first learned to write. Use any color and shade in the areas where writing began.

Coloring Page (Student Page 9)

This Egyptian scribe is carving hieroglyphs into stone.

Projects

Craft Project: Make Cuneiform Tablets

Materials:

    clay
    cuneiform alphabet guide (Student Page 10)
    scrap of paper
    small wedge (a thick Phillips screwdriver would work well)
    drinking straw and heavy string (optional)

Directions:

1. On the scrap of paper, write the message you will be translating and carving into the clay tablet. You could write your name to make a door plaque or a simple message to a friend or relative. Use your mind and imagination to determine what you would like to carve.

2. Roll the clay so it is a flattened rectangle, about ½ - ¾ inch thick. Trim the edges to make them neat.

3. Using your wedge, and following the cuneiform alphabet guide, carve your message into the clay tablet. The further you dig the wedge into the clay, the wider the mark will be. This is how the triangle shapes in the cuneiform alphabet were made by Sumerians. To make a narrower mark, press the wedge in the clay with less pressure. Alternately, if you are using a screwdriver, press the edge into the clay, wiggle it a little bit from side-to-side to get the triangle shape, then drag it straight through the clay to get the straight line. You might want to practise this before beginning your message. Once you are comfortable making the marks, re-roll the clay and begin carving your message.

4. If you want to hang your tablet, use a straw to punch a hole in both top corners.

5. Let the clay tablet dry according to package directions. If you are using clay gathered from outside, you can let it dry in the sun, or bake in the oven at a low temperature until the tablet is hardened and completely dry.

6. If you punched holes into your tablet in order to hang it you will need to thread some heavy string through the holes, and hang.

Craft Project: Make a Hieroglyphic Scroll

Materials:

    firm bristled paint brush
    hieroglyphic letter guide (Student Page 10)
    ink OR paint OR purple berry juice
    ribbon (yarn or string would also work)
    tape, thumb tacks
    lightweight paper (several sheets – computer banner paper would also work well) OR for more
    historical realism, buy some sheets of papyrus paper from a craft/ art supply store
    2 wooden dowels or sticks (slightly longer than the paper)

1. On a piece of paper, plan the hieroglyphs you will use on your scroll. Remember to use the sounds in the words, not the actual letters (that means "Christopher" would be spelled "Kristofer"). You don't need to include silent letters (that means "night" would be spelled "nit"). If you really want to be authentic, check out the internet by doing a search for "Egyptian hieroglyphs."

2. Tape several sheets of paper together, side to side, to make one long strip (you can skip this step if you are using computer banner paper, since it is already one long piece).

3. Using a stiff brush (the Egyptians used reeds with one end crushed into a brush) and the ink, paint, or

berry juice, paint the hieroglyphs onto your scroll.

4. Let the ink dry completely, which shouldn't take very long.

5. Tack each end of the scroll onto a piece of dowel, or a stick.

6. Roll the scroll toward the centre, ensuring roughly half the paper ends up on each pole. The two dowels or sticks should meet in the center.

7. Tie the scroll with a ribbon.

Activity Project: Why Do Clay Tablets Last Longer than Paper?

Materials:

> Hieroglyphic scroll (use directions above; if you use paint or ink, make sure it is water soluble)
>
> clay tablet (use directions for "cuneiform tablet" above)

1. Place the clay tablet and the hieroglyphic scrolls outside. Leave them there for several days.

2. After a week, look at the tablet and the scroll. Are they the same as when you first put them outside? How are they different? Open the scroll and look at the print. Is it changed at all? Depending on the weather, they may have been rained or snowed on, they may have sat under the hot sun's rays, or in the misty fog. The weather will determine how they have changed. If it rained, snowed (which is wet like rain) or was foggy (also wet), the paper scroll is likely soggy. Maybe it is even torn. The print is likely hard to read as well. If it was sitting in the hot sun for many days, the scroll might not look very different. The clay tablet, though, will be the same as the day you set it outside to weather. Even if it is wet, the print will still be easy to read. You won't see any changes in it unless you had a big wind storm, earthquake, or other phenomena that would cause it to fall, and possibly break – even then, you could piece it back together to read it.

3. Next, we will simulate a flood (the Egyptians did live next to the Nile, remember). If you haven't already, roll up the scroll. Take it and the tablet inside. Fill the kitchen sink with water. Put the clay tablet in. Now, put the paper scroll in. Let them sit for 5 minutes (it was a really quick flood – if you leave it longer, the paper might fall apart!) How is the tablet? Wet, but doing OK, right? What about the scroll? Unroll it and look at the print. Can you still make it out? Good for you, if you can.

4. Now, roll up the scroll, if you haven't already. Have an adult put them in the oven for you, at a low temperature (not more than 200F). This part of the experiment is simulating the hot, dry condition of ancient Egypt and Mesopotamia. The paper scrolls and clay tablets of long ago spent many years in hot, dry weather. To speed up the process, we're using the oven (after all, we can't wait years for this experiment!).

5. In half an hour, peek into the oven. If the paper starts to char, turn the oven off immediately (the scroll can remain inside the hot oven, though). In another half an hour, have an adult remove the tablet and scroll from the oven. Does the tablet look any different? Can you still read it as easily as before? What about the scroll? Unroll the scroll and look at the print. Is it any different? Did the paper tear or break at all when it was opened? The hot, dry air in the oven caused any changes you might see. Hot air outside will do the same thing over long periods of time.

6. The clay tablet will be very hot, so let it cool for an hour.

7. While you are waiting for the tablet to cool, re-roll the scroll. Show it to someone (your family pet, baby sibling or parent is fine). Make sure you unroll it when you show it to them. Then roll it up again. Show it to someone else, making sure you unroll it, then roll it up again. Keep showing it to other people (if you run out of live people or animals to show it to, stuffed animals would like to see it, too), making sure you unroll it to show them the hieroglyphs, and re-rolling it after looking. Remember how many times you showed the scroll. After an hour of unrolling and rolling of the scroll, take a look at it. Has it changed in any way? The unrolling and rolling of the scroll simulated the use it might get if it were a real ancient Egyptian document. Did the paper tear or break from all this use?

7. The clay tablet should be cooled by now. If it isn't, use oven mitts to handle it. Now you will simulate the use it might get if it were a real Sumerian clay tablet in ancient Mesopotamia. Show it to the same number of family, friends and stuffed pals as you did with the scroll. (Lucky for you, this won't take as long, since there is no rolling and unrolling involved.) Has the clay tablet changed in any way after showing it so many times? Not at all. Your clay tablet sure is sturdy!

Results:

Likely by this point, your paper scroll isn't looking very healthy (How many pieces is it in?). The clay tablet, on the other hand, is looking pretty much the same way it did before we began this experiment. If you wanted to test if further, have an adult build a campfire, and put the clay tablet in the fire. Even after burning for a several hours, it would still be in good shape. It might be black and sooty, but that can easily be wiped off (at least enough to read the print). If you put the scroll in the fire, I think you know it would burn within minutes. While a real ancient scroll and tablet wouldn't be dunked in the water or baked in the oven, they would be exposed to the weather, including floods and the hot, dry air of the Middle East. The experiments you did simulated these elements of the weather, and reduced the waiting time (it might takes years for nature to do this much damage to a paper scroll). Now, you know why the ancient clay tablets lasted much longer than the ancient paper scrolls.

REVIEW CARDS (Student Page 11)

Every four chapters, you should take one history class to prepare your history review cards. Photocopy the history cards (use stiff cardstock for longer-lasting cards) and cut them out; have the student color the picture. After the cards are completed, use them once or twice a week to review material already covered.

CHAPTER FOUR
The Old Kingdom of Egypt

UBWH 18-21, *UILH* 116-117
KIHW 26, 45, *KHE* 10-11

Review Questions, Making Mummies

What does "embalming" do? *It preserves a body.*

What did priests do to a body to make a mummy? *They took the insides out, preserved the body with salt and spices, wrapped it in linen and put it into a coffin.*

Why did the Egyptians think it was important to preserve dead bodies? *So that dead people could go on to the next world*

What did the Egyptians bury with their mummies? *Everything a dead person would need: food, clothes, toys, games, jewelry, furniture*

What was this time in Egyptian history called? *The Old Kingdom*

Narration Exercise, Making Mummies

"The Egyptians thought that people couldn't go to heaven if they didn't have their bodies. So they made mummies out of the bodies. They did this during the Old Kingdom." OR

"The Old Kingdom was when the Egyptians made mummies out of dead bodies. They put all their insides into jars and put the mummies in special coffins."

Review Questions, Egyptian Pyramids
What kinds of tombs did pharaohs have? *Pyramids*
What were they made out of? *Stone. The child can also add that they were covered with white stone and capped with gold.*
What was Cheops's pyramid called? *The Great Pyramid*
How long did it take to build it? *Twenty years*
How did the Egyptians build the pyramids? *Thousands of workers built them by hand.*
What does the Great Sphinx look like? *It is half lion, half man.*
Did the Great Pyramid keep robbers out? *No, Cheops's mummy and treasures were still stolen.*

Narration Exercise, Egyptian Mummies
"Cheops built the Great Pyramid out of stone. It was supposed to keep him safe, but robbers stole his treasure anyway." OR
" The Egyptians built pyramids for their pharaohs. They thought pharaohs were gods."

Additional History Reading

Who Built the Pyramids?, by Jane Chisholm (EDC Publishing 1996). An Usborne guide to life in ancient Egypt, written for first through third grade. (RA for all but the most advanced readers)

Mummies Made in Egypt by Aliki (HarperCollins, 1979). A very simple guide to the mummy-making process. (RA)

Mummies: A Strange Science Book, by Sylvia Funston. (Owl Books, 2000). A book about mummies around the world; includes illustrations, photographs, a game and an activity to complete. (RA)

Look Inside: An Egyptian Tomb, by Brian Moses (Wayland Publishers, 1997). Everything a child might want to know about an Egyptian tomb, illustrated with photographs of real objects and paintings. (RA)

Cat Mummies, by Kelly Trumble (Clarion Books, 1996). Why were cats important to the ancient Egyptians? This illustrated guide explains. (RA)

Corresponding Literature Suggestions

I Am the Mummy Heb-Nefert, by Eve Bunting (Voyager, 2000). An Egyptian mummy looks back on her days as queen. (IR for many children, RA for beginners)

Easy to Read Mummy Riddles, by Katie Hill (Puffin Books, 1997). Nothing but mummy-humour in this book of kid's jokes. (IR for many children, RA for beginners)

Magic Tree House: Mummies in the Morning, by Mary Pope Osbourne (Random House Children's Publishing, 1993). Jack and Annie find themselves whisked away to ancient Egypt, where they come face to face with a dead queen—and her 1,000-year-old mummy! (RA)

Magic Tree House Research Guide #3: Mummies and Pyramids, by Mary Pope Osbourne and Will Osbourne (Random House Children's Publishing, 2001). Jack and Annie's very own guide to the secrets of ancient Egypt. Includes information on hieroglyphics, how mummies were made, tomb treasures and robbers, Egyptian gods and goddesses, and much more! (RA)

Map Work (Student Page 8)

Using the map from the last lesson, find Egypt. Cheop's pyramid was located on the left side of the Nile River, where the straight part of the river breaks into the smaller rivers of the delta. On your map, draw a golden pyramid where Cheop's Great Pyramid and Sphinx were located.

Coloring Page (Student Page 12)
The Sphinx

Projects

Activity Project: Make a Chicken Mummy

Materials:

  baking powder (3 cans)
  baking soda (3 boxes)
  chicken (small is good)
  freezer bags (large and lots)
  paper towels
  plastic gloves (chicken harbours nasty germs)
  rubbing alcohol (or any alcohol you may have – the Egyptians used wine)
  salt (several boxes)
  scented oil (recipe below – you can use unscented, if you prefer, and just rub the
      chicken with the spices when the oil is used)
  various spices (cinnamon, allspice, cloves, nutmeg, etc) - optional
  water, white glue
  white linen fabric (or other fabric you have on hand)

Directions:

1. Put on your gloves! Chicken (and other poultry) can harbour bacteria that can make you sick.

2. Remove the neck and package of liver, heart, gizzard, etc. You can mummify these, but they continue to smell, even after being dried. It's your choice. If you do mummify them, the heart is usually wrapped in linen, and stuffed back inside the body. The other parts are put in canopic jars. Dry them following the same method as for the chicken.

3. Wash the chicken well in hot running water. Pat dry with paper towels. Wash again with the alcohol and pat dry. Don't forget to wash inside the cavity of the chicken as well. This helps to reduce the amount of bacteria that will grow on the bird. Dry the bird as much as possible before continuing with step 4.

4. Mix ½ a box of baking soda with ½ can of baking powder and 2 boxes of salt. The addition of baking soda and powder will increase the acidity of the salt mixture, reducing the amount of bacteria that grows… the salt mixture will also be more similar to the natron salt that the ancient Egyptians used (which consisted of the three salts we are using, plus sodium sulfate). If you like, you can add spices to the mixture as well, to make it smell a bit nicer.

5. Pour some of this mixture into the cavity of the chicken until it is full. Then, pour some into a large freezer bag. Put the chicken in the bag, and add the rest of the salt mixture. The chicken should be completely covered. If it isn't, add more salt. Seal the bag. Put the sealed bag into a second freezer bag and seal.

6. Check the chicken every day for the first week. If the salt is wet, put on some gloves, remove the chicken from the bag, dust off the salt, and repeat step 4. You will likely need to do this after one day, then again two days later, and 2-4 days after that.

7. After the first week, check the chicken only once per week. If the salt is wet, put on some gloves, remove the chicken from the bag, dust off the salt, and repeat step 4. Likely you will need to do this at the end of the second and fourth weeks (usually every 5-10 days).

8. At the end of the sixth week, put on your gloves, remove the chicken from the bag, dust off the salt as completely as you can. Wet a paper towel and wipe any remaining salt off the bird. Be sure to dry it immediately afterwards with paper towels.

9. Rub the fragrance oil into the chicken, inside and out. If you are using unscented oil, you may rub spices into the chicken before rubbing in the oil.

10. Stuff the inside of the bird with fabric (or sawdust) and spices, if you like.

12. Now we begin the wrapping process. Tear the linen into 1" strips. Mix white glue and water (1-2 parts water to 1 part glue).

13. Dip the strips of linen into the glue, then begin wrapping. Wrap the wings and legs separately from the body. Once that is complete, wrap the body. It should be wrapped in at least 2-3 layers. If you like, wrap a few amulets into the mummy like the Egyptians did. Let it dry completely.

Scented Oil

Materials:
> jar with lid
> oil (any cooking or baby oil is suitable)
> spices (any that you like – a combination of 3 or 4 is good)

Directions:
1. Fill a jar to the top with spices.
2. Add oil to fill the jar.
3. Set it in a sunny location for a week. Shake the jar well 2-3 times per day.
4. Drain the oil. Repeat steps 1-4 for a stronger scent.
5. Use as a perfume as the Egyptians did, and in the mummy-making process.

Canopic Jars

Materials:
> 4 jars with screw top lids
> paints and brushes
> paper (any scraps will do)
> water
> white glue
> > Alternately: instead of paper, water, and glue, you could purchase ready-made paper mache mixture or "paper clay" (a premixed paper mache mix) at a local art or craft supply store.

Directions:
1. Clean the labels off the jars, using hot, soapy water. If they are set well, try soaking overnight.
2. Put the paper and water into a blender and puree. If you are using a premixed pulp, follow package directions. Once mixed, continue with step 4.
3. Remove, drain excess water, mix in glue by hand or with a spoon.
4. Mould pulp onto jar lids into the shapes of the head's of Horus's four sons: human (Imsety, who protected the liver), jackel (Duamutef, who looked after the stomach), baboon (Hapy, who cared for the lungs) and falcon (Qebhsemuf, who tended the intestines). Let your creations dry completely.
5. Paint details onto the heads and let the paint dry. Decorate the jars, if you wish, with hieroglyphics or pictures.
6. Fill your jars with anything you like and enjoy.

Craft Project: Sand-Cube Step Pyramid

Materials:

     cardboard

     plastic cling wrap

     sand

     white glue

(Alternatively, you could use 55 square sugar cubes OR 55 square lego blocks)

Directions:

1. Mix the sand with the glue, until it forms a thick, firm, moldable mixture. If you would rather, you can use sugar cubes or square legos instead of home-made sand cubes (more realistic, and bugs won't try to eat it). If you choose this route, you can jump to step 5.

2. Spread the sand-glue mixture onto the cling wrap. It should be flat, and about a ¾ inch thick. Let it set for 30-45 minutes – don't let it dry completely, or the next step will be more difficult.

3. Cut the slightly dried sand mixture into ¾ inch squares. A ruler could be used to do this, by pressing into the sand with the long, thin edge. You don't need to separate the blocks at this point. In total, you will need 55 cubes. Let the cubes dry another 24 hours.

4. Check to see if the cubes are dry. If they are, cut them apart again and continue with step 5. If they are not yet dry, re-cut the cubes, following the same cut marks from step 3, thereby ensuring they won't be completely glued together when you are ready to use them. Check the cubes again every 3-6 hours. Once they are dry, cut them apart and continue with step 5.

5. Now, you will need to count out 25 cubes for the base of the pyramid, 16 cubes for the second level, 9 cubes for the third level, four cubes for the next level, and one cube for the peak.

6. On the piece of cardboard, spread glue in the center, to form a square roughly 4 inches by 4 inches. Set the first 25 blocks on this square, in a grid of 5x5.

7. Spread glue on top of the base layer. Set 16 cubes in a 4x4 block square in the center of the bottom layer.

8. Spread glue on top of the second layer. Set 9 cubes in a 3x3 block square in the center of the second layer.

9. Spread glue on top of the third layer. Set 4 cubes in a 2x2 block square in the center of the third layer.

10. Spread glue on the final cube and place in the center of the fourth layer. Let the glue dry.

CHAPTER FIVE
The First Sumerian Dictator

UBWH 8-9, 30, *UILE* 113

KIHW 24-25, *KHE* 9

Review Questions, The First Sumerian Dictator

Do you remember what "Mesopotamia" means? *You may need to prompt the child for the answer: "Between the rivers."*

What two rivers is Mesopotamia between? *The Tigris and the Euphrates*

Were the cities in Sumer friends with each other? *No, they fought each other.*

What did Sargon do? *He conquered all the city-states and made them into one country.*

What was his country called? *Akkadia, or the Akkadian Empire*

How did he keep control of it? *He made harsh laws and put his soldiers in the conquered cities to make them obey.*

What do we call it when a ruler uses an army to make sure that people obey without questions? *A military dictatorship. It's fine to prompt the child for this answer – this is a new concept! We'll be returning to it again.*

Narration Exercise, The First Sumerian Dictator

If the child uses the words "military dictatorship" in the narration, make sure he understands what this means! It isn't necessary to use this phrase in the narration since this is only the first introduction to this concept.

"The cities in Sumer all fought with each other. Sargon conquered them all. He made one empire out of them."

OR "Sargon used soldiers to make people obey. The soldiers went to cities in Sumer. They made the cities follow Sargon."

Additional History Reading

Ancient Egyptians and Their Neighbors: An Activity Guide, by Marian Broida (Chicago Review Press, 1999). There are very few elementary-level books about Sargon and the Akkadian Empire, but this book has appropriate age-level readings and activities centered on the Akkadian people. (Also recommended for Chapters Seven and Eight.)

Corresponding Literature Suggestions

The Golden Sandal (A Middle Eastern Cinderella Story), by Rebecca Hickox (Holiday House, 1998). A retelling of the Cinderella story in a Mesopotamian context. (RA)

The Three Princes: A Tale From the Middle East, by Eric Kimmel, illus. Leonard Everett Fisher (Holiday House, 1994). A princess sets her three suitors a task to find out which is most worthy. (RA)

Arabian Nights: Three Tales, by Deborah Lattimore (HarperCollins, 2000). "Aladdin," "The Queen of the Serpents," and "Ubar, the Lost City of Brass" retold, with a full-page illustration for every page of text. (RA)

Map Work (Student Page 13)

1. On the black line map provided , locate the important city of Ur.
2. Locate and name the two important rivers that Sargon's people depended on.
3. Use a red crayon or pencil to color in the area that Sargon conquered and named Akkadia.

Coloring Page (Student Page 14)

Projects

Art Project: Make a Sumerian Seal

In the old days, very few people knew how to write their names. Instead, they made special seals that they pressed into wet clay. Each person's seal was different, so that people did not get confused.

Materials:

    Air-drying clay

    Rolling pin, sculpting tool or sharp pencil

    White glue and water

Directions:

1. Roll out a piece of air-drying clay to the desired size, and about ½" thick.

2. With the sculpting tool, carve a pattern into the clay. Be sure to make it deep enough so that it can make a nice impression in the wet clay. Leave it to dry.

3. Roll out another piece of clay that is a bit larger than the seal and about ½" thick. When this is done, gently press the dried seal into the wet clay leaving a clear impression.

4. To make your impression into a pendant, use a toothpick to make a hole at the top for the string. Let this piece dry completely. If you want to, you can paint your pendant after that.

5. To give the pendant a nice shine, paint it with a mixture of 2 parts white glue to 1 part water. Brush over the entire piece and let dry. After the pendant has dried, cut a piece of soft cord to the desired length and thread it through the hole in the pendant and tie a knot at the end.

6. You could also use a colored stamp pad with your seal to make cards or decorative stationary.

Word Search Puzzle: Sumerian Inventions (Student Page 15)

CHAPTER SIX
The Jewish People

UBWH N/A, *UILE* 142-143
KIHW 50-51, *KHE* 24-25

Review Questions, God Speaks to Abraham

In our story, why did Terah want to leave Ur? *He was afraid a war would start.*

What was Terah's son named? *Abram ["Abraham" is also acceptable]*

Terah and his family went to another city in Mesopotamia – Haran. Why did Abram decide to leave Haran and go to Canaan? *God told him to.*

What did God promise Abraham? *That he would have a son*

Do you remember the name of Abraham's wife? It means "princess." *Sarah*

In the story, how old was Sarah when she had her baby, Isaac? *One hundred years old!*

Narration Exercise, God Speaks to Abraham

Ask the child to summarize the history lesson in 2-4 sentences. You can prompt him with the questions above. The narration should include the information that Abraham went to Canaan because God told him to. The child can use the name "Abraham" throughout his narration. Acceptable narrations might include:

"Abraham lived in Ur with his father. God told him to go to Canaan. Then he had a baby when his wife was 100." OR

"Abraham and Sarah went to Canaan. God told them to obey him and they would have a baby. Abraham laughed because he was so old, but they had a baby."

Review Questions, Joseph Goes to Egypt

What did Jacob give Joseph to show that he loved him? *A coat of many colors*

What did Joseph's brothers think about this? *They were jealous; they didn't like it.*

What country did Joseph's brothers send him to? *Egypt*

Joseph was the son of Jacob, and Jacob was the son of Isaac. Who was Isaac's father? *Abraham*

What did the Pharaoh dream about? *Seven fat cows and seven skinny cows*

What did his dream mean? *Seven good years would come, then seven years of famine*

After Joseph told him the answers to his dream, what did Pharaoh do? *Made him second in command in Egypt*

At the end of the story, where did the Israelites live? *In Egypt*

Narration Exercise, Joseph Goes to Egypt

"Joseph's brothers sold him to Egypt. He was thrown in jail. Then Joseph told the Pharaoh what his dream meant. Pharaoh made him second in command. Joseph's brothers came to get food. Then Joseph told them to all come to Egypt." OR

"Joseph's father loved him best and gave him a colored coat. Joseph's brothers were jealous. They sold him as a slave. Joseph told Pharaoh there would be a famine. He helped Pharaoh get grain and keep it. Joseph's brothers were hungry too. Joseph gave them food and they came to live in Egypt."

Additional History Reading

Joseph and His Brothers, by Mary Auld (Franklin Watts, 1999). A simple paperback retelling of the beginning of the Joseph story. (IR for most readers, RA for beginners)

The Jewish Children's Bible: Genesis, by Sheryl Prenzlau (Pitspopany Press, 1996). Read the Story of Joseph from Genesis itself. (RA)

Dance, Sing, Remember: A Celebration of Jewish Holidays (HarperCollins Juvenile Books, 2000). A page or two of text explains the significance and traditions of each of 11 holidays included in the book – a crash course in basic Jewish history! Most include a story, song, activity or recipe. (RA)

Old Testament Days: An Activity Guide, by Nancy I. Sanders (Chicago Review Press, 1999). Basic information and easy activity about life in Old Testament times. (RA)

Corresponding Literature Suggestions

Angels, Prophets, Rabbis & Kings from the Stories of the Jewish People, by Jose Patterson (Peter Bedrick Books, 1991). Retells stories selected from many periods of Jewish history, with attractive illustrations. (RA)

Abraham's Great Discovery, by Bernard Zlotowitz (Nightingale Resources, 1991). A new rendition of the traditional patriarch Abraham smashing his father's idols and recognizing the one true god. (IR)

Map Work (Student Page 16)

1. Locate Babylon on the map. Circle the name in red, since the threat of war between Babylon and Ur was the reason Terah and his family left their home along the river.

2. Draw a line in blue from Ur up to Haran. This is the journey Terah and his family took.

3. Draw a line from Haran over to Canaan. Abraham left Haran and went to Canaan.

4. Once Abraham and Sarah were in Canaan, they had a child, Isaac. Isaac had a son named Jacob. Jacob had twelve sons. Joseph was Jacob's favorite son, and one of his youngest. He was sold as a slave by his older brothers and later became a governor of Egypt. Then all of his relatives moved from Canaan down to Egypt. Draw a green line from Canaan down to Egypt, to show the path that the Israelites took.

Projects

Art Project: Make Joseph's Coat

Materials:

      construction paper

      glue, fabric scraps (optional)

      large sheet of butcher's paper (or smaller sheets taped together)

      markers, crayons or colored pencils

Directions:

1. Have an adult or older sibling trace your body, wearing a robe, onto the large piece of butcher's paper.

2. Decorate the coat with fabric scraps or with coloured pencils, markers or crayons.
3. Draw a face for Joseph. Hang on the wall, or on a door.

Craft Project: Make Joseph's More Realistic Coat of Many Colors
Materials:
> button down shirt (If oversized, it will drape down the body more. Buy one
> inexpensively at a thrift store if needed.)
> paint (fabric paint that is painted on would be best, but tempera paint can be used – it
> will be more rigid, though)
> scissors

Directions:
1. Cut the collar off the shirt.
2. Paint the shirt in many colors. Let it dry completely.
3. Put it on, and pretend to be Joseph.
   > Alternatively, you could:
   > 1. Cut a large paper grocery bag into a vest, instead of using a shirt.
   > 2. Use fabric scraps instead of paint. Sew or glue them in place.

Activity Puzzle: The Jewish People Word Search (Student Pages 17-18)

Activity Project: Color Your Own Comic Book! (Student Pages 19-20) C

CHAPTER SEVEN
Hammurabi and the Babylonians

UBWH 9, 30-31, UILE 132-133
KIHW 47, KHE 21

Review Questions, Hammurabi and the Babylonians
Why did Hammurabi want to be king? *So that people would be treated fairly*
What city did Hammurabi rule? *Babylon*
What did Hammurabi write down on a stone monument? *Laws*
What were these laws called? *The Code of Hammurabi*
Who had to obey these laws? *Everyone in Babylonia*
Can you tell me about one of these laws? *Allow the child to summarize any of the laws in the chapter.*

Narration Exercise, Hammurabi and the Babylonians
Ask the child to summarize the history lesson in 2-4 sentences. You can prompt him with the questions above. The narration should include the information that Hammurabi was a king of Babylon who wrote laws. Appropriate narrations might be:
"Hammurabi lived in Babylon. He built an empire like Sargon. But he wanted to be fair." OR
"Babylon was a city in Mesopotamia. The king was Hammurabi. He made the Code of Hammurabi. These were laws for everyone to obey."

Additional History Reading

Ancient Egyptians and Their Neighbors: An Activity Guide, by Marian Broida (Chicago Review Press, 1999). There are no easy-to-locate books about Hammurabi written on an elementary level, but this book (also recommended for Chapters Five and Eight) contains age-appropriate information and activities centered on the early Babylonian civilization.

Corresponding Literature Suggestions

The Tale of Ali Baba and the Forty Thieves, by Eric Kimmel (Holiday House, 1996). A poor woodcutter discovers the hidden treasures of a band of robbers, survives great danger, and brings riches to his whole family. (RA)

Abu Ali: Three Tales of the Middle East, by Dorothy Van Woerkom (Crown, 1976). Three tales about Abu Ali, who counts his donkeys, fools his friends and finally fools himself. **Out of print (check your local library).** (IR)

Map Work (Student Page 21)

1. On the black line map provided, locate Hammurabi's city of Babylon and circle it in red.
2. Use a blue crayon or pencil to color in the area that Hammurabi conquered and named Babylonia. Babylonia combined the old kingdoms of Sumer, Akkadia and Babylon.

Coloring Page (Student Page 22)

Using your crayons, color the picture of the Ziggurat of Ur. This temple was originally built by the Sumerians as a place to worship their god Nanna – God of the Moon.

Projects

Art Project: Make Your Own Law Code Stele

A stele is a carved stone. Hammurabi had many of these markers carved to display his Law Code around his empire. This way his people would know what the laws were and would obey them. So, how about making one for yourself that shows the rules you follow at your house? You can even draw a picture at the top showing your mother, seated in a chair handing them to you – just like Hammurabi received them from the god of justice, Shamash. A children's book called *The Rules*, by Marty Kelley (Zino Press, 2000), might be fun to read before doing this project.

Materials:

> Large sheet of paper (10"x18")
> Scissors, saucer, ruler, colored pencils or crayons

Directions:

1. Using a saucer, or other round object, draw a curved line on the corners at the top of the paper. Use scissors to trim the pointed parts off.

2. Measure down 9" from the top of the page and draw a straight line across the page with your ruler. The top curved portion of the page will be where you draw your picture and the bottom portion will be where you write your rules. Drawing extra lines with your ruler on the bottom portion of the page will make it easier to keep your writing straight.

3. When you're finished, hang your stele in your room so that you don't forget the rules!

Craft Project: Make A Ziggurat Temple

Materials:

     4-5 different sized light cardboard boxes (e.g., cereal boxes)

     Glue, scissors

     Poster paints or spray paint

Directions:

1. Place the largest box on the bottom and glue the next largest box on top of it. Take your third and fourth boxes and continue to glue them down to make your ziggurat.

2. Once the glue has dried, take your ziggurat outside and paint it with a reddish-brown color to simulate the look of dried mud bricks. You can either use the poster or spray paint, whichever you prefer.

3. Take another cardboard box and cut out 2" strips that can be used for the steps. The steps should run from the ground to the top floor of the ziggurat.

4. If you don't have a lot of empty boxes sitting around the house, use your Lego or wooden building blocks instead. You can still use the strips of cardboard for your stairs on your project.

Activity Crossword Puzzle: Name That Place (Student Page 23)

(Answers: Akkadia, Ur, Jericho, Babylon, Tigris, Kish)

REVIEW CARDS
Chapters Four, Five, Six, Seven
(Student Page 24)

CHAPTER EIGHT
The Assyrians

UBWH 52-53, 56-57, UILE 146-149
KIHW 48-49, KHE 22-23

Review Questions, Shamshi-Adad, King of the Whole World

What Assyrian king did we read about? *Shamshi-Adad*

What city did he live in? *Assur*

What was the name of his empire? *The Assyrian Empire*

How did he build his empire? *Through conquering other cities, through cruelty, through fear*

How was the Assyrian king, Shamshi-Adad, different from the Babylonian king, Hammurabi? *Discuss the answer with the child: Shamshi-Adad was a* dictator *who ruled by fear and cruelty. Hammurabi ruled by a code of laws. Which kind of king is better?*

Narration Exercise, Shamshi-Adad, King of the Whole World

Ask the child to tell the history lesson back to you in 2-4 sentences. The narration should include the information that Assyria was a cruel empire, and that it was eventually conquered by the Babylonians. It isn't necessary to remember the name of Shamshi-Adad! Acceptable narrations might be:

"The king of Assyria was a dictator. He made people obey him. Assyria became part of Babylon." OR "Shamshi-Adad wanted to be king of the whole world. He conquered cities and was very cruel. Then Hammurabi took his kingdom."

Review Questions, The Story of Gilgamesh

Was Gilgamesh a good king, or a bad king? *He was a bad king (although he was very strong).*

When Gilgamesh's people asked Anu the sky-god for help, what did he send? *The monster Enkidu*

Enkidu was half man and half what? *Animal*

What did the trapper's son do when he met Enkidu? *Took him home, taught him how to talk, eat, wear clothes*

When Enkidu and Gilgamesh fought, who won? *Gilgamesh, but he was too tired to keep fighting!*

What did Enkidu do to make the gods angry? *He killed the bull of the gods.*

Why did Gilgamesh decide to go see Utnapishtim, the only immortal man on earth? *He wanted to find the secret of eternal life,* or *He wanted to beat death.*

What is the first thing Utnapishtim told Gilgamesh to do, so that he would live forever? *Stay awake for six days and seven nights* or *Stay awake for a very long time*

Did Gilgamesh stay awake? *No*

What did Utnapishtim tell Gilgamesh to do then? *Pick a magic plant from the bottom of the sea*

Who ate the magic plant after Gilgamesh picked it? *A snake*

Narration Exercise, The Story of Gilgamesh

This is a long and complex story for a young child to remember! Ask your child to tell you about Gilgamesh and Enkidu, or about Gilgamesh and Utnapishtim, but don't require her to do both. Remind her what the characters are named, since these names are strange and unfamiliar.

"Gilgamesh was a strong king, but he was very bad. The sky god sent a monster down to punish him. The monster was Enkidu. He learned how to talk. He almost beat Gilgamesh at a fight. They got to be friends. Enkidu got sick because he killed the bull of heaven." OR

"Gilgamesh was sad because his friend was dead. He went to see a man who had lived forever. The man (Utnapishtim) told him to stay awake for a week. He couldn't. So the man told him to pick a magic plant. He did, but a snake ate it, so he got old and died like everyone else."

Additional History Reading

Ancient Egyptians and Their Neighbors: An Activity Guide, by Marian Broida (Chicago Review Press, 1999). Early Assyria, like early Babylonia and Akkadia, isn't popular with the publishers of children's books, but this activity book (also recommended for Chapters Five and Seven) contains good basic information about the earliest Assyrian people.

Corresponding Literature Suggestions

Gilgamesh the King, by Ludmila Zeman (Tundra, 1993). The cruel tyrant, Gilgamesh, learns the true meaning of friendship from Enkidu. (RA)

The Revenge of Ishtar, by Ludmila Zeman (Tundra, 1993). When Gilgamesh and Enkidu slay monsters that threaten the city of Uruk, the goddess Ishtar becomes angry. (RA)

The Last Quest of Gilgamesh, by Ludmila Zeman (Tundra, 1993). Gilgamesh sets out on a quest to conquer death. (RA)

Map Work (Student Page 25)

1. On the black line map provided, locate Shamshi-Adad's city of Assur.
2. Use a red crayon or pencil to color in the area that Shamshi-Adad conquered and named Assyria.

Coloring Page (Student Page 26)

This picture is based on a carving sixteen feet high, found in Assyria at the entrance of a doorway.

Projects

Art Project: Draw A Picture of Enkidu 🄲

     Now that you have heard the story of the very first fairy tale, use your imagination and draw a picture of what you think Enkidu looked like. Remember, Enkidu was supposed to be half man and half animal, so don't forget to add some fur and claws!

Writing Project: Compose Your Own Fairy Tale 🄲

     Use your imagination and write a fairy tale of your very own. Your story could be another adventure for Gilgamesh and Enkidu to embark on. Or, you could start from scratch and make up completely new characters and adventures. When you have decided what your tale will be about, tell a parent and they will write it down for you. To make your fairy tale complete, draw a picture to go with it. When you are done, be sure to place your finished story in your notebook to keep it safe.

CHAPTER NINE
The First Cities of India

UBWH 28-29, UILE 118-119
KIHW 32-33, KHE 14-15

Review Questions, The River-Road

Why did ancient people use the river as a road? *Acceptable answers: It was easier than traveling on sand or rocks; it was faster than walking or using carts pulled by cows.*

Why did people in ancient Mesopotamia and India build cities near rivers? *Acceptable answers: There was plenty of water for drinking and for crops; it was easier to send food and other things down the water; the rivers were good roads for trade; the rivers were good for fishing.*

Narration Exercise, The River-Road

"People lived near rivers. They used the rivers to travel on. One of these rivers was the Indus River in India."

OR "People built cities in the Indus Valley. It is in India. They used the river to get around. Sailing on the river was easier than going over the mountains."

Review Questions, The Mystery of Mohenjo-Daro

What is a citadel? *A stronghold at the center of a city*

Tell me some of the things that the people of the Indus Valley built. *Citadels, drains, houses from mud bricks, toilets, public baths*

What happened to the citadel cities? *No one knows for sure, but they were deserted.*

What did the quail decide to do, so that they could escape the hunter? *Stay all together*

Did it work? *Yes!*

Did the quail keep on cooperating with each other? *No, they started to argue and scattered.*

What did the hunter do then? *Caught them for supper*

Narration Exercise, The Mystery of Mohenjo-Daro

Ask your child to tell you about Mohenjo-Daro OR to tell you the story of the hunter and the quail – not both! Acceptable narrations might include:

"People in the Indus Valley built big cities. They had wells, baths, and citadels. One of the cities was Mohenjo-Daro. Then all the cities disappeared, but we don't know why."

OR "The quail wanted to escape from a hunter and his net. They decided to stay together in one bunch. When the hunter threw his net on them, they all flew up together and got away. But then they started to fight with each other and the hunter caught them one at a time."

Additional History Reading

We Come From India, by David Cumming (Steck Vaughn, 2000). A guide to the people (and children) of present-day India. (RA)

Exploration into India, by Anita Ganeri (Chelsea House, 2000). Plenty of photographs of Indian cities, countryside, and the Indus river in this elementary survey of India. (RA)

Corresponding Literature Suggestions

One Grain of Rice, by Demi (Scholastic, 1997). A reward of one grain of rice doubles day by day into millions of grains of rice when a selfish raja is outwitted by a clever village girl. (RA)

The Little Brown Jay: A Tale from India, by Elizabeth Claire (Mondo, 1995). A story of generosity. (RA)

Once a Mouse, by Marcia Brown (Aladdin, 1989). As it changes from mouse, to cat, to dog, to tiger, the pet of an Indian hermit becomes increasingly vain. (IR for strong readers)

Map Work (Student Page 27)

1. On the black line map provided, locate the Indus River and trace its route with a blue crayon.
2. Locate the towns of Mohenjo-daro and Harrapa. Circle their names in red.

NOTE: This map is reprinted from Terri Johnson's "Blackline Maps of Ancient History" set, with her kind permission. For a full set of blackline maps, coordinated to *The Story of the World*, visit Knowledge Quest Maps at http://www.knowledgequestmaps.com, or contact Knowledge Quest at 7722 SE 282nd Avenue, Gresham, OR 97080 (503/663-1210). Or buy these maps directly from Peace Hill Press (http://www.peacehillpress.com).

Coloring Page (Student Page 28)

This picture of the Indus King is based on a sculpture found at Mohenjo-daro.

Projects

Science Project: What Does It Take to Make a Brick?

This experiment is to find the combination of materials that are needed to make a brick from mud. Have the child mix up different ratios of dirt, sand and straw to find what makes the "best" mud. Remember that too much clay in the dirt will cause the brick to crack when it dries. Because it is coarse, sand keeps the brick from shrinking when it dries – but too much sand makes a brittle brick. See what works best with the type of soils you have in your area. All soils need different combinations.

Materials:

     Dirt and sand

     Straw, grass or thin twigs

     Water, bucket and mold (small box or milk carton).

Directions:

1. Place the dirt, sand and clay material in a large bucket for mixing. Add pieces of straw, grass or thin twigs to the dirt. These will act as a bonding agent. Use your hands to mix the ingredients before adding the water.

2. Add the water slowly and continue mixing the dirt mixture until you get a thick, sturdy mud. You will probably have to experiment to find the best combination of ingredients.

3. Place the mud in any rectangular-shaped container. A small shoebox will work well, as will a milk container cut in half. Place the brick in a very warm place for about 2 weeks. When it appears to be thoroughly dry, remove the brick from the containers.

Craft Project: Make a Mohenjo-Daro Dwelling

Materials:

> Large amount of air-drying clay
> Rolling pin, sculpting tool or blunt knife
> White glue, ruler, paint brush, thin cardboard
> Reddish-brown paint

Directions:

1. Roll the clay out to a ½" thickness and start cutting out bricks. You might find that using a ruler as a straight edge and cutting the clay into ½" strips first will help. Then, cut 1" bricks from the strips.

2. Place the cut bricks on wax paper and let air-dry. When this is done, start building. The houses in Mohenjo-daro were small rectangular buildings, with flat roofs. Many of them had no windows at all. White glue can be used as cement to hold your building together. Use a piece of thin cardboard for the roof. For a more realistic mud-brick look, paint your building with a brownish colored paint.

Writing Project: What Happened at Mohenjo-Daro? C

> "It was a dark and windy night as the town of Mohenjo-Daro slept. Little did anyone know that this was their last night…"

> No one knows what happened to the people of Mohenjo-daro. Why did they leave their beautiful city and never return? Was it a flood? Was it an earthquake? Or, was it an invading army? Only you know the answer.

> Use your imagination and decide what happened to the people of Mohenjo-daro. When you've decided what your story will be about, tell a parent and they will write it down for you. Make your tale complete by drawing a picture to go with it.

CHAPTER TEN
The Far East: Ancient China

UBWH 62, UILE 164-165
KIHOW 42-43, KHE 18-19

Review Questions, Lei Zu and the Silkworm

Why is China called "the Far East"? *Because it is all the way to the east on the map, if you live in the Fertile Crescent*

The Chinese people lived between two rivers. Do you remember the name of one of them? *The child can answer either "The Yellow River" or "The Yangtze River"; be sure to tell the child the name of the river she doesn't guess.*

What was their valley called? *The Yellow River Valley*

The Chinese first settled in many small villages. Do you remember the name of the emperor who united them into one empire? *Huang Di (be sure to supply the answer if the child can't remember)*

What did Huang Di's wife, Lei Zu, discover? *She discovered the silkworm and learned how to make silk.*

Narration Exercise, Lei Zu and the Silkworm

Ask the child to tell you in her own words how the Empress discovered silk. An acceptable narration might be, "The Empress was eating in the garden. A worm fell into her tea. It was covered with threads! Then the Chinese people learned how to make silk from the threads."

Review Questions, The Pictograms of Ancient China

What Chinese dynasty did we read about today? *The Shang dynasty*

What is a dynasty? *A family that rules one country for years and years*

How long did the Shang dynasty rule? *Around 500 years*

During the Shang dynasty, the Chinese people began to use a special kind of writing. Do you remember what it is called? *Pictograms*

In pictograms, what do words look like? *Pictures!*

Do you remember any of the pictograms we looked at? *Sun, water*

What kind of writing did the Shang dynasty use? *Pictograms – where a picture represents a word*

Narration Exercise, The Pictograms of Ancient China

Rather than asking the child to do a regular narration exercise, have him draw one or two of the pictograms from the lesson above.

Review Questions, Farming in Ancient China

What valley did Chin live in? *The Yellow River Valley*

What two rivers ran on either side of the Yellow River Valley? *The Yellow River and the Yangtze River*

What crop did the ancient farmers of China grow? *Rice*

Why did Chin get up so early in the morning? *He was going to help his father in the fields for the first time.*

What kind of ground did the rice grow in? *Wet ground*

What was Chin supposed to do for his father, first thing in the morning? *Find out whether his father was well, whether he needed food or water*

What story did Chin's grandfather tell? *About a time when the Yellow River flooded*

Narration Exercise, Farming in Ancient China

An acceptable narration for the last part of the chapter might be, "Chin lived in ancient China. He helped his father grow rice. The rice grew where the river flooded."

Additional History Reading

Ancient China (Nature Company Discoveries), by Judith Simpson (Time Life, 1996). Some of this text will be too difficult for elementary children, but the pictures and projects are excellent. (RA)

We Come From China, by Julia Waterlow (Steck Vaughn, 2000). Modern-day China illustrated, with references to China's history. (RA)

D is for Doufu: An Alphabet Book of Chinese Culture, by Maywan Shen Krach (Shen's Books, 1997). An introduction to elements of modern and ancient Chinese culture. (RA)

Growing Up in Ancient China, by Ken Teague (Troll, 1993). The story of a seven-year-old child who lives in ancient China. (RA)

Corresponding Literature Suggestions

Maples in the Mist: Poems for Children from the Tang Dynasty, by Minfong Ho (Lothrop, Lee and Shepard, 1996). Actual poems from the ancient Chinese, accessible to young children. (RA)

The Story About Ping, by Marjorie Flack (Viking, 1983). A classic children's story; Ping is an adventurous duck who lives on the Yangtze River. (RA, possible IR for some advanced readers)

Tikki Tikki Tembo, by Arleene Mosel (Henry Holt, 1989) – What is in a name? A great deal, according to the Chinese long ago. Great fun to read aloud. (RA)

The Dragon's Tale and Other Animal Tales of the Chinese Zodiac, by Demi (Henry Holt, 1986). A collection of fables about twelve mythical Chinese animals. (RA)

Map Work (Student Page 29)

1. On the black line map provided, locate the Yellow River and the Yangtze River. Use a blue crayon to trace the course of the rivers. Color in the South China Sea.

2. Use a green crayon to color in the area between the two rivers. This is the place where the first Chinese settled down and started to farm.

Coloring Page (Student Page 30)

Using your crayons, color in the picture of Chin and his father going off to tend their rice fields.

Projects

Art Project: Make a Blue and White Ming Bowl

Materials:

    Large piece of air-drying clay, plastic wrap

    Small round plastic bowl, Rolling pin, sculpting tool or blunt knife

    Blue paint, white glue and paint brush

Directions:

1. Roll the clay out into a large square that is about a ¼" thick. The square should be large enough to completely cover the plastic bowl and extend about ½" around it.

2. Wrap the bowl in plastic wrap and place it upside down on a piece of scrap cardboard or foil. Lay the clay over the upturned bowl and press the clay to the bowl. Use the sculpting tool to trim away the excess clay. Or, you can leave it there so that your bowl has a rim around it. You will need to use your sculpting tool to cut away the straight edges and make a smooth curve. Allow the piece to air-dry over night.

3. The clay bowl can now be removed from the form and painted. Chinese pottery was usually decorated with pictures of birds, flowers and outdoor scenes. Use the blue paint to create any design that you like. When you have finished, set the bowl to one side to dry completely.

4. To give your bowl a shiny finish, use 2 parts white glue to 1 part water to make the glaze. Paint the glaze over the entire bowl. This can be done in two steps. First paint the outside, and after it has dried, glaze the inside of the bowl.

Writing Project: Make Your Own Pictograms

Materials:

    Black poster paint

    Thin paintbrush

    White cardboard or construction page

Directions:

Ancient Chinese pictograms looked like the things they stood for. What would the pictogram for "table" look like? How about pictograms for "brother," "sister," or "dog"? Make up your own pictograms and paint them in black paint on the white paper. Can your parents figure out what the pictograms stand for?

CHAPTER ELEVEN
Ancient Africa

UBWH 82, UILE 172-173
KIHOW 58-59, KHE 30-31

Review Questions, Ancient Peoples of West Africa

Do you remember what a *continent* is? *A large piece of land with many countries on it*

What continent is the Nile River in? *Africa*

Do you remember the name of the large desert in West Africa? *The Sahara Desert*

Was the desert always hot and sandy? *No, once it had water and grass and animals in it.*

What did archaeologists find when they dug down into the hard, dry dirt of the Sahara? *Pollen, seeds, bones of animals, turtle shells*

Why did the people of ancient Africa go south? *Because the Sahara began to dry up*

Narration Exercise, Ancient Peoples of West Africa

Ask the child to tell you three things that he has learned about ancient West Africa. These might include (among others):

"The Nile River is in Africa."

"The Sahara Desert is in Africa."

"The Sahara Desert used to be grassy and have water in it."

"People in Africa had to go south when their land dried up."

"Archaeologists found seeds and animal bones in the desert."

"People in Africa made cave paintings."

Review Questions, Anansi and Turtle

What are yams like? *Sweet potatoes*

Why didn't Anansi want to share with Turtle? *He was too hungry!*

What did Anansi tell Turtle to do before he ate? *Wash his hands*

Where did Turtle set his supper table when Anansi came to visit him? *Under the water*

How did Anansi get down to the bottom of the water? *He put rocks in the pockets of his coat.*

What did Turtle tell him to do? *Take his jacket off before he ate*

What happened when Anansi took his coat off? *He popped back up to the surface of the water!*

Narration Exercise, Anansi and Turtle

Ask the child to retell the story in his own words. An acceptable narration might be:

"Anansi the Spider didn't want to share his supper with Turtle. He told Turtle to keep washing his hands until the supper was all gone. Then Anansi went to see Turtle. Turtle didn't want to share either! He put his supper at the bottom of the river. Anansi couldn't get down to the bottom to eat it!"

Review Questions, Anansi and the Make Believe Food

Do you remember the three kinds of food that Anansi found in the villages? *If necessary, prompt the child for the answers: Cassava, plantains and rice.*

What do cassava look like? *Potatoes*

What do plantains look like? *Bananas*

Why did Anansi keep on leaving the villages to go to the next one? *Because he thought he would find something better*

Did he get a wonderful meal at the end of the story? *No, he didn't get anything!*

What was the moral of this tale? *Don't be greedy – eat what you're given.*

Narration Exercise, Anansi and the Make Believe Food

Instead of asking the child to tell you the story again, have her draw a picture of Anansi the Spider with a banana, a potato, and several grains of rice. Should the food have faces?

Additional History Reading

Great African Kingdoms, by Sean Sheehan (Raintree Steck-Vaughn, 1999). This book gives a
great overview of the first kingdoms of Africa; a timeline and glossary are also included. (RA)

Look Who Lives In: The Desert, by Alan Baker (Peter Bedrick Books, 1999). Large illustrations
and easy text makes it fun to learn about some of the animals that live in the desert. (RA)

Animals of the Desert, by Stephen Savage. (Raintree Steck-Vaughn, 1997). This book includes
a map of the deserts of the world, a description of what a desert is, and pictures of an array of
animals that spend their lives living in the desert. (RA)

Corresponding Literature Suggestions

Misoso: Once Upon a Time Tales from Africa, by Verna Aardema (Knopf, 1994). Twelve African
tales from Angola to Zanzibar, beautifully and vibrantly illustrated. A map of Africa detailing the
origin of each story, notes on each tale, and a glossary are included. (RA)

Anansi the Spider: A Tale from the Ashanti, by Gerald McDermott (Scholastic, 1993). This tale,
which tells how mischievous Anansi and his six brave sons helped place the moon in the
sky, won a Caldecott Honor Award. (IR for most readers, RA for beginners)

Zomo the Rabbit: A Trickster Tale from West Africa, by Gerald McDermott (Harcourt Brace
Jovanovich, 1992). Zomo the rabbit, an African trickster, sets out to gain wisdom. This
tale originated in Nigeria. The pictures are colorful and enticing, adding to the
excitement of the story. (RA)

Too Much Talk, by Angela Shelf Medearis (Candlewick Press, 1995), A retelling of a traditional
Ghanaian tale about a king who refuses to believe that yams, fish, and cloth can talk until
his throne agrees with him. The illustrations are warm and reflective of the West African
origins of the story. Silly – and great fun to read. (RA)

Rhinos for Lunch and Elephants for Supper! A Maasai Tale, by Tololwa Mollel (Oxford
University Press, 1991). A tale from East Africa; the animals are frightened by the horrible-
sounding monster who has taken over the hare's cave, until a clever frog solves the problem.
(RA)

Map Work (Student Page 31)

1. On the blackline map provided, put your finger between the Tigris and Euphrates Rivers.

2. Move your finger to the right, to the edge of the map. Put an S in the location of Sumer, a B in the area of Babylonia and an A in the location of Assyria after you have crossed those areas with your finger. You can find these on the maps you've done for previous chapters if you need a reminder.

3. Keep going to the right – that's *east* on your map. Stop when you reach India. Find the Indus River, and color the Indus Valley green. Remember – the first cities of India were built here.

4. Draw an arrow pointing right off the map. Write "China" above the arrow (your mother or father can help). This note tells you that China is further in that direction.

5. Now go back to the Tigris and Euphrates Rivers. The area between the rivers is called "Mesopotamia." Color this area green. Nomads first settled here.

6. Now put your finger on Mesopotamia and go left – that's *west* on your map. You'll run into a big sea. What is this sea called?

7. Follow the shore of the Mediterranean Sea down to the Nile River. Circle the label on the map which identifies Egypt. Draw a little pyramid next to the name "Egypt."

8. If you keep moving your finger down the Nile River, out of Egypt, you will notice that the Nile River is very small compared to the size of the landmass, or continent, that it runs through! Down at the bottom of the Nile River, write AFRICA in capital letters: that is the name of this continent.

9. Now, put your finger back on the Nile River, in the area of Egypt. Move your finger to the left. This area is the Sahara Desert. Shade in the area of this vast desert with a sandy colored pencil, crayon or marker. To remind yourself that this location used to be full of trees and water, draw a tree in the midst of the desert.

Coloring Page (Student Page 32)
Color the picture of Anansi being tricked by Turtle.

Projects

Craft Project: Paper Bead Necklace

Materials:
> colored paper (magazine pages, construction paper, wallpaper samples)
> glue stick
> pencil, scissors, string

Directions:
1. Cut several triangles out of the colored paper. The width of the base should be between one and two inches, and the height should be around four to six inches. The wider the base, the easier it is to work with.
2. Starting with the base of the triangle, roll the paper around the pencil. Put some glue on the point of the triangle and press down firmly.
3. Remove the bead from the pencil and continue making beads until there are enough to thread onto the necklace.
4. Cut a length of string (long enough to easily fit over child's head when completed). Tie a large knot at one end of the string. Thread the beads onto the necklace. Tie the ends together when the necklace is complete.

Craft Project: Make Anansi the Spider

Materials:
> 1 - 1 inch styrofoam ball
> 1- 2 inch styrofoam ball
> glue, scissors
> googly eyes
> paint
> pipe cleaners
> toothpick

Directions:
1. Paint (with brush or spray paint) both styrofoam balls. Let them dry.
2. Attach the smaller ball (head) to the larger ball (body) using part of a toothpick and/or glue.
3. Cut the pipe cleaners into eight appropriate lengths. Attach four per side to the body of the spider and shape them to look like legs.
4. Glue on the eyes and draw or paint a mouth.

Art Project: Painted Hands C

Many African peoples painted their hands, feet and other body parts, usually with geometric designs, on special occasions.

Materials:

> construction paper
> paint and brush

Directions:

1. Have an adult or older sibling trace your hands and feet onto the paper. For more fun, ask if you can trace their hands, too.

2. Paint a geometric pattern (squares, triangles, rectangles, diamonds) onto the hands and feet. Let them dry.

3. Decorate your walls, door or dresser with these hands (ask an adult first!). Or hang them in a mobile by taping colored yarn onto the backs of the hands and feet and tying them to a metal or plastic clothes hanger.

Cooking Project: African Feast

Choose which recipes you would like to include in your feast. Follow the directions to prepare the food. An adult should be present to supervise and assist when necessary, for safety reasons. For a festive touch, decorate your hands (see Henna Hands, above) and make some musical instruments to celebrate with. Instructions for a variety of instruments are included below. Have fun!

Chicken with Figs

Ingredients:

3-4 pounds chicken legs
1 lemon
¼ Cup brown sugar
¼ Cup vinegar
¼ Cup water
1-2 Tbsp lemon juice
8-16 ounces dried figs
salt to taste
parsley

Directions:

1. Preheat oven to 400°.
2. Peel and slice the lemon. Place lemon slices and figs in the bottom of a 9x13 baking pan. Add the chicken legs.
3. In mixing bowl, combine the brown sugar, vinegar, water, and lemon juice.
4. Pour mixture over the chicken. Sprinkle chicken with salt and parsley.
5. Bake, covered with foil, for about 40 minutes. Remove foil and bake for approximately 20-30 minutes longer or until chicken begins to brown. Baste frequently during the last 20-30 minutes. Remove chicken, figs, and lemon slices and place on a serving tray.
6. Skim off any fat and use the remaining juices as a sauce for the chicken.

Papaya Stir Fried Rice

Ingredients:

1 can chopped papaya, reserve the juice
1 red bell pepper, chopped
½ red onion, chopped
2 Tbsp dried parsley

1 Tbsp olive oil (can substitute water)

salt to taste

instant rice (4-6 servings)

Directions:

1. Prepare the rice as directed on the package, substituting the papaya juice for an equal amount of water.
2. While the rice is being prepared, combine the papaya, red pepper, onion, parsley and salt in a medium sized bowl.
3. In a large skillet, heat the oil over medium heat. Add the papaya mixture and stir fry until onions are tender.
4. Add the cooked rice to the papaya mixture, and stir fry an additional 2 minutes. Serve immediately.

Fried Plantains

Ingredients:

¼ cup cooking oil

1 plantain

Directions:

1. Preheat the oil in a large skillet over medium high heat.
2. Cut the plantain into rounds, a bit thicker than ¼ inch.
3. Very carefully, fry the pieces till the edges are very lightly golden brown. Flip them over, and fry the other side. As a guideline, one minute per side should be sufficient. Don't let them get too dark.
4. Remove excess oil with a paper towel. Serve immediately. Add salt and/or garlic to taste.

Date and Banana Bars

Ingredients:

¼ cup margarine

¾ cup sugar

1 egg

1 tsp vanilla

2 med. bananas

1 cup flour

¼ tsp baking soda

½ tsp baking powder

¼ tsp salt

½ cup chopped dates

Optional: ¼ cup almonds

Icing:

2 Tbsp margarine

1 Tbsp lemon juice

½ tsp vanilla

¾ Cup powdered sugar

Directions:

1. Cream together the margarine and sugar.
2. Add the egg and vanilla.
3. Stir in the bananas and dry ingredients.
4. Add the dates and almonds.
5. Bake in an 8x8 pan at 350° for about 30 minutes or until edges are turning brown.

Date Chewies
Ingredients:
1 Cup chopped dates
2 eggs
1 Cup sugar
¾ Cup flour
1 tsp baking powder
1 Cup pecans, ground
¼ Cup powdered sugar
Directions:
1. In a blender, blend eggs and dates together. Set aside.
2. In mixing bowl, combine sugar, flour, baking powder, and pecans. Add in egg mixture.
3. Pour into ungreased cookie sheets. Press the mixture down so it will be as thin as possible.
4. Bake at 350° for 15-20 minutes. Remove from oven and cut into bars while hot.
5. Roll into balls and then roll in the powdered sugar as soon as the chewies are cool enough to handle.

Music Project: Make Instruments for an African Concert
Plate Shakers
Materials:
> 2 paper plates or bowls of the same size
> beans, rice, lentils, pebbles, or small pasta pieces
> tape and/or stapler

Directions:
1. Fill one plate or bowl with beans, rice, lentils, pebbles, or small pasta pieces. (Each will make a slightly different sound, so if you make more than one, fill each with something different).
2. Place the second plate or bowl on top of the first (the bottom of it should be facing you), rims touching. Staple and/or tape the plates together.
3. Decorate. Then, make music.

Cup Shakers
Materials:
> aluminum foil, cling wrap, paper, or balloon
> beans, lentils, rice, pebbles, or small pasta pieces
> rubber band
> plastic cup

Directions:
1. Fill the cup half full with beans, lentils, rice, pebbles, or small pasta pieces. If using pasta, make sure there are no sharp edges or points (in other words, don't use broken spaghetti noodles). Each will make a slightly different sound against the plastic cup. This shaker will sound different from the plate shaker, as well.
2. To cover the cup, you have some options, each of which will alter the sound slightly. You can cover it with a double layer of foil or cling wrap, a single layer of paper (writing paper, or from a magazine), or you can stretch a balloon across the top. Whichever you use, secure it to the cup with a rubber band.

Rustler Shaker Bells
Materials:
> nail

several metal bottle lids

string

Directions:

1. With the nail, have an adult punch a hole into each metal lid.
2. Tie a short piece of string to each lid, through the hole.
3. Bunch all the strings together and tie with a knot.
4. Make some music by shaking these rustling bells.

One-Stringed Plucker

Materials:

facial tissue box

rubber band

Directions:

1. Wrap the rubber band around the tissue box, so it goes over the opening in the top.
2. Decorate. Pluck your one-stringed plucker. For variety, add more rubber bands of different widths.

REVIEW CARDS
Chapters Eight, Nine, Ten, Eleven
(Student Page 33)

CHAPTER TWELVE
The Middle Kingdom of Egypt

UBWH 16-23, *UILE* 114-117
KIHOW 26-27, *KHE* 10-11

Review Questions, Egypt Invades Nubia

What happened to the Old Kingdom of Egypt? *It became weak and powerless.*

When Amenemhet became pharaoh, what country did he decide to conquer? *Nubia*

Why was Nubia valuable to the Egyptians? *It had gold.*

What new name did the Egyptians give to Nubia? *Kush*

What do we call this time in Egyptian history? *The Middle Kingdom of Egypt*

Narration Exercise, Egypt Invades Nubia

"Egypt was weak. Then it became strong again. This was called the Middle Kingdom. The Egyptians conquered Nubia." OR

"The Egyptians invaded part of Africa. It was called Nubia. It had iron and gold in it. This was during the Middle Kingdom of Egypt." OR

"The Egyptians took over part of Africa. They called it Kush. Then the people of Kush became Egyptian. Some even became pharaohs!"

Review Questions, The Hyksos Invade Egypt

What happened to the Middle Kingdom of Egypt? *It became weak because of bad pharaohs.*

Who invaded Egypt and took over the Egyptian throne? *Wandering nomads [It is nice but not essential if the child can remember the name Hyksos.]*

Where were they from? *Canaan*

Did the Egyptians like having the Hyksos for kings? *No! They thought the Hyksos were unclean shepherds*
How did the Egyptians get rid of the Hyksos? *Egyptian princes got together and used the Hyksos' own weapons to drive them out*

Narration Exercise, The Hyksos Invade Egypt
"Egypt became weak again. Nomads came from Canaan and took over. They had good weapons and fought with chariots. Then the Egyptians chased them out." OR
"The Middle Kingdom ended because nomads invaded. They ruled Egypt. Then Egyptians used bows and arrows and chariots to drive them out."

Additional History Reading

The Pharaohs of Ancient Egypt, by Elizabeth Payne (Random House, 1998). This read-aloud book has a brief chapter about the life of each important pharaoh of Egypt. (RA)

Life in Ancient Egypt: A Coloring Book, by John Green (Dover, 1989). Detailed and interesting pictures of life in ancient Egypt, along with brief descriptions. (RA and activity)

Growing Up in Ancient Egypt, by Rosalie David (Troll, 1993). What was it like to be a child in ancient Egypt? Find out in this simple read-aloud book. (RA)

Ancient Egypt (Ms. Frizzle's Adventures, by Joanna Cole (Scholastic, 2001). Ms. Frizzle takes a vacation from the Magic School Bus – and ends up in ancient Egypt. (RA)

Corresponding Literature Suggestions

Rimonah of the Flashing Sword: A North African Tale, by Eric Kimmel (Holiday House, 1995). This story of princesses and heroes mixes African and Egyptian elements. (RA)

Temple Cat, by Andrew Clements (Clarion, 2001). A temple cat in ancient Egypt runs away from his temple and catches fish like a normal cat. (RA)

Sten Gizzle, Time Traveller: The Egyptian Adventure, by Scott May (Long Hill, 2000). A silly (but entertaining) voyage into the Middle Kingdom of Egypt. (RA)

Egyptian Gods and Goddesses, by Henry Barker (Grossett & Dunlap, 1999). An All Aboard Reading Level 2 book with stories about the most important gods and goddesses of Egypt's Middle Kingdom. (RA, but probably an IR for advanced readers)

Map Work (Student Page 34)

1. On the map provided, circle the area around the Nile (Egypt) with a red crayon.
2. Nubia is south of Egypt, in Africa. Label Nubia at the bottom of your map, just to the left of the Nile River.
3. Find Canaan. Draw an H for Hyksos in Canaan, and then draw a line from Canaan down into Egypt. The Hyksos took this route into Egypt when they conquered it!

Coloring Page (Student Page 35)

Projects

Craft Project: Make a Monkey Doll
Materials:
  clean, old sock
  dried beans, peas or seeds
  fabric paint or permanent markers

felt or fabric scraps (brown, if you want a monkey with brown arms, legs and tail)
glue (hot glue works best)
ribbon

Directions:

1. Fill the sock with beans, peas or seeds. Tie the end tightly with the ribbon.

2. Cut out four strips from the felt (for arms and legs), plus one longer strip (for the tail). Glue these parts to the filled sock to make arms, legs and a tail.

3. Cut out two ear shapes from the felt, and glue to the head of your monkey.

4. Paint or draw a face onto your monkey.

5. Now you can deliver your gift to the Egyptians, or pretend you are the Egyptian and thank the Nubian for such a wonderful gift.

Craft Project: Make a Golden Bracelet

Materials:

gold paint and brushes
scissors
toilet paper tube

Directions:

1. Cut the toilet paper tube in half, making two shorter tubes.

2. Cut each of the smaller tubes lengthwise (end to end).

3. Paint the outside of the tubes gold. Let them dry completely.

4. To wear your gold bracelets, gently open the tube, where it has been split, and wrap around your upper arm. It will fit tightly enough that it shouldn't fall off. If it is too tight, take it off, and gently open the tube wider, bending the cardboard a bit. Try it on again. Wear one bracelet on each arm. What a nice gift from the Nubians!

Activity Project: Burn Incense

Materials:

Incense (can be purchased at some grocery and drug stores, and at many gift stores)
matches
adult supervision (Do NOT do this activity without an adult supervising)
flat, wide candle stick (to hold incense cone) or incense holder (any fire and heat proof surface would be suitable)

Directions:

1. Tomb pictures show Nubians carrying incense, among other things, to the Egyptians to give as gifts. Have an adult light the incense with the matches, as directed on the package. After burning, be sure to put out the ember completely. If the package doesn't direct you as to the best way to do this, douse it in water.

2. With the assistance of an adult, try a few different scents of incense. Which do you like best?

Activity Project: Make an Egyptian Chariot and Horse

Materials:

dowel (3 pieces)
hot glue
plastic horse
small gift box (without the lid) OR pint milk carton (one side removed)
wooden wheels (from a craft store)

Directions:

1. Poke one of the dowel pieces through the box or milk carton. Hot glue a wooden wheel to each end of the dowel. Be sure you don't glue the dowel to the box side.

2. Take the two remaining dowel pieces, glue one dowel rod on opposite sides of the box above the wheels, letting them extend forward.

3. Back the horse in, between the dowel rods. Then, tape the rods to the horse's sides.

4. Put a plastic person in the chariot and join the Egyptian Princes who rebelled against the Hyksos.

CHAPTER THIRTEEN
The New Kingdom of Egypt

UBWH 33-39, UILE 135-137
KIHOW 54-55, KHE 26-27

Review Questions, The General and the Woman Pharaoh

We've already learned about the Old Kingdom and the Middle Kingdom of Egypt. What is this time in Egypt's history called? *The New Kingdom*

We read about two pharaohs today. Do you remember their names? *Prompt the child if necessary: Thutmose and Hatshepsut*

What did Thutmose do? *He made Egypt bigger.*

What did Hatshepsut do? *She became pharaoh even though she was a woman.*

What did Hatshepsut wear? *Men's clothes and a false beard!*

Narration Exercise, The General and the Woman Pharaoh

Ask the child to retell the story of EITHER Thutmose OR Hatshepsut. Acceptable narrations might include:

"Thutmose wanted to make Egypt bigger. He fought the Nubians and he even fought the Hyksos. He made Egypt twice as big!" OR

"Hatshepsut wanted to be pharaoh. The Egyptians didn't think a woman could be pharaoh. So Hatshepsut pretended to be a man. She put on a false beard and fought with her army."

Review Questions, Amenhotep and King Tut

What is polytheism? *The worship of many different gods*

What is monotheism? *The worship of just one god*

Did the Egyptians worship just one god, or many gods? *Many gods.* That means that they were polytheists.

Did Amenhotep worship just one god, or many gods? *Just one god*

Did the Egyptians like this? *No! They wanted all their gods back*

Where was King Tut buried? *In the Valley of the Kings*

Who discovered his tomb? *A man named Howard Carter.*

Did robbers steal Tut's treasure? *No.* Why not? *They couldn't find his tomb.*

Why did people think there was a curse on the tomb? *Because some people who opened it died, and Howard Carter's canary was swallowed by a cobra*

Narration Exercise, Amenhotep and King Tut

Ask the child to retell the story of Amenhotep.

"The Egyptians worshipped many different gods. One pharaoh wanted them to worship just one god. But they didn't want to." OR

"Polytheism means having lots of gods. The Egyptians had lots of gods. A pharaoh tried to make them be monotheists. That means having just one god." OR

Ask the child to draw a picture of King Tut's mummy or of Howard Carter discovering the tomb full of treasure. Ask him to describe the picture to you. Write the description on the bottom of the picture.

Additional History Reading

The Pharoahs of Ancient Egypt, by Elizabeth Payne (Random House, 1998). This read-aloud book has a brief chapter about the life of each important pharoah of Egypt. (RA)

Tut's Mummy – Lost, and Found, by Judy Donnelly (Random House, 1988). A simple account of the mummy's discovery. (IR for many readers, RA for beginners)

Pharaohs and Pyramids (Time Traveler Series), by Tony Allan and Philippa Wingate (EDC Publications, 1998). An Usborne book about the days of the pharaohs; simple text and good pictures.

Look What Came from Egypt (Machines at Work), by Miles Harvey (Franklin Watts, 1999). Oriented towards the science of ancient Egypt. (RA)

Tutankhamun: The Life and Death of the Pharaoh (Discover Series), by David Murdoch (Dorling Kindersley, 1998). Covers the life and death of King Tut, the first discovery of the tomb, its opening, and its contents. Includes photos and realistic drawings. (RA)

Corresponding Literature Suggestions

Hatshepsut: His Majesty, Herself, by Catherine M. Andronik (Atheneum, 2001). A picture-book story about Hatshepsut, the ancient Egyptian queen who declared herself King and ruled for more than twenty years. (RA)

His Majesty, Queen Hatshepsut, by Dorothy Sharp Carter (Lippincott, Williams & Wilkins, 1987). The story of the thirteen-year-old Hatshepsut; more detailed and longer than the above title, but still possible as a read-aloud. (RA)

Tutankhamen's Gift, by Robert Sabuda (Atheneum, 1994). The story of King Tut's childhood – especially good for the youngest children in the family who may feel left out at times. (RA)

Tut, Tut (The Time Warp Trio), by Jon Scieszka (Puffin, 1998). A silly but entertaining trip through time. For advanced readers to tackle alone. (IR for advanced readers)

Mara, Daughter of the Nile, by Eloise McGraw (Viking Press, 1990). Mara is a young slave girl who escapes from her cruel master and finds herself in the hands of two new enemies. Too long to read in one day, but this might make a good family reading project, especially if an older child can take on the project of reading to the younger ones. (RA)

Map Work (Student Page 36)

1. On the map provided, circle the area that is known as the Valley of the Kings.
2. Review the locations of Canaan, Mediterranean Sea and the Red Sea.

NOTE: This map is reprinted from Terri Johnson's "Blackline Maps of Ancient History" set, with her kind permission. For a full set of blackline maps, coordinated to *The Story of the World*, visit Knowledge Quest Maps at http://www.knowledgequestmaps.com, or contact Knowledge Quest at 7722 SE 282nd Avenue, Gresham, OR 97080 (503/663-1210). Or buy directly from Peace Hill Press (http://www.peacehillpress.com).

Coloring Page (Student Page 37)
The Golden Mask of King Tut

Projects

Craft Project: Make Hatshepsut's False Beard

Materials:

> colored tissue paper
> fabric elastic, ¼ to ½ inch width (the sort used in clothing)
> white craft glue
> paint brush (for glue)
> scrap paper
> toilet paper tube

Directions:

1. The toilet paper tube will be the "base" for your false beard. Cover it with thin strips of tissue paper, glued to the tube at one end and hanging free at the other. To avoid getting your hands sticky, you can use a paint brush to paint glue onto the tissue paper, and to apply the tissue to the tube. Let the beard dry by setting one end of the tube on a piece of cling wrap or scrap paper.

2. Once the beard is dry, punch two holes opposite each other at one end of the tube. Thread the fabric elastic through one hole, and tie a knot on the inside of the tube.

3. Put the beard up to your chin, and measure how long the elastic needs to be to reach around your head to the other side of the tube. An older sibling or adult could help you with this task. Cut the elastic at the appropriate length (this will keep the beard on your face, so you don't want it to be too loose or too tight).

4. Thread the free end of the elastic into the open hole in the tube. Tie a knot on the inside of the tube. Try the beard on. If it is too loose, pull the knot tighter. You may need to undo the original knot first, or perhaps just tie a second knot to take up the slack.

5. Wear your beard and pretend to be Hatshepsut, the first woman Pharaoh.

Craft Project: Make One of Hatshepsut's Monuments

During Queen Hatshepsut's reign, she had many monuments built. Do you know what a monument is? A monument is usually built to serve as a memorial to a person or group of people who have died. An ancient monument could be a statue of a person, a statue of a god, a large building, a pillar with a story written on it, or a large stone with words carved on it. In ancient times, monuments were often statues of people; sometimes they were also large buildings, or pillars with words written on them.

Imagine that you are a king or queen in ancient times. What important things have happened in your country? (Look back over the chapters you've already read, if you can't remember.) What event or person would you like to make a monument to?

Optional Idea: Think of something that is important to you. This could be someone special, a favorite toy, or a favorite activity. Make a monument (model) of it.

Materials:

> glue (optional: paint)
> white bread
> mixing bowl

Directions:

1. Mix together bread and glue, using one tablespoon of glue for every two slices of white bread. Mix together until the consistency of clay is reached. It will eventually pull away from the sides of the bowl and will not be sticky.

2. Shape mixture into a monument. Mix more dough if you want to make a larger monument.

3. Most ancient monuments are made of plain stone – but some of them may have been painted, in colors that have now worn away. If you want to, paint your monument in bright colors.

Craft Project: Make an Egyptian Death Mask

Kings, queens, and other people of nobility and high class in ancient Egypt were mummified and buried in highly decorated coffins. Each mummy wore a "death mask" which was made in the likeness of the person being buried. The Egyptians believed that every person had a spirit called "ka" which separated from the body at death. To live in the afterlife, the ka would need to find the body it belonged to. The death masks (and the coffins, which were also crafted to look like the person within) helped the ka to recognize the body it belonged with.

Materials:

> circular balloon
> cling wrap covered bowl
> newspaper
> paste (made of glue and water, or salt, flour, and water)
> scissors
> paint, gold glitter, etc. (optional)

Directions:

1. Make the paste. You can use a glue and water mixture (1-2 parts glue to 1 part water) or a flour paste mixture (1 part water with two parts flour and a little salt OR 1 part flour to 5 parts water – for both mixtures, boil three minutes and then cool before using).

2. Blow up balloon. Place it on cling wrap-covered bowl.

3. Cut strips of newspaper. Cover entire front surface of balloon by dipping strips into paste and then carefully putting on balloon. Let dry completely.

4. Add facial features (with string, crumpled paper, foil, buttons, etc). Use masking tape to hold in place.

5. Add 2-3 more layers of paper mache over the features. Allow each layer to dry before adding the next.

6. Pop balloon. You can now paint the mask with bright colors and gold glitter, so that it resembles the death mask of a pharaoh (optional).

Activity Project: Play Tomb Discovery

Archaeologist Howard Carter discovered King Tut's tombs and its treasures after years of searching. Pretend to be an archaeologist discovering a tomb! You'll need a parent or older sibling to help you out.

1. PARENT OR OLDER SIBLING: Choose a small, out-of-the-way, secret place in the house (or out-doors, if the weather is nice) to be "King Tut's Tomb." Select a number of small treasures from around the house (toys from the child's room, stuffed animals, small pieces of candy or other approved treats – a new toy is nice but not essential). Don't choose too many treasures, since the child will need to draw pictures of the treasures as soon as he finds them. Arrange these treasures in the "tomb." Make a simple map for the child to follow, and tell him to go find the tomb!

2. CHILD: Before an archaeologist can move anything in a tomb, he has to draw a picture of its original place. When you discover your "tomb," don't touch any of the treasures! Instead, get a piece of paper and a crayon or pencil. Draw each item in the tomb, just as you see it. (Ask your parent or sibling for help.) After you've drawn your "tomb picture," you can play with the treasures!

CHAPTER FOURTEEN
The Israelites Leave Egypt

UBWH N/A, UILE 142
KIHOW 50-51, KHE 24

Review Questions, The Baby Moses

Who were the Israelites descended from? *Abraham. [Take a moment to talk about what a "descendant" is, if necessary.]*

Did the Israelites worship one god or many gods? *One God.* Were they monotheists or polytheists? *Monotheists*

Why did they go to Egypt? *Because of a famine in Canaan*

What happened to them in Egypt? *They became slaves.*

Who led them back out of Egypt? *Moses*

What terrible command did the pharaoh give? *To kill all the baby boys of the Israelites*

What did Moses's mother do to save his life? *Put him in the Nile River in a basket*

Who took him out? *The princess of Egypt*

Narration Exercise, The Baby Moses

The narration should EITHER say that the Israelites went to Egypt, and were made into slaves by the pharaoh, OR should retell the story of Moses. (If the child wants to include both parts of the lesson in the narration, that's fine, but don't require this.)

"The Israelites went to Egypt because of a famine. There were many of them and the Egyptians were afraid of them. The Egyptians made them into slaves." OR

"Moses's mother wanted to keep him safe. She hid him. Then she put him in a basket on the river. The daughter of the pharaoh found him. Then his mother got to take care of him again."

Review Questions, The Exodus from Egypt

How many plagues did God send on Egypt? *Ten*

Did the pharaoh finally let the Israelites go? *Yes*

What happened when they got to the Red Sea? *The water parted* OR *God parted the water* OR *Moses parted the water.*

What was this great escape from Egypt called? *The Exodus*

Where did the Israelites go next? *Back to Canaan!*

Narration Exercise, The Exodus from Egypt

Ask the child to tell you about the Israelite flight from Egypt. Prompt her to use the word "Exodus." Acceptable narrations might include:

"The Israelites were in Egypt. The pharaoh didn't want to let them go, so God made them have plagues. Then they left Egypt. This was called the Exodus." OR

"Israel was in Egypt. They were slaves. Moses led them out of Egypt to Canaan. They went across the Red Sea. This was the Exodus."

Additional History Reading

Exodus from Egypt, by Mary Auld (Franklin Watts, 2000). A simple and straightforward
    retelling of the Exodus story, told on a level that most children can read independently. (RA, but
    IR for children who are not yet reading independently)

Exodus, by Brian Wildsmith (Eerdmans, 1999). Another simple retelling; the sentences are
    more difficult than those in the Auld book, but the illustrations are spectacular. (RA)

Israel (Countries of the World) by Frederick Fisher (Gareth Stevens, 2000). A simple guide to the Israel today, with a brief glance backwards at Israel's history as a nation. (RA, and some of the text you'll want to skip altogether because of complexity)

Eyewitness: Bible Lands, by Jonathan N. Tubb (DK Publishing, 2000). A guide to the geography, customs, and history of Israel. Much of the text is too difficult for elementary children, but the pictures are beautiful. (RA)

Corresponding Literature Suggestions

Moses, by Leonard Fisher (Holiday House, 1995). The complete story of Moses' life, with the beautiful, full-color illustrations Fisher is famous for. Includes a map and Moses' family tree. (RA)

Moses Parts the Sea, by Theresa Morin (Barbour & Co., 2000). Simplistic text and cartoonish drawings – but most children can read this independently, so it may be worth your while. (IR)

The Passover Journey: A Seder Companion, by Barbara Diamond Goldin (Viking, 1994). A Wonderful retelling of the story of Israel in Egypt, including the ten plagues and the Exodus, along with the story of the first Passover. (RA)

Exodus, by Miriam Chaikin (Holiday House, 1987). Another retelling of the Israelite exodus from Egypt, with interesting pictures full of movement. (RA)

Map Work (Student Page 34)

1. Using the map from Chapter Twelve, draw a line from Egypt up to Canaan. The Israelites fled from slavery in Egypt up to Canaan, the land God promised to Abraham.
2. Color in the Red Sea with a blue crayon.

Coloring Page (Student Page 38)
Moses Parting the Sea

Optional Coloring Page Activity: Puzzle

Materials:

       completed color page

       cardboard

       glue

       scissors

       pen

Directions:

1. Turn completed color page over and cover entire surface with glue. Glue the color page onto a piece of cardboard or construction paper.
2. Let dry completely.
3. Turn picture over and draw jigsaw lines on the back of the construction paper. Cut out the shapes.
4. Reassemble the puzzle.

Projects

Craft Project: Make Baby Moses's Basket

Materials:

       newspaper

       scissors

       glue or glue stick, tape or stapler

paints and brushes

Directions:

1. Take 8 sheets of 13 ½" X 22" newspaper and roll each sheet into a tight tube. Start at the long edge. Glue the open edge to the rest of the tube and flatten the roll. These will be the reeds for your basket.

2. Lay four of the reeds side by side on the table. Weave the remaining four through the first four. Manipulate the strips until they fit tightly together and form a bottom for the basket. Fold the leftover ends of the reeds up to form the sides or spokes of your basket.

3. Cut newspaper sheets into four 11" X 27" rectangles. Roll these into tight tubes starting with the long end first. Tape or staple the end of a reed to the bottom of a spoke reed. Weave the reed in and out of the spokes working your way around the basket.

4. Tuck the end behind a spoke and fasten with glue or stapler. Weave in the other reeds, working your way up and around the basket. Fold the leftover tops of the spokes into the basket and tuck them behind a reed.

5. Now paint your basket inside and out. A coat or two of polyurethane will preserve your basket.

Craft Project: Make a Red Sea Diorama

Materials:

> large shoebox
> construction paper and tissue paper
> crayons and markers
> glue and tape
> string, scissors
> small rocks and clipart
> small plastic figures (plastic soldiers will do in a pinch!)

Directions:

1. Decorate the inside of your shoebox to look like the Red Sea — glue blue construction paper onto the walls of your box, or color them blue with markers (or paint).

2. Add brown paper on the shoebox bottom, for the sea floor.

3. Glue or tape down a few rocks on your sea floor. Draw fish on the walls and floor, if you want to.

4. Glue the feet of the small plastic figures in a line down the middle of the shoebox. These are the Israelites, walking through the sea. (If you use plastic soldiers, you might want to cut or twist their weapons off!)

5. Cut a small square hole in one end of the shoebox, to use for a peephole.

6. Cut a larger square hole in the far end of the shoebox. Glue or tape one layer of tissue paper across it. (This allows light to come in.)

7. Put the shoebox lid on. Now hold the shoebox up to a light and peer in. You'll see an underwater scene!

Activity Project: Moses and the Ten Plagues Stickerbook

Materials:

> colored pencils
> scissors
> Bible
> photocopy of "Somewhere in Egypt" page (Student Page 39) – you may want to have this laminated) contact paper (available at office supply stores)
> photocopy of the three sticker pages (Student Pages 40-42), copied onto label sheets such as Avery's Removable Laser Labels (8 ½" x 11" full sheet). These can be found at office supply

stores or on the web at http://www.vikingop.com.

Directions:

1. Color the "Somewhere in Egypt" page with colored pencils. Cover it with contact paper when it is finished. (Optional: when it is finished, have it laminated in thick plastic at a copy store such as Kinko's. This is a cheap and simple procedure.)

2. Read through the appropriate sections of the Biblical story (Exodus 2-15; try a modern translation such as the New International Version or a children's version such as the Living Bible). As you read, follow the directions on the sticker pages. Cut out each sticker and place it on the "Somewhere in Egypt" page, as directed.

NOTE: The Avery Removable Labels work best with this project, although the regular Avery Labels will also do. Make sure you photocopy onto the laser labels and not the ink jet labels, as the ink jet copy will peel off. The tenth plague does not have a sticker. This plague was a very somber one, which the Israelites remembered long after it happened, and you should use your own discretion in explaining this plague to small children. Read Exodus 11-12:35 to hear about the end of the plagues and the beginning of the Hebrew nation.

Activity Project: Famine Experiment

(Please note, this experiment will take a few weeks!)

Discuss the famine in Canaan. Ask the child to explain why there was a shortage of food, why animals might have died, etc.

Materials:

>   Two small disposable containers
>   Potting soil
>   Handful of bean seeds

Directions:

1. Cut a few drain holes in the bottom of the containers. Mark one container with a W and one with an F. The one marked W stands for water. The one marked F stands for famine.

2. Fill containers with potting soil.

3. Plant a couple of bean seeds per container.

4. Place both containers on a tray and leave in a warm location.

5. Water the W container frequently. Water the F container no more than once a week, adding only a small amount of water.

6. After a few weeks, discuss the differences in the plants and why there are differences.

CHAPTER FIFTEEN
The Phoenicians

UBWH 50-51, *UILE* 144-145
KIHOW 56-57, KHE 28-29

Review Questions, Phoenician Traders

Where did the Phoenicians live? *In Canaan*

What were they good at? *Sailing their boats*

The Phoenicians made glass. Do you remember what two things they made glass from? *Sand and lye*

What special way of shaping glass did the Phoenicians invent? *Glass blowing*

What did they make their purple dye from? *Snails*

Why was purple called "the color of kings"? *Because it was so expensive*

Narration Exercise, Phoenician Traders

Ask the child to list four things that the Phoenicians sold to other countries. Acceptable answers include: cedar trees, logs, beautiful furniture, salt, dried fish, embroidered cloth, tin, metals, glass , purple dye and purple cloth.

Review Questions, The Founding of Carthage

What is a colony? *Prompt child for the answer: a little settlement of people.*

Do you remember the name of the little Phoenician colony that grew into a big city? *Carthage*

What queen helped to start Carthage? *Dido*

Why did Dido have to leave her home? *She was afraid of her brother.*

Why did Dido want to start the city of Carthage near the water? *So that ships would visit her city and trade with her*

Narration Exercise, The Founding of Carthage

Ask the child, "How did Dido use the bull-hide to get the land she wanted?" An acceptable answer might be, "She told the man who owned the land that she only wanted enough to go under a bull hide. Then she cut it up into lots of small pieces and laid it all around a big piece of land."

Additional History Reading

Eyewitness Anthologies: Ancient Civilizations, by James, Pearson and Tubb (Dorling Kindersley, 1998). This book contains one section ("The Phoenicians," pp. 18-19) that includes pictures of artifacts from ancient Phoenicia (seal, pots, motifs, glassware, etc.).

Ancient Arts Stained Glass: Create Five Original Designs Inspired by Masterpieces from Around the World, by Sarah Brown (Running Press, 1999). More activity than reading, and you'll probably have to order this (the cover price is $19.95), but this book/kit includes fascinating information on ancient glassmaking. (RA – do with the help of an adult)

Fire Into Ice: Adventures in Glass Making, by James Houston (Tundra Books, 1998). One craftsman's process of making glass sculptures. Beautiful pictures. (RA)

Corresponding Literature Suggestions

In Search of a Homeland: The Story of the Aeneid, by Penelope Lively, illus. Ian Andrews (Delacorte Press, 2001). Aeneas meets Dido, among other adventures; you may not want to read all of the text to a young child, but the illustrations are lovely. (RA)

Map Work (Student Page 43)

1. On the black line map provided, find the Phoenician cities of Tyre and Carthage and circle their names using a red pencil.

2. With a green pencil, color in the areas that were controlled by the Phoenicians (these areas are marked by the dotted lines).

3. Use a blue pencil to color in the Mediterranean Sea. This was where the Phoenician sailors did most of their trading. (The solid lines show the paths along the sea that the Phoenicians used to sail to their colonies.)

NOTE: This map is reprinted from Terri Johnson's "Blackline Maps of Ancient History" set, with her kind permission. For a full set of blackline maps, coordinated to *The Story of the World*, visit Knowledge Quest Maps at http://www.knowledgequestmaps.com, or contact Knowledge Quest at 7722 SE 282ⁿᵈ Avenue, Gresham, OR 97080 (503/663-1210). You can also purchase these maps from Peace Hill Press at http://www.peacehillpress.com.

Coloring Page (Student Page 44)

A Phoenician Ship

Projects

Craft Project: Make Pretend Colored Glass

Materials:

      wax paper

      crayon shavings – red, blue and yellow

      colored threads

      a picture (see below)

      iron, ironing board and old newspapers

Directions:

1. Choose a picture to encase in your project. This could be a drawing, a picture from a magazine, a coloring page, a photocopied illustration from your favorite book, or even a sticker or stamp.

2. Cut out two identical shapes from the wax paper. The shape can be anything of your choosing- a circle, a square, a rectangle, or even a hexagon. Be sure that the shapes of wax paper are larger than the picture.

3. Place one piece of wax paper on the table. Place the picture on the wax paper. Add the crayon shavings and colored threads and then place other piece of wax paper over the top.

4. Set up the ironing board and place a layer or two of newspaper over the ironing board. Place colored glass project on the newspaper and then add more layers of newspaper. Using a low level of heat, iron project (carefully) until crayon shavings have melted. This step needs to be done by an adult.

5. When project has cooled, trim up any rough edges. Hang in window or put in history notebook.

Craft Project: Make Purple Dye

The Phoenicians used snails, but you can use fruits and vegetables for a short cut!

Method One:

    Materials:

      head of purple cabbage

      alum (at most grocery stores)

    Directions:

    1. Chop the cabbage into small pieces.

    2. In large saucepan, boil cabbage for about an hour.

    3. After the cabbage is partially cooled, drain colored water from cabbage. Discard cabbage. Water will be turquoise in color.

    4. Add about a tablespoon of alum to the colored water. You may need more or less depending upon the quantity of water. This will turn the colored water into a nice shade of purple.

    5. Use the dye to color any cotton material – a shirt, cotton yarn to use in a project, a handkerchief.

    6. Try to set the dye using cold salt water. (This will not always work and color will fade.)

Method Two:

    Materials:

      1 package of frozen blueberries

    Directions:

1. In saucepan, boil whole blueberries for about an hour.
2. After partially cooled, drain colored water from blueberries. Discard berries.
3. Colored water is ready for dyeing.

Optional: Use dye to make a **Colored Pasta Necklace**
Materials:

dye water from cabbage or blueberries

string or yarn

elbow macaroni or pasta shapes (such as hearts or Christmas trees – which are available during the holiday seasons)

Directions:
1. In bowl, pour a cup or two of the dye and add a handful of pasta. Keep pasta in the dye until it has changed its color. This will take a few minutes.
2. Remove pasta from dye and set to dry in a safe place.
3. Add more pasta to the dye and continue process until there is enough colored pasta to make a necklace.
4. After pasta is completely dried, string onto a length of yarn that is long enough to easily fit over child's head.
5. Securely tie the ends together.

Cooking Project: Make Phoenician Bread (Pita Bread)
Ingredients:

6 cups Flour

2 tsp. Salt

1 T Yeast

2 cups Warm water

1 T Honey

(Some butter and extra flour for preparation)

Directions:
1. Let the yeast dissolve in the warm water. Stir the honey in the water and yeast mixture. Then add the salt and flour, slowly. Stir until it becomes tough to mix.
2. Put the dough on a surface lightly covered with flour.
3. Knead for about 10 minutes. Then place the dough in a buttered bowl (make sure all sides are buttered). Cover the bowl with plastic wrap or a damp dishtowel.
4. Let dough rise for about 2 hours. Should double in size.
5. After punching down the dough, shape it into 10 balls.
6. Set them aside for about 15 minutes, then shape into approx. 6 or 7-inch round shapes (like mini pizza crusts).
7. Preheat oven to 450 degrees. Place dough on a cookie sheet. Bake for 10 to 12 minutes on the lowest rack in the oven. Makes about 10 Pita Bread rounds.

REVIEW CARDS
Chapters Twelve, Thirteen, Fourteen, Fifteen
(Student Page 45)

CHAPTER SIXTEEN
The Return of Assyria

UBWH 50-51, UILE 144-145
KIHOW 56-57, KHE 28-29

Review Questions, Ashurbanipal's Attack

Can you tell me two countries that Assyria conquered? *Egypt, Canaan [the answers Mesopotamia, Babylon, and Asia Minor are also acceptable].*

What did Ashurbanipal like to do for fun? *Hunt lions with bows and arrows*

What kind of shields did the Assyrians use? *Basket shields tied together with leather*

How did the Assyrian soldiers break through city walls? *They built ramps out of dirt and pushed wooden towers on wheels up the ramps.*

Did the people in the Assyrian empire like their king? *No, they hated him for his cruelty.*

Narration Exercise, Ashurbanipal's Attack

"The Assyrians wanted to make their empire big again. They conquered everyone around them. Their king knew how to break into cities with walls. The Assyrians were very cruel to the cities they beat."

Review Questions, The Library of Nineveh

What city did Ashurbanipal live in? *Nineveh*

Can you tell me two things that Ashurbanipal did to make Nineveh beautiful? *He built a beautiful palace, decorated the gates of the city, planted gardens, made sculptures.*

Why did Ashurbanipal decide to collect a library? *So that people would remember him*

Were the library books made out of paper? *No, they were made out of clay.*

Some of the clay tablets had the history of Assyria written on them. Can you tell me two other kinds of writing from Ashurbanipal's library? *Stories, prayers, facts about the sun, moon and sky, medicine, law, and science*

Can we still read Ashurbanipal's library today? *Yes, some of the clay tablets can still be read today.*

Narration Exercise, The Library of Nineveh

"Ashurbanipal lived in Nineveh. It was a beautiful city with gardens in it. He wanted to be remembered. He made a library out of clay tablets." OR "The first library was in Nineveh. The king collected stories and other writings. He kept them in big rooms so that people could read them a long time afterwards."

Additional History Reading

Ancient Egyptians and Their Neighbors: An Activity Guide, by Marian Broida (Chicago Review Press, 1999). This book contains a few activities related to ancient Assyria – very little is available for elementary children on this subject. (RA)

Corresponding Literature Suggestions

The Story of Jonah, by Mary Auld (Franklin Watts, 1999). Jonah was sent to Assyria's capital city, Nineveh, but he didn't want to go! (IR)

Illustrated Jewish Bible for Children, by Selina Hastings (DK Publishing, 1997). A beautifully illustrated version of Jonah's journey to Nineveh.

The Seven Voyages of Sinbad the Sailor, by John Yeoman, illus. Quentin Blake (Margaret McElderry, 1997). Sinbad's mythical voyages took place around the time of Nineveh's height. (RA)

Map Work (Student Page 46)

1. On the black line map provided, locate Ashurbanipal's city, Nineveh, and circle the name in red.
2. Use a green crayon or pencil to color in the area that Ashurbanipal ruled under the name Assyria.
3. Use a blue crayon to color in all of the seas. See if you can read their names.

Coloring Page (Student Page 47)

Using your crayons, color the picture of King Ashurbanipal fighting a lion. This picture was based on a relief found in his palace.

Projects

Craft Project: Make an Assyrian Siege Tower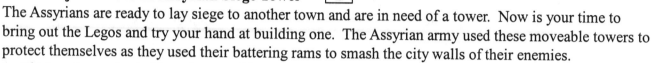

The Assyrians are ready to lay siege to another town and are in need of a tower. Now is your time to bring out the Legos and try your hand at building one. The Assyrian army used these moveable towers to protect themselves as they used their battering rams to smash the city walls of their enemies.

1. First, make a wheeled base by attaching your Lego wheels to a flat Lego base.
2. Next, build a three-sided tower on top of the base. The siege tower was built on a wheeled base and had a three-sided tower built on the front portion of the vehicle. The archers stood inside the tower and shot arrows as the tower was pushed closer and closer to the city walls.
3. Add a battering ram — a long Lego, sticking out from the front of your tower, as the battering ram.

Writing Project: Make a Book for Ashurbanipal's Library

Ashurbanipal was the first king to start collecting stories and putting then in one place, his library at Nineveh. You can make a book too and add it to his collection.

Materials:

    2 sheets blank paper (8 ½ x 11)
    1 sheet of colored paper
    Markers, crayons, stickers and glitter
    Length of ribbon or cord

Directions:

1. Take two sheets of blank paper (8 ½ x 11) and fold them in half.
2. Take a sheet of colored construction paper and fold it in half also. Place the folded blank paper inside the folded colored paper.
3. Punch two holes along the folded edge, spacing them about 3" apart. Get a piece of ribbon, thread it through the holes and tie a bow. This will help keep your book together. If you prefer, you can place three staples along the folded edge instead.
4. On the outside cover of your book, write a title. For example it could be titled "My Favorite Things."
5. Ancient peoples often told stories through pictures. Once that is done, get out the markers, crayons, stickers and glitter and draw away!

CHAPTER SEVENTEEN
Babylon Takes Over Again!

UBWH 58-59, *UILE* 150-151
KIHOW 70-71, *KHE* 36-37

Review Questions, Nebuchadnezzar's Madness

What did the Assyrians do to Babylon when they conquered it? *They flooded it (destroyed it).*

What did the Babylonians do to Nineveh when they conquered Assyria? *They destroyed it and smashed some of Ashurbanipal's clay tablets.*

Was the Babylonian empire as big as the Assyrian empire? *No*

Do you remember the name of Babylon's most famous king? He built the Ishtar Gate in Babylon. *Nebuchadnezzar*

What happened to Nebuchadnezzar after he thought he was a god? *He went mad (thought he was an animal).*

Did he get better? *Yes*

Narration Exercise, Nebuchadnezzar's Madness

"Assyria was destroyed by Babylon. The king of Babylon thought he was a god. Then he went mad and ate grass like a cow. Finally he got better again." OR

"Nebuchadnezzar was the king of Babylon. He was a great king, but he thought he was greater than God. So he lost his mind. He thought he was an animal. When he said that he was only a man, he got better."

Review Questions, The Hanging Gardens of Babylon

Why was Nebuchadnezzar afraid of Persia? *He thought Persia would attack him.*

Why was Persia afraid of Nebuchadnezzar? *The Persians thought Nebuchadnezzar would attack them.*

Why was Amytis homesick? *Because she missed the mountains.*

What did Nebuchadnezzar build to make Amytis happy? *The Hanging Gardens of Babylon.*

We've studied two of the Seven Wonders of the Ancient World. What two have we learned about? *The Great Pyramid and the Hanging Gardens of Babylon.*

Narration Exercise, The Hanging Gardens of Babylon

"Nebuchadnezzar married a princess who missed her home. He built her a big garden on a hill to make her happy. It was called the Hanging Gardens of Babylon." OR

Ask your child to draw a picture of the Hanging Gardens of Babylon and to describe the picture to you. Write the description on the bottom of the picture.

Additional History Reading

Great Wonders of the World, by Russell Ash (DK Publishing, 2000). The ancient wonders, including the Hanging Gardens of Babylon, beautifully illustrated and explained; also includes modern and natural wonders of the world. (RA)

The Seven Wonders of the Ancient World, by Reg Cox and Neil Morris, illus. James Field (Chelsea House, 2000). Links the Seven Wonders to broader cultural developments, including those in Babylon. (RA)

Literature Suggestions

Forty Fortunes: A Tale of Iran , by Aaron Shepard (Clarion Books, 1999). A well-intentioned fortune-telling peasant unwittingly tricks a band of local thieves into returning the king's stolen treasure; set in the area of ancient Babylonia. (RA)

1001 Arabian Nights (*Oxford Story Collections*), by Geraldine McCaughrean, illus. Rosamund Fowler (Oxford University Press Childrens' Books, 2000). A long and fascinating collection of stories from the ancient Near East. (RA)

King Nimrod's Tower, by Leon Garfield (Lothrop, Lee & Shepard, 1982). Against a background of the building of the Tower of Babel, a boy tries to train a stray dog—and God watches over all. **Out of print; check your library for availability.** (RA)

The King in the Garden, by Leon Garfield (Lothrop, Lee & Shepard, 1984). A little girl named Abigail finds mad King Nebuchadnezzar eating the flowers in her garden and helps him return to his palace and to God. **Out of print; check your library for availability**. (RA)

Map Work (Student Page 48)

1. On the black line map provided, locate Nebuchadnezzer's city of Babylon and circle it in red.
2. Use a green crayon or pencil to color in the area that Nebuchadnezzar ruled under the name Babylon (the area within the dashed lines).
3. Find the city of Jerusalem, which was destroyed by Nebuchadnezzar, and circle it in red.

Coloring Page (Student Page 49)

This picture of the Babylonian god of creation, Marduk, was based on an ancient Babylonian relief.

Projects

Art Project: Draw a Picture of the Hanging Gardens of Babylon

You have just finished reading the story of why Nebuchadnezzar built the Hanging Gardens in Babylon. But no one knows what the gardens actually looked like. We only know of their existence because we have copies of ancient Greek and Rome texts that describe them. Many people believe that the gardens were made up of terraces stacked one on top of another. It probably resembled a ziggurat with plants! Trees, shrubs and flowers were brought in from all around the vast empire and planted in the garden. The finished result was a magnificent green emerald in the desert landscape.

Use your crayons and a great deal of imagination to draw a picture of how you think the Hanging Gardens of Babylon looked. Your drawing just might be the one that best depicts how the gardens really looked so long ago.

Science Project: Build a Babylonian Mountain Garden
Materials:

dirt, water and large bucket
large square of cardboard
grass seeds
wild flower seeds (optional)

Directions:
1. Fill a large bucket with dirt. Add water and mix with your hands until you form a wet, but not mushy, clay-dirt mixture. Let the mixture sit in the bucket for a day.
2. Place a stiff piece of cardboard (about three times larger than the mouth of the bucket) on top of the bucket. Place one hand on top of the cardboard and the other hand under the bucket. Then turn you hands over quickly so that the dirt will slide out of the bucket onto the cardboard. Put the cardboard and bucket on the ground. Slowly lift the bucket off of your mountain. Use your hands to pat down any dirt that didn't stay formed to your mountain.
3. Sprinkle grass seeds all over the mountain (follow the seed pack instructions). Use your hands to gently press the seeds to the sides of your mountain, so that they will adhere. If you want, you can sprinkle wild flower seeds on the top.
4. Be sure to gently water your mountain daily and keep it outside in a sunny place. Behold, a Babylonian Mountain Garden

CHAPTER EIGHTEEN
Life in Early Crete

UBWH 24-27, UILE 124-127
KIHOW 38-39, KHE 16

Review Questions, Bull-jumpers and Sailors

Why did the Minoans hold bull-jumping festivals? *To honor the gods of Crete*

Were the bull-jumpers treated well? *Yes; they were given food, beautiful clothes, jewelry, and gold.*

Was bull-jumping dangerous? *Yes; bull-jumpers were often killed.*

What did pirates do in the Mediterranean Sea? *They attacked and robbed people who tried to sail on the sea.*

What did the Minoans build to get rid of the pirates? *Ships*

What is a navy? *An army that fights on water*

Narration Exercise, Bull-Jumpers and Sailors

 "The Minoans lived on Crete. They jumped over bulls to worship their gods. The king of the Minoans wanted a navy. He built ships to drive pirates away."

Review Questions, King Minos and the Minotaur

What kind of monster was the Minotaur? *Half man and half bull*

Why did King Minos tell Athens to send him seven girls and boys every year? *To feed them to the Minotaur*

Where did the Minotaur live? *Under the palace, in a maze*

How did Theseus get out of the maze? *With a ball of wool that Ariadne gave him*

What color sail was Theseus supposed to put on his ship? *A white sail*

What happened when he forgot to put on the white sail? *His father jumped off a cliff.*

The father of Theseus was called King Aegeus. What sea was named after him? *The Aegean Sea*

Narration Exercise, King Minos and the Minotaur

Ask the child to retell the story of Theseus and the Minotaur to you. Aim for a narration of 4-6 sentences; if the child wants to include every detail, suggest a more condensed version of the story. (For example, if the child says, "Theseus went down to the seaside. He found out that people were being sent to Athens for the Minotaur to eat. He said he wanted to go. His father didn't want him to go," suggest, "We could just say, "Theseus wanted to go to Athens, even though his father told him not to.")

OR

Ask the child to draw a scene from the story and to describe the picture to you. Write this description at the bottom of the page.

Review Questions, The Mysterious End of the Minoans

Why did the Minoans leave Crete? *Because a volcano erupted nearby.*

What island did the volcano erupt on? *Thera*

What happened to Thera? *It sank beneath the sea.*

What did the volcano do to the air and land of Crete? *A tidal wave hit Crete; ash, dust, and rock covered the fields and towns, so that people couldn't breathe and crops couldn't grow.*

Narration Exercise, The Mysterious End of the Minoans

Ask the child to tell you why the Minoans had to leave Crete. Acceptable narrations might include, "A volcano erupted near Crete. All the people on Crete had to leave." OR

"A volcano blew up the island of Thera. The ash and the dust fell all over Crete, and the people couldn't grow crops any more. So they had to leave."

Additional Reading

In Search of Knossos: The Quest for the Minotaur's Labyrinth, by Giovanni Caselli (Peter Bedrick Books, 1999). Some of this text is too detailed for elementary children, but the illustrations and captions alone give an interesting account of ancient Cretan life.

The Minotaur of Knossos: A Journey Through Time by Roberta Angeletti (Oxford University Press; 1999). Information about ancient Crete mixed with the Minotaur story.

Where Was Atlantis? by Brian Innes (Raintree/Steck Vaughn, 1998). The legend of Atlantis may have been based on the destruction of the island of Thera; this book (along with others that may be at your library) discusses this factual foundation. (RA)

Ancient Aegean [videorecording], produced and directed by JWM Productions (Schlessinger Media, 1998.) Join archaeologist Arizona Smith and a young detective in training as they explore the mysteries of the ancient Minoan civilization. You can buy this video from Amazon.com, but check your local library first.

Corresponding Literature Suggestions

Theseus and the Minotaur, by Warwick Hutton (Holiday House, 1992) A very simple retelling. (RA)

Monster in the Maze: The Story of the Minotaur (All Aboard Reading, Level 2), by Stephanie Spinner (Grossett and Dunlap, 2001). This version can be read independently by advanced readers, and even beginners should be able to read a page or two alone. (IR/RA)

Greek Myths, by Geraldine McCaughrean (Margaret K. McElderry Books, 1993). A slightly more complex (and scary) telling of Theseus and the Minotaur, along with other ancient Greek myths. (RA)

Atlantis: The Legend of a Lost City, by Christina Balit (Henry Holt, 2000). A retelling of the ancient Greek legend about the creation of Atlantis by Zeus, and its sinking to the bottom of the sea. (RA)

Map Work (Student Page 50)

1. On your blackline map, color the Aegean Sea in blue.
2. Find the island of Crete and color it yellow.
2. Find Athens and circle it in green. Draw a line from Athens to Crete. This is the path that Theseus took!
3. Can you find the island of Thera? Circle it in red to remind you that a volcano erupted there!

Coloring Page (Student Page 51)

Projects

Activity Project: Maze (Student Page 52) C

Help Theseus slay the Minotaur — color the maze and help Theseus find his way through the labyrinth to the Minotaur at the center.

Craft Project: Build Your Own Labyrinth
Materials:
    cardboard sheet
    clay (variation: Legos or building blocks)

Directions:
1. Roll the clay into long, skinny (snake-like) pieces.
2. Place the clay on the cardboard to make your own Labyrinth.
3. Tape a piece of string at the start and wind it through your Labyrinth so you can find your way out.
Variation: Use your Legos or blocks instead of clay.

Craft Project: Build a Minoan Ship: *Note: Archaeologists disagree over whether most Minoan boats had sails.*
Suggested Materials (many different things will work for this project):
    styrofoam or plastic container (takeout, or from grocery store meat counter)
    styrofoam floral arranger
    styrofoam plate
    small wooden dowel
    hot glue
    paints (optional)
Directions:
1. Wash the container well. This is the hull of your boat. If you plan to paint it, do that now.
2. Glue a 1½-inch thick piece of styrofoam floral arranger to the inside floor of the hull. This will hold the mast up.
3. Push the dowel rod into the styrofoam floral arranger and glue. This is the mast for your boat.
4. Cut a rectangular shape sail from the styrofoam plate.
5. Poke a small hole in the top and bottom of the sail. Gently push the dowel rod through the bottom hole then through the top hole.

Take this project a step further and make some oars for your ship.
Materials:
    thin dowel rod or 3 bamboo skewers
    1 package of "Woodsies," small, medium and large circles, teardrops and ovals (available at craft stores)
    wood glue
Directions:
1. Cut the dowel rod or skewers into 6-inch lengths. These are the oars.

2. Glue a large oval Woodsie on the end of each oar to make the paddle end.

3. Carefully poke three evenly spaced holes on each side of the hull.

4. Poke the ends of the oars through the holes so the paddles are outside the hull.

5. Glue a small oval Woodsie on the end of each oar for a handle.

Craft Project: Make an Erupting Volcano

(a little messy, a lot of fun)

Materials:

    plaster of paris or self-hardening clay

    8oz drink bottle

    pie tin or plastic plant saucer

    water proof paint

    baking soda and vinegar

    red and yellow food coloring

    liquid dish soap

    funnel

    water

Directions

1. Spread newspapers and wax paper over work area.

2. Mix plaster of paris with just enough water to make thick clay.

3. Working quickly, shape the plaster of paris or clay around the bottle to resemble a mountain. Use small amounts of water to smooth the surface. Let volcano dry completely.

4. Paint your volcano, let it dry, and then put it in the pie plate or plant saucer.

5. Use the funnel to pour ¼ cup of water and 1 or 2 tablespoons of baking soda into the bottle. Add about three drops of yellow food coloring.

6. Mix red food coloring and liquid soap with ½ cup of vinegar.

*7. **Quickly** pour vinegar mixture into the bottle and stand back!*

What's happening here? The baking soda reacts with the vinegar and carbon dioxide gas is produced. As the gas bubbles build up in the bottle the liquid or "lava" is forced out. Experiment with different mixtures of the ingredients to create different effects.

Take this one step further and make an ancient city out of clay to place at the foot of your volcano.

CHAPTER NINETEEN
The Early Greeks

UBWH 42-45, UILE 128-131
KIHOW 40-41, KHE 17

Review Questions, The Mycenaeans

What were the people who came from Greece to conquer Crete called? *The Mycenaeans.*

What were the Mycenaeans good at? *Fighting.*

Where did the Myceneans build colonies? *Around the Aegean Sea.*

Can you tell me a little bit about how the Mycenean Greeks lived? *Prompt the child if necessary for the following answers: they lived in houses, had jobs, went to school.*

Narration Exercise, The Mycenaeans

"After the volcano erupted near Crete, other people took over. They were called Mycenaeans. They used helmets and shields and chariots to fight."

Review Questions, The Greek Dark Ages

How did the barbarians live? *Prompt the child if necessary for the following answers: they wandered around, couldn't read or write, and spent their time fighting other people.*

What did the Mycenaean Greeks have that made them such strong fighters? *Bronze weapons and chariots*

What kind of weapons did the barbarians have? *Iron weapons that were stronger than bronze weapons.*

When the Greeks and the barbarians fought, who won? *The barbarians.*

Do you remember why we call this time the Dark Ages? *Because the barbarians didn't leave us any written history or records about the time that they lived in Greece.*

Narration Exercise, The Greeek Dark Ages

If necessary, prompt the child to use the phrase "Dark Ages."

"The Greeks thought they were strong. But barbarians were stronger. They took over Greece. This was the 'Dark Ages,' when they didn't write anything." OR

"Greeks lived like regular people. Barbarians wandered around fighting. The barbarians conquered the Greeks, but they didn't keep histories. This was the 'Dark Ages.'"

Additional History Reading

Growing Up in Ancient Greece by Chris Chelepi (Troll, 1994). Presents an interesting, simplified view of ancient Greek society. (RA)

Footsteps in Time: The Greeks by Sally Hewitt (Children's Press, 1998). Introduces young children to ancient Greece using crafts and activities. (RA)

How Would You Survive as an Ancient Greek? by Fiona MacDonald (Franklin Watts, Incorporated, 1996). Presents an account of everyday life in Ancient Greece. (RA)

Ancient Greeks at a Glance by John Malam (Peter Bedrick Books, 1998). This site-seeing guide to Ancient Greece uses simple sentences and concepts. (RA, some parts may be IR for advanced readers)

Ancient Greece (Nature Company Discover Libraries), by Louise Schofield (Time Life, 1997). Spectacular pictures and information about the earliest Greeks. (RA)

Corresponding Literature Suggestions

Usborne Greek Myths for Young Children by Heather Amery (Usborne, 1999). Simplified retelling of Greek myths. (RA, possible IR for advanced readers)

D'Aulaire's Book of Greek Myths by Edgar Parin d'Aulaire (Bantam Doubleday Dell, 1962). A classic in its own right, this introduction to the gods and goddesses of Ancient Greece has beautiful illustrations by Caldecott Award winners.

The Trojan Horse, by Emily Little (Random House, 1988). The Greek assault on Troy took place during the Mycenean period; this retelling can be read independently by strong readers. (IR, RA for beginners)

The Trojan Horse, by Warwick Hutton (Margaret K. McElderry Books, 1987). This picture-book retelling is **out of print**, but still remains a classic (and is stocked by most libraries). (RA)

Map Work (Student Page 50)

1. Look at your map from the last chapter. Find the cities of Mycenae, Thebes and Athens.
2. Choose your favorite color, and color Greece.

Coloring Page (Student Page 53)

This picture of a warrior in his chariot is based on a fresco found in Pylos.

Projects

Craft Project: Make an Easy Mycenaean Helmet

Materials:

cardboard box the size of your head

scissors

paints

Directions:

1. Cut eyeholes so you can see out of your helmet when it's on your head.
2. Paint the box bronze.

3. Get ready for battle!

Craft Project: Make a Realistic Mycenaean Helmet

Some Mycenaean helmets were made of bronze. Bronze is a metal made by mixing tin and copper.

Materials:
>   old cap with bill cut off
>   heavy cardboard
>   paper mache clay (Celluclay, available at craft stores)
>   masking tape, scissors
>   sealer paint (optional)
>   bronze paint
>   polyurethane (optional)

Note: Make this helmet a little too large all the way around to allow for shrinkage.

Directions:

1. Put the cap on and attach cardboard to the bottom of the cap from the back of your head to your ears. Attach another section of cardboard around your face. Use wedges of cardboard to attach the back section to the front. Make sure the bottom of the helmet is a little bigger around than the top.

2. With a pin, mark places for eyeholes and mouth. After you cut out the mouth and eyeholes, it should look like this.

3. Cover the outside of the cap with strips of masking tape.

4. Stuff the cap with tightly wadded up newspaper or plastic bags and prop up your helmet so it is not touching the table.

5. Mix the paper mache clay according to directions and spread over the outside of helmet. Use water on your hands to help smooth the clay. The surface will have a rough hammered appearance. Let this dry completely.

6. When the outside of the helmet is completely dry, turn it over and apply paper mache clay to the inside. Do not cover the cap on the inside of the helmet. Let this dry completely.

7. Apply sealer paint (optional), then bronze paint, then polyurethane (optional) letting each coat dry completely before applying the next one.

8. Take it a step further and line your helmet like the Mycenaeans did. Glue cloth or fake fur inside. Paint gold trim around the edges. Your finished helmet will look something like this.

Craft Project: Make a Shield (to go with your helmet)

Materials:
>   cardboard
>   scissors, glue
>   paint

Directions:

1. Draw a circle or oval shape on a heavy piece of cardboard and cut it out.
2. You need two handles on the back of your shield, one for your hand to hold on to and another to put your forearm through. Lay your arm across the back of the shield and measure where the handles should go.

handles

3. Glue or tape the handles onto the shield
4. Paint and decorate your shield. (Some Mycenaean warriors painted scary faces or animals on their shields and some warriors had bronze shields.)

Craft Project: Make a simple Greek vase: C

Much of what we know about the Ancient Greeks comes from the pictures they painted on their beautiful pottery.

Materials:

    copy of vase outline (Student Page 54)

    colors and or paints

    construction paper

Directions:

1. Draw a design onto the vase outline.
2. Cut out and decorate your vase using colors, paints or construction paper.

Craft Project: Make a Realistic Greek vase:

Materials:

    7" balloon

    newspaper torn into 2" by 4" strips

    glue (white school glue or wallpaper paste)

    small plastic cup

    jar lid, foam brushes, paints

    polyurethane

Directions:

1. Blow up the balloon and tape the jar lid on the bottom so it stands upright.
2. Spread glue on the balloon with a foam brush.
3. Put strips of newspaper on the balloon and brush glue on top. Cover the entire balloon and jar lid. Continue layering newspapers and glue until you have about 6 layers of newspaper on balloon.
4. Tie a string around the knot in the balloon and hang up to dry.
5. When the vase is completely dry cut a hole in the top of the balloon and let the air out. The balloon should come right out.
6. Carefully cut a hole in the top of the vase and fit the plastic cup into the hole.
7. Cover the plastic cup with several layers of newspaper and glue. Set aside to dry.
8. Paint and decorate your vase. Spray a coat of polyurethane on your vase for durability.

REVIEW CARDS
Chapters Sixteen, Seventeen, Eighteen, Nineteen
(Student Page 55)

CHAPTER TWENTY
Greece Gets Civilized Again

UBWH 64, UILE 141, 154, 156-157
KIHOW 72, KHE 38

Review Questions, Greece Gets an Alphabet

What happened to the barbarians who lived in Greece? *They became civilized – built houses, learned how to read, etc. (any details the child wants to repeat from the lesson are fine).*

Did they kill their neighbors for fun? *No.* What did they do instead? *Wrestled, raced, danced*

Did the women go out and find food? *No, they stayed indoors.*

The barbarians were now called Greeks. They learned to read and write. Can you tell me about the letters that they used? *Ask the child to point back to some of the Greek letters and tell you what they represent.*

Narration Exercise, Greece Gets an Alphabet

Instead of a narration exercise today, help the child to write her first name (middle and last name is optional) in Greek letters. (Greek Alphabet- Appendix p. 56)

Review Questions, The Stories of Homer

What hero is the Odyssey named after? *Odysseus*

Why did Poseidon get angry at Odysseus and his men? *Because they forgot to thank him for their victory over Troy*

What was the one-eyed monster called? *A Cyclops*

How did the Greeks know the stories of Odysseus and Troy, in the days when they couldn't read and write? *They told them to their children and grandchildren*

Who first wrote down these stories? *The poet Homer*

How did Odysseus get revenge on the Cyclops? *He blinded him/put his eye out.*

How did the men get out of the cave? *They held on to the Cyclops' sheep when he let them out in the morning.*

Why did Odysseus tell the Cyclops that his name was Noman? *So that anyone who came to rescue the Cyclops would think that no man was hurting him*

After Odysseus made fun of the Cyclops, what did the Cyclops do? *Asked Poiseidon to keep him from reaching home*

Why do you think Odysseus decided to make fun of the Cyclops? Why didn't he just sail quietly away? *Discuss this with the child. Possible answers: pride, foolishness, he wanted to boast.* Would it have been better if he'd just left without making any more noise? *Yes*

Narration Exercise, The Stories of Homer

"Odysseus and his men were headed home. They landed on an island where a monster lived. The monster ate two of the men. Odysseus tricked the monster into going to sleep and put his eye out. Then he and his men sneaked out of the cave. The Cyclops cursed Odysseus before he left." OR

"Odysseus landed on an island. A monster who lived there ate two of his men. Odysseus was trapped in the monster's cave and couldn't get out. Odysseus told the monster that his name was Noman, and then put out his eye. The monster told everyone that Noman was killing him. Then Odysseus and his men held onto the sheep to get out of the cave."

Review Questions, The First Olympic Games

What god was honored by the first Olympic games? *Zeus, the king of the gods*

What mountain was the Olympics named after? *Mount Olympus, where the gods were supposed to live*

What is a virtue? *Something good about a person*

What virtues did the Olympic Games reward? *Strength and courage*
Who was allowed to compete in the Olympic games? *Men from Greece*
Narration Exercise, The First Olympic Games
Ask the child to draw a picture of an Olympic competition. She should describe the picture to you; write the description on the bottom of the picture, and put it into the History Notebook.
OR
Ask the child to tell you three things about the Olympic games. Write them down and put them into the History Notebook. Sample narrations might include:
"The Olympics started in ancient Greece. They were held to worship Zeus. Only men could go." OR "The Olympics started because two cities made peace. They were held every four years. The winners got olive branches for medals."

Additional History Reading

I Wonder Why Greeks Built Temples and Other Questions About Ancient Greece by Fiona McDonald (Kingfisher, 1997). Presents information in a question-and-answer format using double-page spreads and large, full-color illustration.

Count Your Way through Greece by Jim Haskins and Kathleen Benson (Chrorhoda Books, 1996). The authors use the numbers one through ten to explain Greek history and culture. (RA)

The Ancient Greek Olympics, by Richard Woff (Oxford University Press Childrens' Books, 2000). Describes the five-day celebration of the ancient Greeks, comparing it to the modern Olympic festival. Written for first and second graders; short and simple. (RA)

The Original Olympics (Ancient Greece), by Stewart Ross (Peter Bedrick Books, 1999). This is a slightly more detailed and longer look at the Olympic games; Ross uses stories to move the fact-filled narrative along. (RA)

Footsteps in Time: The Greeks, by Sally Hewitt (Children's Press, 1998). Introduces young children to ancient Greece using crafts and activities. (RA/activity)

A Coloring Book of the Trojan War: The Iliad, Vol. 2, illus. (from vase paintings of ancient Greece) by Nancy Conkle, story by John K. Anderson (Bellerophon Books, 1995). Detailed pictures based on original Greek sources; also contains some Greek text. (RA/activity)

Start Exploring Bulfinch's Mythology, by Steven Zorn, illus. Helen I. Driggs (Running Press, 1989). A fact-filled coloring book – fun to color, fun to read. (RA/activity)

Corresponding Literature Suggestions

The Librarian Who Measured the Earth, by Kathryn Lasky (Joy Street Books, 1994). Describes the life and work of Eratosthenes, the Greek geographer and astronomer who accurately measured the circumference of the Earth. (RA)

How the Greeks Won the War: Step Into Reading, by Emily Little (Random House, 1988). A retelling of the Trojan War with simple sentences and vocabulary (on a second-third grade reading level). (RA, IR for advanced readers)

Black Ships Before Troy: The Story of the Iliad, by Rosemary Sutcliff (Delacorte, 1993). A simple and beautifully illustrated (but lengthy) retelling of the Trojan War; good for a read-aloud project that extends over a couple of weeks. (RA)

The Wanderings of Odysseus: The Story of the Odyssey by Rosemary Sutcliff (Delacorte Press, 1996). Fascinating and beautifully illustrated, but long. Some scary pictures. (RA)

Run With Me, Nike! by Cassandra Case (Soundprints, 1999). This simple picture book tells the story of a young Olympic competitor in ancient times. (RA)

The First Olympic Games : A Gruesome Greek Myth With a Happy Ending, by Jean Richards, illus. Kat Thacker (Millbrook, 2000).   A mythological account of the first Olympics, written for first and second graders. (RA)

Hour of the Olympics (Magic Tree House #16), by Mary Pope Osborne (Random House, 1998). Jack and Annie go to ancient Greece, where they race against time to witness the very first Olympic Games! (RA)

The Twelve Labors of Hercules: Step Into Reading, by Marc A.Cerasini (Random House, 1997). Hercules must use his wits as well as his strength to complete the tasks that the jealous king has in store for him. (RA, IR for advanced readers)

Archimedes Takes a Bath, by Joan M. Lexau (Crowell, 1969). Young Xanthius has the job of seeing that absent-minded Archimedes eats and bathes occasionally. His success has much to do with the formulation of Archimedes' principle. **Out of print (check your local library).**

Audio Books

She and He Adventures in Mythology, by Jim Weiss (Greathall Productions, 1992). Upbeat and exciting yet deeply moving, this unique collection of myths addresses the equality of the sexes and the value of love and honor.

Galileo and the Stargazers, including: Archimedes and the Golden Crown, by Jim Weiss (Greathall Productions, 1999). Adventure, laughter, mystery...amid scientific fact.

Greek Myths, by Jim Weiss (Greathall Productions, 1997). Makes Hercules, King Midas, and Perseus and Medusa understandable to children, with strong emphasis on character over violence.

Map Work (Student Page 57)

1. On your blackline map of Greece, find the country of Greece and color it green.
2. Find Mount Olympus and circle it in red.
3. Find Troy and circle it in blue. What sea did the Greeks cross to fight against the Trojans?
4. Optional: Color all the islands of Greece your favorite color. How many islands are there?

Coloring Page (Student Page 58)
The Cyclops

Projects

Activity Project: Make Greek Instruments
The Greeks loved music and dancing. There are very few records of the songs the Greeks played but we do know about the instruments that they used because they painted pictures of them on pottery.

> **Make a Timpanon:** A timpanon is a tambourine that the Greeks used to provide rhythm. It was made from animal skin stretched tightly over a frame.
> Materials:
>> 2 Styrofoam plates or pie tins
>> glue
>> hole punch
>> ribbon
>> paints
> Directions:
> 1. Glue the two plates together at the rim, so that they form a hollow "shell."

2. Paint or decorate as desired.

3. Punch evenly spaced holes around edges of plates.

4. Lace ribbon through the holes and tie ends together leaving streamers.   Tap your timpanon for rhythm!

Make a Greek Flute:

Materials:

       cardboard roll from toilet paper

       wax paper

       rubber band

       pencil or ice pick

Directions:

1. Punch three holes on one side of the cardboard roll using a pencil or ice pick (adult help required!).

2. Stretch wax paper over one end and fasten with a rubber band.

3. Hum in your flute. Using your fingers, cover the holes one at a time to make different sounds.

Make Finger Cymbals:

Materials:

       2 small metal jar lids

       2 pieces of pipe cleaner

       ice pick

Directions:

1. Punch two holes in each jar lid (make sure that a grown-up helps!).

2. Put a piece of pipe cleaner through holes and fasten the jar lids to your thumb and longest finger. Now put on your favorite music and pretend you are in Ancient Greece. Make up a dance and play your instruments while dancing.

Craft Project: Make a Greek Loom

The Ancient Greeks had to make all their own clothes. They even had to weave their own cloth!

Materials:

    sturdy piece of cardboard or Styrofoam tray

    string

    knife

    all kinds of paper, yarn, ribbon, pipe cleaners — you can even use dried grasses and flowers!

Directions:

1. For an adult: Cut slots or V's all the way down both ends of the cardboard, leaving a space about ½" between each slit.

2. Student: Attach string at top left corner of cardboard and wind it around the V's of the cardboard. Do this from top to bottom. Parallel lines will be formed. Securely attach string at bottom of cardboard.

3. Weave your chosen materials in and out, going over one string then under the next.

4. When finished weaving, carefully cut the strings and tie the ends together. You can attach your woven piece to a dowel rod or a twig and hang it on the wall.

Craft Project: Make an Olympic Wreath

The winners at the ancient Olympic received olive branch wreaths as a prize.

Materials:

      small (green) branches or twigs from trees or bushes or artificial greenery

      floral wire

      hot glue gun

construction paper leaves, real leaves or artificial leaves

1. Bend a tree branch or two, using light pressure, to form a circle. If green enough, they won't snap.
2. Secure the ends by using floral wire.
3. Continue wrapping the rest of the branches around the form until it resembles a wreath. Use floral wire and, if necessary, a hot glue gun (make sure an adult helps out!) to hold all of the branches in place.
4. Glue leaves onto your "olive" branch wreath.

Activity Project: Have an Olympic Games/Greek Feast Party

Invite several friends over to participate in some fun games. Award the winners an olive branch wreath or provide the materials and let each participant make their own wreath. Then enjoy some Greek food and dancing.

Suggested Games:

Crab walk or bear walk to a finish line

Wheel barrow race – hold your partner's ankles like the handles of a wheelbarrow while he uses his hands to race to the finish line.

Skip, hop or jump backward or somersault or cartwheel to the finish line.

Frisbee discus throwing — see who can throw a Frisbee the farthest!

Long jump or high jump

Hula hoop competition – who can keep it going the longest?

Obstacle course race – create an obstacle course and see who can finish it first. The obstacles can be physical (jump a barrier, crawl through a tire) or they can be tasks (stop at each corner and do jumping jacks, pushups, somersaults, etc.).

Greek Food Suggestions:

Hummus
Ingredients:

2 15oz. cans of chick peas rinsed and drained
6 Tbs. tahini (sesame seed butter)
2 to 3 garlic cloves pressed
1/4 cup olive oil
Lemon juice
Salt
Pepper

Directions:

Mix all of the ingredients together in your food processor or mash with a potato masher. Serve with warmed pita bread

Greek Pilaf
Ingredients:

1 ½ cups raw brown rice
2 ¼ cups water or chicken broth
1 ½ Tbs. olive oil
1 ½ cups minced onion
½ cup minced celery
½ cup toasted pine nuts

4 or 5 garlic cloves pressed
2 Tbs lemon juice
salt and pepper

Directions:

1. Place rice and water in a saucepan. Boil, cover and simmer for about 40 min. or until tender.
2. Sauté onion, celery and garlic in olive oil until vegetables are tender. Add salt, pepper and pine nuts and sauté for five minutes.
3. Mix rice with sautéed mixture and add lemon juice.

Stuffed Grape Leaves

Ingredients:

About 24 grape leaves 3 to 4 inches wide (Grape leaves can be found in larger grocery stores or specialty food stores. You can pick your own in the spring when they are tender.)
Greek pilaf
spaghetti sauce

Directions:

1. Preheat oven to 350 degrees and lightly grease a baking dish.
2. Place a heaping spoonful of Greek Pilaf on each leaf and roll it up, tucking in the ends.
3. Place the stuffed leaves in the baking dish and bake for 20 minutes.
4. Serve with spaghetti sauce or squeeze lemon juice on top.

Ekmek

Ingredients:

Syrup:
2 teaspoons honey
2/3 cup inexpensive brandy
1 cup sugar
1 cup water
Cake:
1 package square melba toast (or Jacobsen's Snack Toast)
Ground cinnamon
pudding/custard (such as vanilla instant pudding)
Top Layer:
real whipped cream (NOT Cool Whip)
ground cinnamon
slivered almonds or pistachios

Directions:

Assemble syrup ingredients in a pan and boil for about 15 minutes (while you're making the pudding). Mix the instant pudding. When the pudding is done, remove syrup from heat and let cool. Line a glass dish with melba toast (cake is actually the toast that has soaked up the syrup). Pour cooled syrup over toast (syrup should cover toast slices completely). Sprinkle lightly with cinnamon. Pour instant pudding over toast. Pour whipped cream over pudding. Sprinkle with slivered almonds & cinnamon.

CHAPTER TWENTY-ONE
The Medes and the Persians

UBWH 66, UILE 152-153
KIHOW 74-74, KHE 40-41

Review Questions, A New Empire

What was the name of the shepherd tribe at the edge of Media? *Persia, or the Persians*

What country did the Persians obey? *The Medes, or Media*

Why did the Persian king, Astyges, want to get rid of his grandson? *He dreamed that the baby would grow up and take his throne away.*

What was the baby's name? *Cyrus*

After Cyrus became king of the Persians, what did he do? *He conquered Media too.*

Narration Exercise, A New Empire

The child should know the name Cyrus, but she doesn't need to know the other proper names of characters in the story. Acceptable narrations might include:

"The king of Persia was afraid of his grandson. The baby was named Cyrus. When he grew up, he took over the throne. Then he conquered the Medes." OR

"Cyrus grew up and became king of the Persians. Then he also took over Media. He became a great ruler."

Review Questions, Cyrus the Great

Was Cyrus a good king? *Yes, he was very fair.*

Can you tell me one of the fair things Cyrus did? *He let the Medes have some power in his empire.* OR *He let the Jews go back to Palestine.*

What was King Croesus known for? *His gold — he was richer than anyone else.*

Why did the Babylonians let Cyrus into their city? *Because they did not like their own king*

Narration Exercise, Cyrus the Great

Now ask the child to tell back to you the story of Cyrus's conquests in two to four sentences. Use the above questions to prompt the child if necessary. The narration should include the information that Cyrus conquered Babylon. Acceptable narrations might include:

"Cyrus conquered lots of other nations. One was ruled by a rich king named Croesus. He had lots of gold. He also conquered Babylon." OR

"Cyrus was a good king. His people liked him. Babylon let him in because he was better than their king. Cyrus ruled a large empire."

Additional History Reading

The Persian Empire, by Karen Zinert (Marshall Cavendish, 1997). This descriptive book
> Highlights the history of the Persian empire and its contributions to modern life. Intended for slightly older children; you'll only want to read selected sections. (RA)

The Persian Empire: World History Series, by Don Nardo (Lucent Books, 1998). Like Zinert's book, this has more complexity than a first-grader needs – but you can use the illustrations and selected bits of the narrative to reinforce knowledge of Persia. (RA)

Corresponding Literature Suggestions

King Midas and the Golden Touch, by Charlotte Craft (Morrow, 1999). The legend of King Midas may be based on Croesus, the rich king of Asia Minor. For a longer project, listen to the unabridged audio of Lynn Reid Banks's *The Adventures of King Midas* (try your local library). (RA)

Esther's Story, by Diane Wolkstein (Mulberry, 1998). The story of Esther took place during the expansion of the Persian empire, among the Jews who were in exile in the Persian capital city. (RA)

Queen Esther: The Morning Star , by Mordecai Gersein (Simon & Schuster, 2000). Colorful pictures and a simple story. (RA)

The Legend of the Persian Carpet, by Tomie de Paola and Claire Ewart (Putnam's, 1993). This simple read-aloud has detailed and accurate pictures of Persian architecture. (RA)

The Persian Cinderella, by Shirley Climo and Robert Florczak (HarperCollins, 1999).   This retelling sets the story in ancient Persia, with beautiful detailed paintings for illustrations. (RA)

The King & the Three Thieves: A Persian Tale, by Kristen Balouch (Penguin/Viking, 2000). A story of justice from ancient Persia. (RA)

The Red Lion: A Tale of Ancient Persia, by Diane Wolkstein (Crowell, 1977).   A prince discovers that he can face his fears. (RA)

Map Work (Student Page 59)

1. On the blackline map provided, trace the dotted line that goes all the way around the Persian empire.

2. Find the Persian Gulf and color it blue. Why do you think it is called the "Persian" Gulf?

3. The ancient Persian empire had four rivers in it. Trace each one in blue. What are the names of the four rivers?

4. Three countries that we have already studied – Egypt, Canaan, and Phoenicia – fall within the boundaries of the Persian empire. Find each country. Circle its name in red.

NOTE: This map is adapted from an original map in Terri Johnson's "Blackline Maps of Ancient History" set. It is reprinted here with her kind permission. For a full set of blackline maps, coordinated to *The Story of the World*, visit Knowledge Quest Maps at http:// www.knowledgequestmaps.com, or contact Knowledge Quest at 7722 SE 282nd Avenue, Gresham, OR 97080 (503/663-1210). You can also buy these maps from Peace Hill Press at http:// www.peacehillpress.com

Coloring Page (Student Page 60)

This picture of Cyrus the Great is based on a bas-relief found in Pasargade, the capital city of Persia founded by Cyrus.

Projects

Craft Project: Make "Persian Shoe Strings" (Student Page 61)

Materials:

> one set of new, wide, white shoestrings
> non-washable markers, marker stamps
> piece of white paper and pencil
> old newspaper

Directions:

1. Have you ever heard of a Persian carpet? They are rich in color and design. In myths, Persian carpets are magic – they can fly away to unknown, mysterious places! Persian rugs used patterns from nature – flowers and twisting designs — and bright, magical colors. Draw some patterns of vines and flowers on

your piece of white paper with your pencil. You can copy the illustrations in the appendix on page 61, or make up your own patterns.

2. Now gather your non-washable markers and shoestrings. With newspapers beneath the shoestrings, use the markers to copy your pattern onto the shoestrings. Be sure to do both sides!

OPTIONAL: Use acrylic paints. They will take longer and will create more of a mess, but the colors will be brighter.

Craft Project: Make the Persian Ruler's Silver Plate

The Persian Kingdom was full of silver. To us, silver is valuable. (Do you have anything silver in your home? How about a picture frame, jewelry, or special dinnerware?) Silver was valuable to the Persians as well. Workers of this precious metal made beautiful silver plates and bowls, decorating them with pictures of their favorite warriors or heroes – some of whom were famous hunters. They also made beautiful silver crowns. Some were so heavy that the kings couldn't even wear them!

Materials:
>   cardboard
>   dinner plate
>   foil (Reynolds Wrap works best)
>   pencil, craft knife
>   scratch paper

Directions:

1. Put the dinner plate face down on a large piece of cardboard and trace the plate.

2. Using a craft knife, cut out the plate shape from the cardboard.

3. Wrap the cardboard plate with foil. Tack down the foil on the back of your cardboard plate with glue or tape. Cut away any extra foil, making sure that it lies down flat

4. Using your scratch paper, draw some pictures of heroes: a king on a throne, a hunter, or a warrior on a horse. Stick figures are just fine!

5. When you have a drawing that you like, place the paper on the silver plate, right where you want your picture to be. Trace over the lines of your drawing with your pencil, pushing medium hard so that your pencil tip dents the foil beneath.

6. Take the scratch paper off. See your picture on your Ruler's Plate!

Craft Project: Make Persian Puppets

Materials:
>   several brown paper lunch bags (one for each puppet)
>   crayons, markers, colored pencils, or pastels
>   construction paper, fabric scraps
>   buttons, felt, glitter or sequins
>   yarn
>   glue
>   scissors

Directions:

1. Read over the story of Cyrus and how he became king of the Persians. Decide which characters in the story would make good puppets.

2. Use the paper bags as puppet bases. Put your hand into each one and open and close the fold for a mouth. Draw lips around each "mouth" and use buttons, sequins, or construction paper circles to make eyes.

3. Glue strands of yarn on the top crease of the puppet for hair.

4. Use your other art materials to decorate the puppets.

5. Get behind your sofa, put your hand into the puppet, and push the puppet up above the back of the sofa. Now you have a stage! Act out part of the story of Cyrus for your parents or grandparents.

Activity Project: Play the Conquer Mesopotamia Game (Student Page 62)

Materials:

> The "Conquer Mesopotamia" gameboard
>> The board works best if it is enlarged (to 11x14) and photocopied onto cardstock. You can also color it as an additional art project.
> 1 die (2 dice for faster play)

Directions:

1. Object of the game: Be the first one to the FINISH line!

2. Keep your *Story of the World* nearby for quick answer checks.

3. Players should select different objects to represent them on the board (button, bean, coin, Lego, small plastic animal, etc.) All playing pieces should be placed on START.

4. Roll the die (or dice). Highest number goes first.

5. Going clockwise, each player should throw the dice and move the prescribed number of spaces. When a player lands on a square that contains a symbol, she should check the corresponding symbol and follow the instructions.

CHAPTER TWENTY-TWO
Sparta and Athens

UBWH 67-69, UILE 154-159
KIHOW 82-89, KHE 52-55

Review Questions, Life in Sparta

Did the Greek cities all obey the same king? *No, each city had its own king.*

What did all Spartan boys grow up to be? *Soldiers.*

What did they learn in school? *Acceptable answers: How to fight; how to be tough; how to be strong.*

If you were a Spartan boy and you hurt yourself, what would you do? *Be brave and silent! You wouldn't cry. You would pretend that you were fine.*

What were Spartan girls supposed to do? *Have children who would be good fighters.*

Narration Exercise, Life in Sparta

Ask the child to tell you two important things about Sparta. Prompt him if necessary! Any two of the following are acceptable:

Boys were supposed to be soldiers.

Spartan boys went away to camp to learn how to fight.

Men were supposed to be tough (or brave, or strong, or silent).

Spartans weren't supposed to complain.

The Spartans didn't obey the same king as other Greeks.

Review Questions, Life in Athens

What is a democracy? [Prompt the child for the answer:] *A country where people vote on the laws and on who becomes the leaders.*

Did Athens think fighting was the most important thing for boys to learn? *No.*

What kinds of things did Athenian boys learn in school? *Mathematics, reading, writing, poetry, music.*
What did Athenian girls learn how to do? *Keep house.*
What happens to ignorant people who don't know the laws? *Other people can make them do things.*
Why is it important to be educated? [Discuss the answer with your child:] *So that you know what the laws are; so that you know how to vote on laws and leaders; so that tyrants can't tell you what to do.*

Narration Exercise, Life in Athens

Ask the child to tell you two important things about Athens. Prompt him if necessary! Any two of the following are acceptable:

Athens was a democracy.

In Athens, people voted on the laws and on the leaders.

People in Athens were educated.

Boys learned how to read and write (or do math, or play music, or memorize poetry).

Girls learned how to keep house.

Plato was a famous man in Athens.

They didn't want tyrants to be in charge.

Additional History Reading

Time Traveler: Children Through Time (DK Eyewitness Reader), by Angela Bull (Dorling Kindersley, 1999). Colorful, interesting book that draws children into the ancient cultures, including the Greeks! Part of a series that focuses on encouraging young readers. (RA for beginning readers, IR for advanced).

Ancient Greece: DK Eyewitness, by Anne Pearson (Dorling Kindersley, 2000). This book is packed with information bites that make it a good reference. Descriptive of many aspects of ancient Greece, using pictures, drawings, actors dressed up and more. Fantastic pictures of artifacts! (RA)

How Would You Survive As An Ancient Greek? by Fiona Macdonald (Franklin Watts, 1995). A creative look at life as a Greek, complete with questions leading you on a journey to find the answer. Illustrations are enticing. Read the main text quickly, or spend more time studying details. (RA)

"Paper" Through the Ages, by Shaaron Cosner. Carolrhoda Books, 1984. Easy reading with expressive illustrations. Special section on wax tablets. Includes a recipe for writing a secret message! (RA)

A Coloring Book of Ancient Greece (Bellerophon Books, 2000) is available at www.bellerphonbooks.com. Real Greek art, simplified for young artists to color, along with interesting explanatory text. (RA/activity)

Spend the Day in Ancient Greece! Projects and Activities That Bring the Past to Life, by Linda Honan (John Wiley & Sons, 1998). Weave on a loom, paint an amphora, build a racing chariot. These are a few of the fun projects taught in this book. Each section centers around a child in ancient Greece and tasks he or she has to do. (RA/activity)

Ancient Greece! 40 Hands-On Activities to Experience This Wondrous Age by Avery Hart and Paul Mantell (Williamson Publishing, 1999). This collection of activities and information that can be used with older children if you are multi-leveling. (RA/activity)

Corresponding Literature Suggestions

D'Aulaire's Book of Greek Myths, by Edgar Parin d'Aulaire (Bantam Doubleday Dell, 1962). This introduction to the gods and goddesses of Ancient Greece has beautiful illustrations by Caldecott Award winners. (RA)

Mr. Semolina-Semolinus : A Greek Folktale, by Anthony Manna and Christodoula Mitakidou (Atheneum, 1997). Take a break from myths and read another old Greek story – a folktale about a princess who makes the perfect man out of cookie dough (since she can't find one in real life). (RA)

Bright-Eyed Athena: Stories from Ancient Greece, by Richard Woff (Getty Museum Publications, 1999).
A group of weaving women in Athens tell stories about the city's protector. (RA)

Megan in Ancient Greece (Magic Attic Club), by Susan Korman (Magic Attic Press, 1998). A longer read aloud project, about a girl who travels back to Greece and finds herself grappling with the restricted roles women can play. (RA)

Map Work (Student Page 57)

1. Get out the blackline map of Greece that you used in Chapter Twenty. Can you circle Athens in red?
2. Now circle Sparta in yellow.
3. The Athenians and Spartans could reach each other in two ways – by land and by sea. Draw a blue line to show the *sea route* between the two. If the Athenians wanted to sail over to Sparta, they would use this path.
4. Now draw a green line to show the *land route* between the two. If the Spartans wanted to march an army over to Athens, they would use this path.

Coloring Page (Student Page 63)

Projects

Craft Project: Make a Greek Bowl

Materials:

 terracotta clay (available at craft stores) or Sculpey clay
 small round bowl that can be baked in the oven
  foil
  baking sheet
  red and black acrylic paint

Directions:

1. Place the bowl on the baking sheet and spread a piece of foil over it.
2. Break the clay up in small chunks about half the size of a child's hand. Flatten these pieces, but not too thin. Place each piece on the inside of the bowl, smoothing the edges together with water. When the bowl is completely covered, smooth off the top edge.
3. Bake following terracotta or Sculpey clay instructions.
4. After your clay pot has cooled, take it out of the small round bowl.
5. Paint a design on the sides using black and red paint!

Activity Project: Write on an Athenian Wax Tablet

Materials:

 a small brick of lard or shortening
 plastic lid from a yogurt or margarine tub
 table knife
  toothpicks

Directions:

1. An hour before you plan to use your wax tablet, spread the lard the inside of the plastic lid so that the edges provide a frame for your tablet. Place in the refrigerator and let it solidify.
2. When you're ready, take out and write a message, or draw a picture on the lard with a toothpick.

3. When you're finished, smooth it over with the knife and write something new. This is similar to how the sturdy wax tablets were used. The Greek boys used them at school and the Greek girls used them in their housework.

Craft Project: Make "No-Sew" Greek Clothes

How do we know how the Greeks dressed in ancient days? Archeologists get a pretty good picture from the art work that has been left to us. Bowls, beautifully carved statues and also letters found give us peeks into their daily lives. Spartan soldiers were depicted in their uniforms. Their long red cloak was their most prized possession. If you want to be a Spartan, make sure you use a old red T-shirt!

Materials:
> old white pillowcase
> Dad or Mom's old colorful T-shirt
> scissors
> jute rope or twine

Directions:

1. Place a white pillowcase flat on a table. Cut out a hole in the middle of the folded edge on the short side. This will be the neck hole.

2. On the longer, folded sides, cut out arm holes at the top corner edge on the side close to the neck hole. Slip it over your head. Voila! Your *chiton*.

3. Use the rope as a belt for the chiton.

4. Do your hair like a Greek! Girls often wore their hair in pony-tales or buns. Sometimes they would wrap a ribbon in a criss-cross fashion around their heads. Boys wore a band of material around their heads.

5. To make your cloak, use the old T-shirt and make a cut down the middle front, from the neck to the bottom seam. Slip it on over your chiton. Add sandals and you're ready to visit ancient Greece!

Craft Project: Make Greek Stickers (Student Page 64)

Using the stencils provided, pick one of the following options. Put your stickers on your bike helmet, in your scrapbook, or anywhere else you're allowed to stick them!

Homemade Greek Stickers:

Materials:
> 2 envelopes unflavored gelatin
>> 1 cup water
>> 1/2 teaspoon peppermint extract
>> small saucepan
>> photocopy of the Greek stencils (Student Page 64)

To make the lickable sticky-gum for the backs:

1. Mix the gelatin and the water together in a pan. Heat the mix over medium heat until the gelatin is dissolved. Add the peppermint extract and let cool.

2. Color the Greek stencils with colored pencils, markers or crayons. Once done, cut them out. Paint a thin layer of the homemade sticky-gum on the back of your pictures and let dry. Now your Greek stencils are ready to be licked and stuck! (Ask mom for suggestions on where to stick them!)

Regular Greek Stickers:

1. Photocopy Greek stencils on a sheet of Avery 8 1/2 x 11 full sheet of sticky-back paper.

2. Color and cut them out. Peel off the backs whenever you're ready to stick your stickers.

Craft Project: Greek Charm Bracelet (OR Shrinking Greek Stencils!)

Materials:

> photocopy of the stencils
>> hole punch, colored pencils
>> sandpaper
>> elastic gold cording (in the bead section of your craft store)
>> deli plastic containers, #6 recyclable, flat sides cut out for use
>>> Or use "Rough and Ready" plastic shrinkable sheets (found at a craft store)

Directions:

1. Cut up a deli plastic container, freeing the useable top and bottom. Sand one side of the plastic until it is cloudy and you can feel the roughness on every part of it (delete this step if using the "Rough and Ready" shrinkable sheets). This is so that the color will stick.

2. Lay the plastic on top of the stencil pattern. Trace it on to the plastic, making sure you are working on the scratched side. Then fill in the stencil with the colored pencils. You can use markers as well, but the pencils seem to work best.

3. Decide where you want to punch your hole for the "charm" to hang from your bracelet, and use the hole punch to create the hole.

4. Once you are finished, cut the stencil out and place on a cookie sheet. Bake at 250 degrees for about 15 minutes. Check often. Burning plastic is not good for you to breathe. Take out when the charms are lying flat and are thicker. Your charms will shrink and the color will intensify.

5. Use your elastic cording and measure around your wrist or around your neck. Leave enough string to knot each charm to your cording. (You may need to repunch some of the holes.) String the charm and make a knot so it will stay put. Finish by tying the elastic cord ends together.

Activity Project: Make Greek Tattoos

Materials:

> pure henna (from health food stores) or henna hair coloring that is 100% henna
>> stencils photocopied on to cardstock and cut out (use the cardstock with the empty spaces)
>> small paint brush, non-toxic body crayons (optional)

Directions:

1. Mix the henna with boiling hot water until it is like wet sand and let cool.

2. Put cut-out stencil outline over skin. Brush the henna in the stenciled area. Let sit for a few minutes. This washes off after a few washings. Add details with non-toxic body crayons, if available.

*Note: Most people are not allergic to henna. Though it is natural, we recommend that new users put a very small amount on their skin first as a test. If skin gets red or irritated, do not use.

Activity Project: Make Spartan and Greek Paper Dolls (Student Pages 65-67)

Materials:

> Colored pencils, scissors, Scotch Removable Double Stick Tape
> Photocopy of the paper dolls on card stock, and clothes on regular white paper

Directions:

1. Color the Greek figures and their clothes and then cut them all out. The Spartan soldier's pride was his flaming red wool cloak and the helmets of the Greek soldiers were passed down from generation to generation.

2. Use the Scotch Removable Double Stick Tape to keep the outfits on your dolls.

3. Options: Laminate your dolls and their clothes (stick-on laminate sheets are available at most office

supply stores). Or attach dolls to thin balsam wood and cut out using a craft knife. Photocopy the dolls and clothes twice or more for a family or army.

CHAPTER TWENTY-THREE
The Greek Gods

UBWH N/A, *UILE* N/A
KIHOW N/A, *KHE* 48 (just one illustration)

Review Questions, The Greek Gods

Were the Greeks monotheists? *No.*

Were they polytheists? *Yes.*

Does a polytheist believe in one God or many gods? *Many gods.*

Why did Zeus start a war on earth? *Because there were too many people on earth.*

Can you name any of the other gods from the story? *Hera, Aphrodite, Athena, Eris, Poseidon.*

Narration Exercise, The Greek Gods

Ask the child to retell the story. An acceptable narration might read, "Zeus wanted to get rid of some of the people on earth. So he started a war on earth. All the gods took sides." OR

"Paris had to say which goddess was the most beautiful. He picked Aphrodite. The other goddesses got mad. A war started."

Additional Historical Reading

An Ancient Greek Temple:The Story of the Building of the Temples of Ancient Greece, by John Malam, illus. Mark Bergin (Peter Bedrick Books, 2001). Beautifully illustrated look at the building of a Greek temple from the quarry to the finished product. (RA)

Trojan Horse: The World's Greatest Adventure, *A DK Eyewitness Reader*, by David Clement-Davies (Dorling Kindersley, 1999). Wonderfully crafted paperback with detailed information on side bars of each page. Pictures of gold coins and the pipes are some of the features making this book a terrific read! (RA)

Corresponding Literature Suggestions

Greek Gods and Goddesses, by Geraldine McCaughrean (Margaret McElderry Books, 1997). McCaughrean's paraphrases are always interesting and sometimes surprising. (RA)

The Gods and Goddesses of Olympus, by Aliki (HarperCollins, 1994). Colorful pictures and lively, short tales of the central Greek gods. (RA) **This book is the basis for one of the Activity Projects in this chapter.**

The Robber Baby: Stories From the Greek Myths, by Anne Rockwell (Greenwillow Books, 1994). A bright and whimsical way of retelling these old myths in short chapter form. Should stir up all kinds of discussions! (RA)

Hercules, by Robert Burleigh (Harcourt Brace, 1999). A poetic presentation of the last of Hercules' seven labors. Excellent illustrations. (RA

Medusa, by Deborah Nourse Lattimore (Joanna Cotler Books, 2000). This book has dramatic pictures to illustrate a well written retelling of this familiar tale. (RA)

Max and Ruby's First Greek Myth: Pandora's Box, by Rosemary Wells (Dial Books for Young Readers, 1993). Two bunnies, sister and brother, explore the Greek myth of Pandora's Box and how it applies to their situation. Very fun! (RA)

Max and Ruby's Midas: Another Greek Myth, by Rosemary Wells (Dial Books for Young Readers, 1995).
Bunny brother and sister deal with yet another situation that calls for an old Greek tale! (RA)

The Illustrated Book of Myths: Tales and Legends of the World, by Neil Philip (Dorling Kindersley, 1995).

This book has examples of myths from several cultures, divided into subjects. Philip weaves in several enjoyable Greek myths. Short chapters are well-illustrated. (RA)

Map Work (Student Page 68)

Your map is the same map of Greece you have seen in the last few lessons – but the names are missing! Can you fill them in? Try to find:

The country of Greece

The island of Crete

The Aegean Sea

The city of Athens

The city of Sparta

The city of Troy

Mount Olympus

(PARENT: You can offer a small reward — a chocolate chip, for example — for each name the child can identify. Offer the student a chance to look back at the map of Greece before trying to identify places on the new map.)

Coloring Page (Student Page 69)

The three goddesses are arguing about which one is the most beautiful!

Projects

Activity Project: Make an Olympus Family Tree [C]

Once you have read through *The Gods and Goddesses of Olympus* by Aliki, consider making a family tree of the Greek and Roman gods and goddesses – a little bit like you did for your family in the beginning of this book! The Greeks thought their gods were like a big, *very* unhappy family.

Materials:

large twig with several branches

small clay pot or empty container (a coffee can works), filled with rocks, sand or clay

green construction paper

string, ribbon or hot glue

double stick tape or glue

Directions:

1. Stabilize your tree branch in a pot using rocks, sand or clay.

2. Go outside and find your favorite leaf shape. Trace one leaf shape onto your green construction paper for each Greek god and goddess you will include.

3. Write the name of the god or goddess on the leaf. You can also draw a picture of the character on the other side of the leaf. Or you may write the Greek name on one side and the Roman name for the god or goddess on the other (use chart on Student Page 70).

4. Using string, ribbon or hot glue, attach the leaf for the god who is in charge, Zeus, at the top of your "tree." Place the other leaves in order, from the most important gods near the treetop down to the least

important near the bottom.

Materials:
>   long sheet of newspaper print (Check with your local newspaper printers for the end roll.
>   Inexpensive and very versatile!)
>   OR a piece of white construction paper, 11x14
>   colored pencils or thin markers
>   ink pad and your thumb

Directions:

1. Imagine what it might be like to live on the top of a mountain. Illustrators for books about the Greek gods and goddesses had to imagine this. Take your piece of paper and think through how you want to set up your home for the Greek gods. You may want to draw it in pencil first. What would you include in your home for the Greek gods? Maybe their thrones, or the fire that Hestia might be stoking, a valley for Pan's sheep, a bed for Hypnos or a long road for Nike to race on? If you need ideas, go through Aliki's book or another of the recommended readings on the Greek gods and goddesses.

2. After you've set up their home, use your thumb-print to make your gods and goddesses. Put your thumb on the ink pad, and then on the paper where you want the head of your character to be.

3. Now add eyes, nose, and mouth with your markers. Add a body to each head with another thumb-print, or draw a body with your markers. Add arms and legs with your markers.

4. Decorate each character so that you remember who they are. Zeus might have a golden crown and a beard; Cupid could have a heart in his hand, while Helios might have sun-rays coming out of his head!

Craft Project: Make a Golden Apple

Materials:
>   small strips of newspaper
>   wad of newspaper squished to the size of an adult fist
>   toothpick, snapped in half
>   masking tape
>   wallpaper paste (NOTE: you can also use a mixture of one part flour to two parts water)
>   gold and brown paint, permanent black marker

Directions:

1. Make sure your wad of newspaper is tightly packed into a round, apple shape.

2. Secure a toothpick, sharp-side into the newspaper ball, on the top of your apple.

3. Use masking tape to secure loose ends of newspaper into place. Put another piece of masking tape over the toothpick so that the toothpick pushes through the tape; this will keep the toothpick in place.

4. Mix wallpaper paste (if you bought it dry) and dip the newspaper strips into it until they are completely wet with the glue, but not dripping heavily. Place the strips over the newspaper ball until it is covered with one layer. Repeat this step until the ball and stem are covered in four layers. Let the apple dry.

5. After the apple is dry, paint your apple gold and print the message Zeus put on his mischievous golden apple: *For the Most Beautiful*, with your black permanent marker. Paint the stem brown.

Activity Project: Greek Gods and Goddesses Wordsearch (Student Page 71)

REVIEW CARDS
Chapters Twenty, Twenty-One, Twenty-Two, Twenty-Three
(Student Page 72)

CHAPTER TWENTY-FOUR
The Wars of the Greeks

UBWH 67, UILE 154-155
KIHOW 80-83, KHE 52-53

Review Questions, Greece's War with Persia

Why did Athens and Sparta decide to be friends and allies? *Because they were afraid of the Persians*

What did the Athenians and Spartans do to the messenger sent by the Persian king? *They threw him down a well.*

What did Persia do then? *Attacked!*

What two armies fought the Battle of Marathon? *Persia and Athens*

Who won? *Athens*

Why didn't the Spartans come help the Athenians? *They were having a religious festival.*

What happened to the runner who took the good news to Athens? *He died of exhaustion.*

Was the Battle of Marathon the end of Greece's war with Persia? *No*

The last battle in the war with Persia was the Battle of Salamis. Who won – the Greeks or the Persians? *The Greek, and the Greek cities stayed independent!*

Narration Exercise, Greece's War with Persia

The narration should include the information that Athens and Sparta united to fight the Persians, and that the Persians eventually lost the war. Acceptable narrations might include:

"Athens and Sparta weren't friends. But they fought the Persians together. They won a famous battle at Marathon. Persia lost the war." OR

"Persia attacked Greece. The Greek cities fought back all together. Persia was defeated. One of the battles was at Marathon."

Review Questions, The Greeks Fight Each Other

What kind of building was the Parthenon? *A temple*

In one of the wall friezes, or carved pictures, inside the Parthenon, Greek soldiers are fighting strange creatures. What were they? *Centaurs – half man, half horse.*

Did the Greeks go on making beautiful art in peace? *No, they fought with each other.*

What two cities fought the Peloponnesian War? *Sparta and Athens*

When Sparta was attacking Athens, what happened inside the city of Athens that made it weaker? *The plague*

Alcibiades led the Athenians out of the city to attack the Spartans. But what did he do when the Athenians lost? *He joined the Spartans. He led the Spartans into Athens.*

Which Greek city won the fight? *Sparta finally conquered Athens.*

Narration Exercise, The Greeks Fight Each Other

The narration should include the information that the Greeks made lifelike art, and that Sparta and Athens fought until both cities were weak. Acceptable narrations might include:

"The Greeks knew how to make statues that looked like real people. They built beautiful buildings. But they kept on fighting with each other." OR

"Athens and Sparta were at peace for a little while. They did beautiful art. Then they started fighting with each other again. They got weak from fighting."

Additional History Reading

The Greeks (Footsteps in Time), by Sally Hewitt (Children's Press, 1998). Covers Greek culture and lifestyles with pretty illustrations and simple text on a first-second grade level. (RA)

The Greek Hoplite, by Martin Windrow (Franklin Watts, 1985). An excellent description of the Greek soldier, his equipment, and his place in the Greek army. (RA)

I Wonder Why the Greeks Built Temples? And Other Questions about Ancient Greece, by Fiona MacDonald (Kingfisher, 1998). Questions and answers about Greek accomplishments, with full-page color illustrations. (RA)

The X-Ray Picture Book of Big Buildings of the Ancient World, by Joanne Jessop (Franklin Watts, 1994). Cutaway diagrams of the Parthenon, as well as the Colosseum, the Great Pyramid, the Forbidden City, and others. (RA)

The Parthenon (Great Buildings), by Peter Chrisp (Steck Vaughn, 1997). Using lively drawings and pictures of carvings and ancient object, this book covers the building of the Parthenon; it even introduces young students to the war betwen the Greeks and the Persians, the reason for the Parthenon's construction. (RA)

Discoveries, Inventions, and Ideas: The Ancient Greeks, by Jane Shuter (Heinemann, 1999). This elementary-level book discusses Greek innovations and their place in Greek life. (RA)

Corresponding Literature Suggestions

The Aesop for Children, by Milo Winter (Scholastic, 1994). The famous moral stories from Greek times in an illustrated, easy-to-read edition. (RA)

Cupid and Psyche, by M. Charlotte Craft (William Morrow, 1996). This child-appropriate retelling of the story of Cupid and Psyche has stunning illustrations. (RA)

The Flying Horse: The Story of Pegasus (All Aboard Reading, Level 1), by Jane B. Mason. A Greek story that most beginners can read alone. (IR)

Apollo & Daphne: Masterpieces of Greek Mythology by Antonia Barber (J. Paul Getty Museum Publications, 1999). Retellings of Greek and Roman myths (intended for slightly older students) are accompanied by great paintings based on these stories. (RA)

Map Work (Student Page 73)

1. On the blackline map provided, find Sparta and Athens. They fought each other. Draw a red line connecting them to show that they were at war.
2. The Persian Empire wanted to conquer Greece. Color the Persian Empire yellow.
3. After the Battle of Marathon, a messenger ran from Marathon to Athens. Draw a blue line to show his path.

Coloring Page (Student Page 74)

The Parthenon was a temple built to honor Athena, the goddess of war.

Projects

Cooking Projects: Ice-Cream Greek Ship and Gingerbread Parthenon

(You don't have to do both of these – choose your favorite!)

Ice Cream Greek Boat

The Greek leader Themistocles went to the Oracle of Delphi and asked her how the Greeks could win the war against the dreaded Persians. Her answer puzzled everyone but this great leader. She said, "The wooden wall will save you." Themoistocles knew what she meant – the Greeks needed to build a whole fleet of wooden ships, and then line them up side by side like a great floating wall to keep the Persians away.

Here is a picture of a Greek fighting ship.

Do you see how the front of the ship is curved? The ships were designed to ram into enemy ships. When the Greeks fought the Persians at Salamis, they rammed into the Persian ships until the Persians were destroyed.

Materials:

        inexpensive box of vanilla ice cream, frozen VERY hard

        table knife and spoon, glass of warm water

        toothpicks

        skewer

        white paper cut in the shape of a sail

        cookie sheet or brownie pan

        heavy whipping cream, whipped up

        blue food coloring

        black, red, and white cans of icing (best choice: Betty Crocker's *Easy Flow Decorating Icing*)

Directions:

1. Open the box of ice cream and peel the paper away from the ice cream block.

2. Ask an adult to use a large knife to cut the block lengthwise into two long rectangles. Put the rectangles end-to-end on the cookie sheet.

3. Work fast! Dip the table knife and spoon in the warm water. Use the knife for carving and the spoon for scooping. Carve sharp ends into your ice cream, and scoop a hollow out of the middle. Use your hands if you need to! Keep dipping the knife and spoon into the warm water. You should also keep a warm damp towel nearby to warm your hands now and then. If the ice cream begins to melt, slide your cookie sheet back into the freezer and take a break until the ice cream refreezes.

4. Refreeze the ice cream at least 15 minutes before the next step. Then, when you have the boat shaped, slide the toothpicks into the sides for "oars."

5. Mix a few drops of blue food coloring with your whipped cream. Spread the whipped cream over the cookie sheet and around the boat for "water."

6. Use the frosting to decorate your ship.   Line the sides and edges; give your ship an eye and mouth, as in the picture above.

7. Slide your paper sail onto the skewer and push the skewer into the middle of the boat.

8. Take a picture (quick!), and then eat!

NOTE TO PARENT: This is an exciting but messy project. A perfectly-shaped boat is impossible, and the frosting tends to slide off, especially if the ice cream is melting.

Gingerbread Parthenon

Once the battle of Marathon was won, the people of Athens wanted to thank their goddess Athena for their victory. So they built her a temple – the Parthenon.

Materials:

        gingerbread dough (recipe below)

        canned or homemade white frosting (1 can for 2 Parthenons)

        rolling pin, greased baking sheet

        photocopy of the Parthenon coloring sheet, with the Parthenon cut out

        toothpicks and table knife

Gingerbread dough

    ¾ cup shortening

    ¾ cup brown sugar

    ¾ cup dark molasses

    ¼ cup cold water

    1 tsp. vanilla

    4 ½ cups all purpose flour

    2 tsp. ground cinnamon

    ½ tsp. ground ginger

    ½ tsp. ground nutmeg

    ¾ tsp. salt

Beat together shortening, sugar, molasses and water. In a separate bowl, mix flour, spices, and salt. Add dry ingredients to the shortening mix and blend together. Take out of the bowl and form a ball. If you are making this ahead of time, put a teaspoon of flour into a ziplock bag and shake. Put the dough in and set in refrigerator up to four days. This is enough dough to make two Parthenons!

Activity Project: Make a "Stone" Sculpture

Stone sculptors were busy people in ancient Greece! They worked hard making beautiful statues and friezes, using tools of different sizes and shapes. They were so good that when Greek towns and cities were conquered, the stone art work was carted off as bounty for the conqueror!

Materials:

    bar of Ivory soap, or another soft soap bar

    table knife

    white paper and pencil

Directions:

1. Place the bar of soap on the white paper and draw around it. Now you can see how much space you have to work with. On the square you traced, draw the design you want to carve.

2. When your design is finished, draw it carefully onto the flat side of the bar of soap.

3. Now use your knife to carefully shave away the soap around the outside lines of your design.

4. Remember: make your designs simple, without too many details! You might want to start with a very simple shape such as a fish. Shave off the edges to make the front rounded. Then carve out triangles on the top side and bottom side to make the back fin. Careful! If you carve too much off, the back fin will fall off. Dig out a place in the front to form the eyes. There's your first statue!

Craft Project: Make Athenian Coins

The Greeks were at war with each other. Money was one cause of this war – Athens tried to force all the other city-states to stop using coins of their own. Instead, they would have to use the special coins Athens made. These coins had the picture of Athena, goddess of war and patron of the city of Athens, on one side, and her symbol, an owl, on the other.

Materials:

    yellow quick-dry clay such as Sculpey (sold by Rainbow Resource Center,

        www.rainbowresource.com, and at craft stores)

    toothpick

    quarter, dime, and nickel

    encyclopedia picture of an owl

Directions

1. Preheat the oven to 250 degrees.

2. Knead clay until it is easy to mold. Roll it out flat, about 1/8" thick.

3. Using the quarter as a guide, cut the clay around it with the point of the toothpick. This will form a round, coin-like shape.

4. Now use the toothpick to draw a picture of a woman's head on one side of the coin. (A round head with eyes, nose, and a mouth is just fine!) You can draw hair or a helmet on her head, and if you have room you can draw a sword beside her. This is Athena, the goddess of war.

5. Turn the clay over and draw the head of an owl on the other side. The owl has big round eyes and triangular ears!

6. Now design a coin of your own. What picture will you draw on the first side? What symbol will you use on the second side? Look at the quarter, dime, and nickel. Whose picture is on each coin? What symbol is on the other side of the coin?

7. Bake your Athenian coins on a glass pie plate for 20 minutes. Allow them to cool.

Activity Project: Play the Peloponnesian War Game (Student Page 75) ⟦C⟧

Materials:

> The "Win the Peloponnesian War" gameboard (Student Page 75)
>> The board works best if it is enlarged (to 11x14) and photocopied onto cardstock. You can also color it as an additional art project.
>
> 1 die (2 dice for faster play)

Directions:

1. Object of the game: Be the first one to the center of the board, after going around it once

2. This game is for two players or teams. Players or teams should select different objects to represent them on the board (button, bean, coin, Lego, small plastic animal, etc.) Each player should have four pieces.

3. One player/team should put all four pieces onto the Athens star; the other player/team should put theirs in the Sparta star (like in the game of Sorry).

4. Take turns rolling the dice (or die). You must roll a one to move one of your pieces out of your star. If you are playing with two dice, you can roll a one on either die (ignore the number on the remaining die if you choose to move a piece out of your star).

5. Move your pieces all around the board in the direction of the arrows. If you land directly on an opponent's piece, you can send it back to its star!

5. Go around the board until you reach your port – the port right in front of your star. The first player to get all four pieces into the right port wins!

CHAPTER TWENTY-FIVE
Alexander the Great

UBWH 70-71, *UILE* 160-161
KIHOW 90-95, *KHE* 56

Review Questions, Philip and His Son

Who attacked the Greek cities? *Philip*

What country did he rule? *Macedonia*

What was the name of Philip's son? *Alexander the Great*

What does "Alexander" mean? *Ruler of men*

Do you remember the name of Alexander's horse? *Bucephalus*

How did Alexander tame his horse? *He turned the horse so that it couldn't see its shadow.*

How did Alexander solve the problem of the Gordian Knot? *He cut it in half.*

Narration Exercise, Philip and His Son

Ask the child to retell the story of Bucephalus OR of the Gordian Knot. 3-4 sentences is long enough. The child can choose to illustrate the story, if she wants to. Appropriate retellings might include: "Alexander's father was going to buy a horse. The horse was too wild for him. Alexander told his father that he would tame the horse. He did, and his father bought the horse for him." OR "Alexander the Great saw a chariot with a huge knot on it. No one could untie the knot. So he cut it in half with his sword. This meant that he would conquer Asia."

Review Questions, Alexander's Invasions

What three Wonders of the Ancient World have we learned about? *The Hanging Gardens of Babylon, the Great Pyramid, the Pharos*

What was the Pharos? *A giant lighthouse*

What was the name of the city Alexander built in Egypt? *Alexandria*

Why did Alexander stop before he conquered all of India? *His soldiers refused to go any further.*

Narration Exercise, Alexander's Invasions

Ask the child: What three things did we learn about in this lesson? Prompt him if necessary for three of these answers:

1. Alexander didn't finish conquering India because his soldiers rebelled.
2. Alexander built a city in Egypt called Alexandria OR Alexander built many new cities.
3. The Pharos was a huge lighthouse in the harbor of Alexandria.

Revew Questions, The Death of Alexander

How did Alexander the Great die? *No one knows why he died. He got weak.*

How many pieces did Alexander's empire get divided into? *Three*

What did Ptolemy do in Egypt? *Finished the city of Alexandria and built a library.*

What is another name for the Seleucids? *The Syrians*

Did the three generals who ruled Alexander's kingdom make friends with each other? *No, they fought.*

Narration Exercise, The Death of Alexander

"Alexander the Great had a huge kingdom. When he died, his generals split it into three parts. Then they all fought with each other."

Additional History Reading

Alexander the Great: The Greatest Ruler of the Ancient World (*What's Their Story*), by Andrew Langley (Oxford University Press Children's Books, 1998). A simple, nicely-illustrated picture-book biography. (RA, but may be IR for strong readers)

The Greek News, by Anton Powell and Philip Steele (Candlewick Press, 1999). The cover story of this "Greek newspaper" (full of silliness and good information) is about Alexander the Great. (RA)

The World in the Time of Alexander the Great, by Fiona MacDonald (Chelsea House, 2000). Covers events in the ancient world during Alexander's rise to power. You won't want to read all of the text to a very young child – pick and choose your pages (RA).

Corresponding Literature Suggestions

Alexander the Great: The Legend of a Warrior King, by Peter Chrisp (Dorling Kindersley, 2000). Stories and legends about Alexander and information about the world he conquered, with stunning illustrations. (RA)

The Great Alexander The Great, by Joe Lasker (Viking Press, 1983). Alexander's life, from the time of the taming of Bucephalus to the end; illustrated, and very easy to read. (IR). **Out of print; check your library.**

Map Work (Student Page 76)

1. On the blackline map provided, find the city that Alexander named after himself. Circle it in red. What country is it in?

2. Trace the Nile River in blue. Don't forget the delta!

3. Trace all the way around the borders of Alexander's empire in red.

4. Find and trace in blue the Tigris, Euphrates, and Indus Rivers. How many rivers were inside Alexander's empire?

NOTE: This map is adapted from Terri Johnson's "Blackline Maps of Ancient History" set, with her kind permission. For a full set of blackline maps, coordinated to *The Story of the World*, visit Knowledge Quest Maps at http://www.knowledgequestmaps.com, or contact Knowledge Quest at 7722 SE 282nd Avenue, Gresham, OR 97080 (503/663-1210). You can also buy these maps from Peace Hill Press at http://www.peacehillpress.com.

Coloring Page (Student Page 77)
Alexander and Bucephalus

Projects

Craft Project: Make a Bucephalus Stick Horse

Materials:

> broomstick (available at hardware stores)
> piece of heavy cardboard
> template of horse's head (Student Page 78; enlarge this for best results)
> glue and yarn
> nylon rope, cotton rope, or old belt
> crayons or paint

Directions:

1. Make two copies of the horse template out of cardboard.

2. Cut out a hole in the horse's mouth on both templates (a rope can be tied here to make reins).

3. Paint or color heads and glue yarn (for the mane) along the inside of one of the necks.

4. Attach cardboard heads together by stapling the edges (leave the bottom open).

5. Set assembled head on broomstick. Staple the bottom of the neck on either side of the broomstick (you can also use duct tape for extra security.

6. Thread cotton or soft nylon rope (or an old leather belt) through the mouth whole. Tie ends together in a loop, long enough for the child to hold while astride the broomstick.

Activity Project: Tie a Gordian Knot (Student Page 78)

Alexander cut the Gordian Knot because it was too complicated for him to untie. If you tie these knots, can you untie them? What if you tie them several different times?

Materials:

> Two heavy pieces of string or rope

Directions:

1. Begin with the bowline knot – a knot in one piece of rope. First, make a loop in the rope and push the free end up through the loop from the bottom (Step One). Next, pass the free end around the rope above the loop (Step Two). Finally, bring the free end back down through the loop and pull it tight (Step Three).

2. Now try a sheet bend. This knot ties two pieces of rope together. First, make a loop in one rope. Pass the end of the second rope through the end loop and then around the first rope further up (Step One). Next, pull the end of the second rope through the loop in the first rope and tighten (Step Two).

Activity Project: Make the Pharos Lighthouse (Student Pages 79-80)
Materials:
  1 11.5 oz mixed nut can (or any can the same size)
  1 small Pringles can
Lighthouse base template (Student Page 80); make two copies on cardstock
  Lighthouse top template (Student Page 79); make one copy on cardstock
  Yellow cling wrap
  Tape, glue, scissors, crayons
Directions:
1. Color pieces of lighthouse.
2. Cut out both pieces of the base template. The bottom will be slightly larger than the middle and you will need both copies of the bottom to go around the nut can. Turn empty nut can upside down. Wrap the two sections around the nut can and cut end to fit. Tape or glue in place with the railing sticking up over the bottom of the can.
3. Cut out the lighthouse middle template. Turn the Pringles can upside down and wrap it with the middle template. Tape or glue in place.
4. Glue top of Pringles can to bottom of nut can.
5. Cut out the lighthouse top template. Cut out windows. Attach yellow cling wrap to the inside of the template. This will make your lighthouse look like it is lit.
6. Fold the top and glue the large tab to the inside to make a rectangular shape. Fold the bottom tabs and tape to the top of the Pringles can. Set your lighthouse in a window so the sunlight will shine through the top.

Story Project: Being Brave
Discuss the reasons why you think Alexander was a brave person. Make a list of the things that made Alexander brave. Then think about a time when you were brave. Draw a picture or narrate a story about that time in your life.

Activity Project: Play the Alexander the Great Game (Student Page 81)
Materials:
  The "Alexander the Great" gameboard
    The board works best if it is enlarged (to 11x14) and photocopied onto cardstock. You can also color it as an additional art project.
  1 die (2 dice for faster play)
Directions:
1. Object of the game: Be the first one to the finish line! Keep your copy of *The Story of the World* close by for quick answer checks.

2. Players should select different objects to represent them on the board (button, bean, coin, Lego, small plastic animal, etc.).

3. All players begin at the START. Roll the dice and the highest number goes first.

4. Roll again and begin the journey through the life of Alexander the Great. When you land on a square that has a symbol, look for the corresponding symbol and follow the instructions.

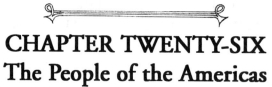

CHAPTER TWENTY-SIX
The People of the Americas

UBWH 63, 80-81, *UILE* 176-181
KIHOW 62-63, 134-135, *KHE* 32, 76-77

Review Questions, The Nazca Drawings

What is a continent? *A big mass of land*

There are three different "Americas." The first is South America; what are the other two? *North America and Central America*

South America has flat land in the middle. What does it have all down one edge? *Mountains*

Do you remember the name of the South American tribe that made drawings on the ground? *The Nazca*

How big were the drawings? *Hundreds of miles across!*

Do you remember what some of the drawings were? *Spider, pelican, hummingbird, flowers, spirals, squares, patterns*

Archaeologists don't know how the Nazcas made their drawings, but they have two guesses. What methods might the Nazca have used to draw these big lines? *They may have used math, or the position of the stars.*

Narration Exercise, The Nazca Drawings

"The Nazca lived in South America. They made big drawings on the ground. Some of the drawings were of birds and flowers." OR

"There are three Americas – North America, Central America, and South America. Tribes lived in South America a long time ago. They hunted and grew things like other people in ancient times. One tribe was called the Nazca."

Review Questions, The Heads of the Olmecs

What does "Meso" mean? *"Between"*

What does "Mesoamerica" mean? *Between the Americas*

What is the other name that we use for "Mesoamerica?" *Central America*

Do you remember the name of the tribe that lived in Central America? *The Olmecs*

Where did the rich Olmec people live? *In the city, up on a hill*

Where did the poor people live? *Down on the plain below*

What kind of pyramid did the Olmecs build in the middle of their city? *A dirt pyramid*

What kind of sculptures did they make? *Giant heads of their rulers*

Narration Exercise, The Heads of the Olmecs

"Central America is in the middle between North America and South America. The Olmec people lived there. They made huge giant stone heads that didn't have any bodies." OR

"The Olmecs lived in a place called Central America. They built a dirt pyramid at the center of their city. The rich people lived up in the city, and the poor people lived down on the ground."

Review Questions, Rabbit Shoots the Sun

What two countries are now in North America? *Canada and the United States*

Way up in the northern part of North America, where it is too cold to grow crops, what did ancient people eat? *Seals, polar bears, birds, caribou, mosses, lichens, whales*

How about people in the middle part of North America – what did they eat? *Corn, wheat, buffalo, fish*

Did the people of North America live in cities? *No, they were nomads.*

In the story of "Rabbit Shoots the Sun," why did Rabbit decide to shoot the sun? *Because it was so hot and dry*

What happened when Rabbit's arrow hit the sun? *Fire came out and started to burn up the world.*

What color did the bush turn when the fire scorched it? *Yellow*

Was Rabbit still brave and bold, at the end of the story? *No, he was timid and shy.*

Did the sun still jump over over the edge of the world in a hurry? *No, it crept up a little at a time.*

Narration Exercise, Rabbit Shoots the Sun

Ask the child to tell you two things about the people who lived in the far northern parts of North America, and two things about the people who lived down in the warmer part of North America. Acceptable answers might be:

"People in the cold part of North America hunted seals and gathered moss to eat. People where it was warmer hunted buffalo and grew corn." OR

"People in North America were nomads. Up where it was cold, they hunted whales and polar bears. Further down they grew corn and wheat, and they went fishing and hunting."

OR

Ask your child to retell the story of "Rabbit Shoots the Sun." An acceptable retelling might be, "Rabbit was mad at the sun for making it so hot and dry. He shot the sun with an arrow, but fire poured out all over the world and made it brown. Rabbit had to hide. Now Rabbit is very shy and the sun is afraid to jump up over the edge of the world."

Additional History Reading

Growing Up in Aztec Times, by Marion Wood (Troll, 1993). Basic information about life in ancient South America, from the perspective of an Aztec child. (RA)

You Wouldn't Want to Be an Aztec Sacrifice!, by Fiona Macdonald (Franklin Watts, 2000). Colorful guide to ancient Aztec civilization. (RA)

Macchu Picchu: The Story of the Amazing Incas and Their City in the Clouds, by Elizabeth Mann (Mikaya Press, 2000). With beautiful paintings of Inca times and photographs of Inca artifacts, this book describes Inca life and explores the building of the greatest Inca city. (RA)

The Incas (See Through History), by Tim Wood (Viking, 1996). Some of the text will be too difficult for first and second graders, but lifting transparent overlays reveals fascinating details of Incan civilization. (RA)

Anasazi, by Leonard Everett Fisher (Atheneum, 1997). A picture-book account of the ancestors of Pueblo Indians, in the American southwest. (RA)

Native Americans (First Discovery Books), by Gallimard Jeunesse (Scholastic, 1998). A very simple and short introduction to ancient North American peoples. (RA, IR for strong readers)

Who Were the First North Americans? by Philippa Wingate (EDC Publications, 1996). This Usborne book has bright, cartoon-like illustrations and a good, brief summary of ancient cultures in North America. (RA)

Life in Ancient Mexico Coloring Book, by John Green (Dover, 1991). Detailed scenes of ancient South American culture.

A Coloring Book of Incas, Aztecs, and Mayans (Bellerophon Books, 1985). All Bellerophon coloring books use simplified adaptations of actual images from the culture under study.

Corresponding Literature Selections

Numerous North, Central and South American tales have been published as picture books; you can use many books other than those listed below for this chapter.

Stories from the Amazon, by Saviour Pirotta (Raintree/Steck Vaughn, 2000). A collection of folk tales from the Central American rain forest region. (RA)

The Two Mountains: An Aztec Legend, by Eric Kimmel (Holiday House, 2000). The children of the sun and moon fall in love, even though their families are opposed. (RA)

Jabuti the Tortoise, by Gerald McDermott (Harcourt, 2001). This very brightly colored picture book version of a South American legend tells how the tortoise's shell was cracked, why the toucan is so bright, and explains a host of other natural phenomenon. (RA)

Thirteen Moons on Turtle's Back: A Native American Year of Moons, by Joseph Bruchac (Paper Star 1997). Tales from a wide range of Native American traditions are beautifully illustrated with watercolors; each story explains the importance of a season to a particular tribe. (RA)

Is My Friend at Home? Pueblo Fireside Tales, by John Bierhorst (Farrar, Straus and Giroux, 2001). Seven stories about friendship; each one also explains some aspect of nature. (RA)

Dancing Drum: A Cherokee Legend, by Terri Cohlene (Troll, 1991). This is a retelling of Dancing Drum's attempt to save his people from the wrath of the Sun. Terri Cohlene has a whole series of books about Native Americans and their legends. All of the books in this series have a section at the end that discusses the historical and cultural aspects of the civilizations. Others in this series include books about the Cheyenne, Algonquian, Eskimo, Makah and the Navajo; any would be appropriate for this lesson (see below). (RA)

Ka-Ha-Si and the Loon: An Eskimo Legend, by Terri Cohlene (Troll, 1991). A boy saves his tribe from disaster. (RA)

Keepers of the Earth: Native American Stories and Environmental Activities for Children, by Michael J. Caduto and Joseph Bruchac (Fulcrum Publishing, 1997). Retellings of 25 legends from 20 different cultures combined with scientific information and hands-on activities. Joseph Bruchac has written many other books concerning Native Americans. (RA)

Map Work (Student Page 82)

1. On the blackline map provided, locate and color South America.
2. Choose another color and shade in Central America.
3. Now use a third color for North America.

Coloring Page (Student Page 83)

For the Student: Color the "Rabbit Shoots the Sun" comic strip while your parent reads the story aloud. Then cut out each frame, shuffle them and see if you can tell the story while you put the frames back in order.

Projects

Craft Project: Make a Seed Mosaic Map C

The foods we eat today come from different places all over the world. Many were first grown in the Americas! Some foods that originated in the Americas are corn, beans, sunflowers, tomatoes, peanuts, peppers, potatoes, pumpkins, squash and strawberries.

Materials:

corn, any kind of beans, peanuts, as well as sunflower, tomato, pepper, pumpkin and squash seeds

copy of the blackline map above

glue

Directions:

1. Brush glue all over your map.

2. Pick out which seeds you want to use on each continent and glue them on. You can use smaller seeds for the flat land and larger seeds for the mountains.

Craft Project: Make a Native American Headband

Materials:

posterboard or lightweight cardboard

scissors and tape (stapler or glue)

crayons, markers, stickers, construction paper, etc.

Directions:

1. Measure around your head with a measuring tape. Now cut a two-inch wide strip of posterboard the same length.

2. Decorate your headband. Fake feathers can be attached or made from construction paper.

3. Tape headband at ends.

Craft Project: Make a Native American Sand Painting

Materials:

sand

food coloring or powder paints

piece of cardboard

Directions:

1. Draw outline of picture on piece of cardboard.

2. Make colored sand by stirring food coloring (3 drops at a time) or powder paints (1 Tbs at a time) into ½ cup of sand. Use a metal spoon and a metal mixing bowl (sometimes coloring will stain plastic).

3. Working with one color at a time, spread glue over appropriate area. Sprinkle on colored sand. Continue until picture is complete.

Activity Project: Make a "Nazca" White Crayon Drawing

Do you remember reading about the huge Nazca line drawings an only be seen from the air? How hard is it to draw a picture if you can't see what you are doing?

Materials:

white crayon

white paper

watercolor paints

Directions:

1. Using the white crayon, draw a picture of your choice on white paper. Notice how difficult it is to draw a picture when you can't see exactly what you are doing. Be sure and press down hard with your crayon.

2 Using watercolor paints, paint over the entire sheet of paper.

3. Let dry. How did your "invisible drawing" turn out?

Cooking Project: Make Tapioca Pudding:

Ingredients:

1/3 cup sugar

1 egg

3 T minute tapioca

2 3/4 cup milk

Directions:

Mix together above ingredients and let stand for five minutes. Cook and stir till mixture comes to a full boil. Remove and add 1 t vanilla.

Microwave directions:

Mix together above ingredients and let stand for five minutes. Microwave on high for approximately 10-12 minutes, stirring every two minutes until the mixture boils.

Cooking Project: Make Navajo Fry Bread

This recipe comes from the ancient people of North America!

Ingredients:

4 cups white flour

1 T baking powder

1 t salt

1 1/2 cups warm water

1 cup shortening

Directions:

1. Mix together flour, baking powder and salt. Add water.
2. Knead until dough is soft and elastic and does not stick to bowl. If necessary add more water.
3. Shape dough into balls. Pat the balls back and forth by hand until dough is about 1/4 inch thick. Dough should be round. Make a small hole in the center.
4. Melt the shortening in a fry pan. Brown on both sides. Pat dry on paper towel.
5. Eat plain, or use these in place of a tortilla and make tacos.

CHAPTER TWENTY-SEVEN
The Rise of Rome

UBWH 86, UILE 184
KIHOW 66-67, 104-105, KHE 34-35

Review Questions, Romulus and Remus

Can you tell me the names of three empires that came before Rome? We have studied about all of them.

Acceptable answers include: Assyria, Babylon, Media, Persia, Greece, Macedon or *Alexander the Great's kingdom*

Who founded the city of Rome in the legend that we read? *Romulus.*

Who raised Romulus? *First a wolf, then a shepherd*

What was Romulus's twin brother named? *Remus*

Why did Romulus name his city Rome? *He named it after himself*, or *Rome sounds like Romulus.*

How many hills was Rome built on? *Seven hills*

Narration Exercise, Romulus and Remus

Now ask the child to retell the story of Romulus and Remus in three to five sentences. Make sure the child includes the information that Rome was named after Romulus. An acceptable story might sound like this:

"Romulus and Remus were twins. A wolf raised them. They built a town at Rome. Romulus killed Remus and became king. He named Rome after himself."

OR Have the child draw a picture of some part of the story of Romulus and Remus. Ask the child to describe the picture to you. Write the child's description on the bottom of the paper. Put the picture in the History Notebook.

Review Questions, The Power of Rome

What important tribe of people lived in Italy? *The Etruscans*

Whose alphabet and gods did they borrow? *The Greeks*

Did the Romans fight with the Etruscans? *Yes*

Did they learn anything from them? *Yes*

Do you remember anything that the Roman kings borrowed from the Etruscans? *Any of the following are acceptable: how to dress, about the Greek gods, painting, music, special robes called togas, the rods with ax blade (fasces)*

In a democracy, who makes the laws and chooses the leaders? *The people*

How do they do this? *They vote.*

What does *monarchy* mean? *Rule by a king*

What two symbols of power did the Roman kings have? *The fasces (bundle of rods with an axe in the middle) and the purple-bordered robe*

How many kings did Rome have? *Seven*

Who ruled Rome once the Romans got rid of their kings? *Two consuls*

Was Rome a democracy? *No*

Narration Exercise, The Power of Rome

Ask the child to tell you about the history lesson in four or five sentences. He should include the information that Rome was ruled by kings first, and that the kings were followed by consuls. Acceptable narrations might include:

"At first Rome had kings. Rome got rid of the kings and had consuls instead. There were two of them."
OR "The Etruscans lived in Italy. They taught the Romans about painting and other things. Rome had kings, but then the people wanted to help with government. They had consuls instead of kings."

Additional History Reading

Who Were the Romans? (Usborne Starting Point History), by Phil Roxbee Cox (EDC Publications, 1994). A very elementary, easy-to-read introduction to Roman culture, put out by Usborne Books. (RA)

Vulcan the Etruscan (Journey Through Time Series), by Roberta Angeletti (Oxford University Press Children's Books, 1991). Slightly more difficult, but one of the few children's books dealing with the Etruscans; a modern child explores a historic site and encounters an ancient inhabitant along the way. (RA)

The Etruscans (British Museum), by Ellen Macnamara (Harvard University Press, 1991). This book, designed for slightly older children, traces the rise and fall of the Etruscans and describes their language, religion, government, economy, dress, and leisure activities. With a younger child, look at the photographs and drawings of Etruscan artifacts and read the captions. (RA)

The Roman News: The Greatest Newspaper in Civilization, by Andrew Langley (Candlewick Press, 1999). "News stories" about ancient Roman life, with silly headlines and colorful illustrations. A good way to introduce young children to Rome. (RA)

Corresponding Literature Suggestions

Romulus and Remus (Ready to Read, Level 2), by Anne Rockwell (Aladdin, 1997). In this young-readers version of the legend of the twin founders of Rome, Romulus does not kill Remus; instead, Remus goes away to hunt with the wolves. (IR for many children, RA for very early beginners)

Myths and Civilization of the Ancient Romans, by John Malam (Peter Bedrick Books, 1999). Colorful and eye-catching, these two page stories retell Roman myths and also describe the culture of Rome. (RA)

The Time Trekkers Visit the Romans, by Antony Mason (Copper Beech Books, 1995). An adventure through ancient Rome, with cartoon-like illustrations and lighthearted text. (RA)

Map Work (Student Page 84)

1. On the blackline map provided, circle Rome with a red crayon.
2. Rome is in Italy, the country shaped like a boot. Shade in Italy with your favorite color.

Adapted from Terri Johnson's "Blackline Maps of Ancient History" set, with her kind permission. For a full set of blackline maps, coordinated to *The Story of the World*, visit Knowledge Quest Maps at http:// www.knowledgequestmaps.com, or contact Knowledge Quest at 7722 SE 282ⁿᵈ Avenue, Gresham, OR 97080 (503/ 663-1210). You can also buy these maps from Peace Hill Press at http://www.peacehillpress.com.

Coloring Page (Student Page 85)
The wolf finds Romulus and Remus.

Projects

Craft Project: Make a Roman Hairpiece

In ancient Rome, fancy hairstyles became very popular. Sometimes it was difficult to get the right look with natural hair – so many Romans wore wigs or hairpieces.

Materials:

> black, brown or yellow (or any color hair you desire) yarn and construction paper
> glue, stapler, scissors
> bobby pins

Directions:

1. Cut yarn into the length of "hair" desired. Braid the yarn into plaits.
2. Cut a strip of construction paper, long enough to fit around the child's head. Staple the ends together.
3. Glue the braids onto the construction paper. Use bobby pins to keep the hairpiece in place.

Craft Project: Make a Fasces

Materials:

> handful of craft sticks, straws, pencils or twigs
> red yarn or ribbon
> cardboard
> aluminum foil

Directions:

1. Cut out the shape of an ax blade from a piece of cardboard.
2. Cover ax blade (both sides) with aluminum foil.
3. Form your craft sticks into a bundle.
4. Starting at the bottom, wrap the yarn completely around the bundle, then wind the yarn up and around the bundle of sticks. Wrap the yarn completely around the top and then glue down wherever

needed.
5. Glue ax blade in between two of the sticks.

Craft Project: Make a Saturnalia Gift

Saturnalia was a festival to honor Saturn, the god of agriculture. Romans celebrated this festival by exchanging gifts and eating. The most common gifts were small clay figures.

Materials:
> easy-bake clay such as Sculpey (available at craft stores or from Rainbow Resource Center,
> > www.rainbowresource.com)
> baking sheet, wax paper
> cookie cutters (small ones, if available — animal shapes work great!)
> rolling pin
> pencil, plastic knife

Directions:
1. Roll out about 1/4 block of clay until flat on wax paper. Use cookie cutter to cut out shape. Trim with plastic knife, if needed.
2. Use a pencil to poke eyes or any details. You may also wish to add small pieces of another color clay for features on your shape.
3. Bake 20 minutes at 275 degrees. For Scupley, see package instructions.

Activity Project: Run a Popinas (Roman take-out restaurant)

Materials:
> "Roman coins" (either make some pretend ones out of aluminum foil, or use pennies)
> poster board and markers
> canned lentil soup
> bread
> olives
> fruit
> grape juice
> bowls, spoons, glasses, serving utensils
> large pot for soup (or crock-pot)

Directions:
1. Paintings outside the popinas advertised what was on the menu. Make posters with pictures of the items you will be selling (bread, soup, fruit, grape juice, olives, etc.)
2. Heat the soup in pan or crock-pot (adult help needed!).
3. Cut up fruit and bread and arrange it on a platter or plate (adult help needed!).
4. Open for business (maybe a family dinner). Be sure to bring lots of coins to pay for the hard work!
5. If you want to, serve the Roman dish below:

> **Cecina**
> Ingredients:
> > olive oil
> > salt
> > basil leaves (dried or fresh)
> > 2 cans chick peas
> Directions:
> 1. Heat oven to 375 degrees.

2. Drain beans, but save the liquid. Mash beans in a bowl.
3. Add 2 Tbs olive oil and enough liquid as needed to make a smooth paste.
4. Oil a cookie sheet or pizza pan with olive oil. Spread batter on the pan, shaping into a circle.
5. Drizzle on a tablespoon or two of olive oil. Sprinkle with basil. Bake for 45 minutes.

REVIEW CARDS
Chapters Twenty-Four, Twenty-Five, Twenty-Six, Twenty-Seven
(Student Page 86)

CHAPTER TWENTY-EIGHT
The Roman Empire

UBWH 86, UILE 188-191
KIHOW 117, 127, KHE 62-63

Review Questions, The Roman Gods

Whose gods did the Romans worship? *The Greek gods, with different names*

Can you tell me any of their names? *Jupiter, Ceres, Proserpine, Hades, Neptune, Mars*

Why did Proserpine have to stay with Hades for six months of the year? *Because she ate some seeds from a pomegranate*

What season of the year comes when Proserpine is underground with Hades? *Winter*

Narration Exercise, The Roman Gods

Ask the child to draw a picture of Proserpine and Ceres, Proserpine and Hades, or Ceres looking for her daughter. Ask the child to describe the picture. Write the description on the bottom of the picture.

Review Questions, The Roman Builders

Can you tell me three things that the Romans built? *Roads, aqueducts, and apartment buildings*

What were the Roman roads made out of? *Sand, gravel, stone, concrete*

Can you still see Roman roads today? *Yes*

What did aqueducts do? *Carried water into the city*

What did the Romans use the water for? *Drinking, cooking, and public baths*

Narration Exercise, The Roman Builders

Ask the child to tell you three things that the Romans built, and to tell you one fact about each of these things. Write these down for the child and put them into the History Notebook. An acceptable answer might be:

"Roads. They were made of sand and gravel."

"Aqueducts. They carried water."

"Apartments. They were made of concrete."

Review Questions, The Roman Gladiators

What did gladiators do? *Fought with each other or with wild animals while an audience watched*

Why did Servius have to be a gladiator? *He didn't have any choice because he was a prisoner.*

Where did Servius learn how to fight? *In the gladiator school*

Did he want to be a fighter? *No*

What happened when he fought in the arena? *He didn't kill his opponent.*

Narration Exercise, The Roman Gladiators

Say to your child, "Can you tell me the story of Servius very briefly – in just a couple of sentences? Begin with 'Servius was captured…' and go from there." Note to parent: This exercise is developing your child's ability to summarize the main points of a story. Talk to the child about the story. Guide her towards a summary that sounds like this: "Servius was captured by Roman soldiers. They took him to Rome and forced him to go to gladiator school."

Review Questions, The Gladiator School

Did Servius feel lucky to be a gladiator? *No, he hated it.*

Do you remember what a *secutor* is? *Prompt child if necessary: a fighter who chases net-fighters*

What did Servius do in his first match when the net-fighter stumbled? *Let him live, let him get away*

Did the Romans like to see gladiators die? *Most of them did. A few, like Seneca, did not.*

Narration Exercise, The Gladiator School

Say to your child, "Can you tell me the end of Servius' story? First, let's read what you told me last time. *Read the child the summary of the first part of the story.* Now can you finish the story?" Note to parent: Aim for 2-3 sentences. An acceptable summary might be: "Servius learned how to fight. But when he went to the arena, he didn't want to kill the other man. So he let him live."

Additional History Reading

Gladiator, by Richard Watkins (Houghton Mifflin, 1997). Dramatic black and white pictures of gladiators, and descriptions of each type of gladiator armor. (RA)

The Roman Colosseum (Wonders of the World) by Elizabeth Mann (Mikaya, 1998). This book is to be "explored," not necessarily read word for word; look at the pictures, read the captions, and read those pages that the child finds most interesting. (RA)

Ancient Rome: The Nature Company Discoveries Library, ed. Paul Roberts (Time Life Books, 1997). Beautiful pictures and illustrations of Roman construction

Rome Antics, by David Macauley (Houghton Mifflin, 1997). Macauley takes a pigeon's-eye view and leads young readers through the streets of early Rome. Beautifully done, like all Macauley's books. (RA)

City: A Story of Roman Planning and Construction, by David Macauley (Houghton Mifflin, 1983). Follow the development of a Roman town from its earliest days. (RA)

The Romans (Illustrated World History), by Anthony Marks (EDC Publications, 1991). An Usborne publication, covering Roman culture and architecture on a very basic level. (RA, may be IR for some strong readers)

Roman Roads and Aqueducts (Building History Series), by Don Nardo (Lucent, 2000). This well-researched account is packed with detailed information about the technical principles of construction and architectural features. Probably best for advanced readers and children with strong engineering interests. (RA)

The Roman Colosseum (Building History Series), by Don Nardo (Lucent, 1998). Detailed information about early Roman stadiums, building methods, and materials. Fairly advanced for first and second graders.

Corresponding Literature Suggestions

Classic Myths to Read Aloud, by William F. Russell (Crown, 1992). A collection of Greek and Roman myths, designed to be read aloud to children aged five and older. (RA)

Androcles and the Lion, by Dennis Nolan (Harcourt Brace, 1997). Picture-book retelling of the classic story of a Roman slave who befriends a lion. (RA)

The Roman Twins, by Roy Gerrard (Farrar Straus & Giroux, 1998). A colorful, interesting adventure story about Roman siblings; the beautiful illustrations show all sorts of Roman architectural detail. (RA)

Asterix the Gladiator, by Rene de Goscinny (Distribooks, 1995). This comic-strip tale of adventure is as much fun for grown-ups as for children. (RA)

See You Later, Gladiator (Time Warp Trio), by Jon Scieszka (Viking Children's Books, 2000). "*Gratias tibi ago quia me gladio tuo non fodisti.*" That's "thank you for not poking me with your sword," a useful phrase for the hapless time-traveling trio, Sam, Fred, and Joe, when they find themselves flunking out of gladiator school in ancient Rome. (RA)

Map Work (Student Page 84)

Look back at last lesson's map. Review the locations of Rome and Italy.

1. Find the island of Sicily. Color it yellow.
2. What is Italy shaped like?
3. What does it look like it is doing to the island of Sicily?

Coloring Page (Student Page 87)

The Gladiators

Projects

Craft Project: Make a Roman Archway and Aqueduct

As the Roman towns grew, the architects put their beautiful archways to use as water-conduits, in structures known as aqueducts. The aqueducts were a series of connected archways built to tilt the water from its source to a holding tank in the town which would distribute the water through out in a piping network, like those in use today.

Materials:

> photocopy of arch pattern (Student Page 88)
> sand dough (recipe follows)
> rolling pin
> table knife
> baking sheet
> cardboard inside roll from paper towels
> empty yogurt cup
> plastic straw
> scissors
> full glass of water

Directions:

1. Pre-heat oven to 250 degrees.
2. Cut out archway pattern from the next page.
3. Divide your sand dough into two parts. Wrap up the dough you are not using to prevent drying. Pat or roll out the first half to one inch thickness and place the archway pattern on top. Using a table knife, cut around the pattern. Save the scraps with the rest of the dough not being used.
4. Carefully lift your first arch on to a baking sheet.
5. Repeat with the other slab of dough, only with the second arch, add 1/4 inch more dough on the top. This is so that when the archways are hooked together, there is a gradual sloping down to the water tank. (You can make additional archways as long as each is slightly taller than the last.)
6. Bake the archways for 20 minutes. Let them cool for 15 minutes.
7. To make your archways stand, lift them one at a time and stand them on the baking sheet. Brace the bottoms with more sand dough built up on the sides slightly. When all are standing, bring them together

and smooth in sand dough between them, hooking them securely.

8. Gather a glob of sand dough the size of two jumbo marbles. Pat it down in the palm of your hand and press it on to the side of a rolling pin. This will create a kind of cradle for the cardboard tube to sit on. Add these cradles to the top of each archway, checking to make sure there is a gradual sloping downward. Bake the aqueduct for another 20 minutes.

9. After your aqueduct has cooled, lay the cardboard tube on the top.

10. On the bottom of the yogurt cup, poke scissors through on three sides. Cut the straw into three parts and insert into the bottom holes of the cup. This is the water tank for the Roman town. Place it under the lower end of your aqueduct.

11. Pour water into the tube at the top of your aqueduct and watch as it travels to your holding tank and out the different pipes to the parts of the town that need it. You are hired as a Roman architect!

Optional: Embellish your Roman archway with columns or scroll work on the top. Use a toothpick to etch decorative borders or use the sand dough and make heads of lions, bears or eagles on the top of the arch.

Sand Dough Recipe

Ingredients:

> 4 cups of play sand (get at any hardware store)
>
> 2 cups of cornstarch
>
> 4 teaspoons of cream of tartar

Directions:

1. Combine in a saucepan and whisk together slowly.

2. When well mixed, add 3 cups of hot water. Place the pot over medium heat and stir constantly until you cannot stir any longer.

3. When it is too stiff to stir, take off the heat and let it cool for 15 minutes. If it feels sticky at this point, put back on medium heat and stir some more. Then take off and let it cool for 15 to 20 minutes.

4. When you are able to handle it, knead it slightly and put unused dough into a resealable bag until it will be used.

5. Soak pan for an hour to wash out the dough residue.

Activity Project: Make a Roman Road Model

The Romans were well known for their roads. One of the most famous Roman roads was known as the Appian Way. You can make a cutaway model of a Roman road in which you can see all of the layers that went into making the final product.

Materials:

> small shoebox lid
>
> glue
>
> sand
>
> small pebbles or aquarium rock
>
> smooth, round rocks (or decorative marbles from a craft store)

Directions:

1. The first step in making a Roman road was to dig a wide ditch. The shoebox lid is going to be our ditch.

2. Then the Romans filled the ditch with sand. Brush a thin layer of glue over the entire inside surface of the shoebox lid. Then sprinkle sand over entire bottom. Let dry.

3. Next they poured small stones on top of the sand. For this step, brush a thin layer of glue over ¾ of the sand. Sprinkle small pebbles or the rock used for fish tanks over the glue.

4. Concrete was the next layer. For this layer, use the sand dough recipe from above or a mixture of glue and sand for the concrete. **Optional:** Add some black paint to make mixture look more like concrete. Spread the concrete over half of the surface of the shoebox lid.

5. Finally, the Romans laid smooth paving stones on top of the concrete. Glue round rocks (or marbles) one at a time over ¼ of the surface of the shoebox lid.

Activity Project: Roman Chariot Races
Materials:

> cardboard box large enough to fit around your child
> packaging tape
> scissors
> markers
> paints
> construction paper
> glitter and anything else you may want to decorate the "chariot" with
> paper plates
> glue

Directions:

1. Use a cardboard box that will fit around your child and provide a little extra "running" room.

2. Cut out the bottom and top of the box. For handles, cut two 4-inch lines, one about 1 1/2 above the other on each side of the box. Reinforce the handles with packaging tape.

3. Make two "wheels" by gluing two paper plates on the chariot, one per side.

4. Decorate your chariot.

5. "Let the races begin!"

CHAPTER TWENTY-NINE
Rome's War with Carthage

UBWH N/A, *UILE* 185-187
KIHOW 106-107, *KHE* 62-63

Review Questions, Rome's War with Carthage

What city did Rome fight? *Carthage.*

What did they fight over? *They wanted to trade with the same cities.*

Was it a long war or a short war? *A long war!*

Do you remember what the wars were called? *The Punic Wars*

Where did they fight – on land or on water? *Mostly on water.*

What are soldiers who fight on water called? *A navy.*

What did Hannibal do? *Fought the Romans with elephants.*

How did General Scipio get Hannibal out of Italy? *He attacked Carthage.*

Who won – Carthage or Rome? *Rome*

What did Hannibal do when Carthage surrendered? *He drank poison.*

Narration Exercise, Rome's War with Carthage

"Rome and Carthage fought a long war. They fought with each other on ships. One Roman general had chickens for good luck! Then Hannibal attacked Rome with elephants. But he lost and drank poison." OR "Rome wanted to rule more land. So did Carthage. They fought the Punic Wars. Hannibal went into Italy with elephants. Then Scipio attacked Carthage, and Hannibal came back to fight him. But Carthage lost."

Additional History Reading

The Roman Army, by John Wilkes (Cambridge, 1973). A good illustrated guide to the arms and organization of the Roman military. (RA)

A Roman Fort: The Inside Story, by Fiona Macdonald (Peter Bedrick Books, 1993). Cutaway views of a Roman fort. (RA)

So You Want to Be a Roman Soldier? by Fiona Macdonald (Twenty First Century Books, 1999). Simple, well-illustrated descriptions of how Roman soldiers lived and worked,. (RA)

Going to War in Ancient Times (Armies of the Past), by Moira Butterfield (Franklin Watts, 2001). Lots of pictures with captions; describes Roman military strategy.

Hannibal, by Robert Green (Franklin Watts, 1996.) The life and military exploits of the famous Carthaginian general. Really too much text for young children, but this is the only "junior biography" of Hannibal available. (RA)

Corresponding Literature Suggestions

Hannibal and his 37 Elephants, by Marilyn Hirsch (Holiday House, 1977). The only available picture-book related to the Punic Wars. Unfortunately, it's **out of print** – check your library. (RA)

The Young Carthaginian, by G. A. Henty. (Lost Classics Book Company, 1998). This historical novel, set during the times of Hannibal and the Punic Wars between Carthage and Rome, is for older children, but could be an extended read-aloud project (especially if you have an older student who could read to the younger ones). An adventure story that describes the campaigns of Hannibal in Iberia, Gaul, Cisalpine Gaul and at Rome's doorstep through the experiences of a young Carthaginian noble. (RA)

Map Work (Student Page 89)

1. On the blackline map provided, underline Carthage with a red crayon.
2. Find Rome and circle it with a red crayon. Color Italy yellow.
3. Color and/or label the Mediterranean Sea with a blue crayon.
4. Find Carthage and circle it with a red crayon. What continent is Carthage in?
5. Draw a line showing how Hannibal and the Carthaginians got to the Alps by going through North Africa, Spain, and Gaul.
6. Now draw a line from the Alps down to Rome. This is the path that Hannibal tried to take with his elephants.

This map is from Terri Johnson's "Blackline Maps of Ancient History" set and is used with her kind permission. For a full set of blackline maps, coordinated to *The Story of the World*, visit Knowledge Quest Maps at http://www.knowledgequestmaps.com, or contact Knowledge Quest at 7722 SE 282nd Avenue, Gresham, OR 97080 (503/663-1210). You can also buy these maps from Peace Hill Press at http://www.peacehillpress.com.

Coloring Page (Student Page 90)
Color Hannibal and his elephant, and then help him get through the Alps!

Projects

Craft Project: Make a Cuff Bracelet (like the Roman soldiers wore)

Materials:

      poster board or lightweight cardboard

      aluminum foil

      permanent marker

Directions:

1. Cut the poster board so that it is about 2 inches wide and fits around the wrist of your child.
2. Cover the poster board with aluminum foil.
3. Write S-P-Q-R on the bracelet with permanent marker.
4. Staple the bracelet together so it fits your child's wrist.

Note: SPQR stood for **Senatus Populus que Romanus** in Latin, which means "The Senate and the Roman People." Roman soldiers were supposed to remember that they served Roman citizens and the Senate.

Craft Project: Make a Coin Ring

The Romans often used money as jewelry. You can too!

Materials:

      pipe cleaner or chenille covered wire

      button with two holes

      glue

      penny or other coin

Directions:

1. Put the pipe cleaner through the holes of the button.
2. Cut and twist together ends to fit your child's finger.
3. Then glue coin on top of the button

Cooking Project: Hannibal's Elephant's Ears

Ingredients:

      package of refrigerated biscuit dough

      cinnamon and sugar, honey, or powdered sugar

Directions:

1. Open can of refrigerated biscuits.
2. Flatten out a little and shape dough into an elephant ear shape (scone).
3. Fry in hot oil, about one minute per side.
4. Remove from oil, and roll in cinnamon and sugar mixture.

Craft Project: Make a Journey of the Elephants Flipbook

Ever wonder what a herd of elephants must have looked like to the Romans who first saw them coming over the Alps? Hannibal hoped that these intimidating animals would help him win the battle against the mighty Romans.

Materials:

      two or more photocopies of the elephant page (Student Pages 91-92)

      scissors, stapler

Directions:

1. Cut out all of the squares along the black line.
2. Keep only one of the #1 squares. This one will be the cover of your flipbook.

3. Now place the square frames behind each other in numerical order. Repeat, starting with #2, as many times as you have copies.

4. Make sure that the right side is lined up evenly.

5. Staple the top left corner.

6. Test out the book by flipping through the pages slowly a couple of times. Realign the book if necessary.

7. Now you are ready to view the journey of Hannibal's elephants. Flip the pages quickly and watch the elephants march down the mountains.

Art Project: Draw Yourself in Ancient Roman Armor
Materials:

> newsprint (from an end roll found at a newspaper printing business), or wide, white butcher paper
> black marker
> crayons
> (Optional: book with pictures of Roman soldiers, from the list above)

Directions:

1. Imagine you are called out of your ripe, farm fields to help defend your country from that menace, Hannibal. You gather together your weapons. You fit your plate armor over your red tunic. Lifting your father's brightly plumed helmet over your head, you check the cheek guards. Then you reach for your javelin and rectangular shield, covered lovingly in goathide. Your family rushes around. One child brings your kit pole, which your wife has already fitted with a hide water bag and mess tins that hang from your food pack. You notice the tight knots. All is made secure for the journey. Another child ceremonially hands you your sword, sheathed securely for your travels. From under your bed, you unwrap your spiked shoes and carefully replace your hide sandals with them. The third child has been busy with your horse. So all is ready. All that is left is to say good-bye.

2. Now lie down on the paper and have your whole body traced on to the newsprint. Carefully lift yourself off.

3. With your crayons, begin dressing yourself for the battle ahead. The Roman soldiers wore a tunic, which is a long shirt that stops above the knee, has short sleeves and is belted at the waist. Often in the pictures, the tunics are red, but you can color yours what ever color you like. But before you color it in, add the plate armor. This was a vest that crossed around the chest and stomach and was held up over the shoulders, kind of like overalls. A large belt-like strap went around the waist and held the sword and other tools the soldier would carry with him. He also would wear his shield and javelin on his back, secured over the shoulder. If the travel was long, he had a long, wooden pole, called a kit pole. It acted like a hobo-stick, only it reached the ground and was thick enough to carry a load.

4. Don't forget your spiked shoes. They looked like sandals with baseball cleats, and made a distinct sound that would strike fear in the heart of an enemy.

5. The Roman helmet was made of thick iron and had cheek guards to protect his face. They did not sport the nose guard like the Greeks did, but a Centurion did have a wide, full plume that went over the helmet's crest like a peacock's feathers spread out. Many soldiers also had the head of wild animals, like a lion or bear, over their helmet so that the teeth rested on the forehead, making the soldiers look fearless and ruthless. What will yours look like?

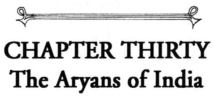

CHAPTER THIRTY
The Aryans of India

UBWH 63, 83, *UILE* 174
KIHOW 64-65, *KHE* 33

Review Questions, Life on the Ganges River

What were the people who settled in ancient India called? *Aryans*

Where did they come from? *Asia*

Do you remember the names of the two big rivers that they settled near? *Ganges and Indus*

Why did they settle near the Ganges and Indus Rivers? *Because they needed water for crops and animals*

What was the name of the chief god of the Indian Aryans? *Shiva*

Why did the river-goddess Ganga get angry at Shiva? *He told her to go down to earth and give water to the people who were thirsty.*

What did Shiva do, when he saw that Ganga was getting ready to jump down on the earth? *He jumped down ahead of her so that she landed on top of him.*

Which river was named after Ganga? *The Ganges*

What do we call people who believed in Shiva and Ganga? *Hindus*

Narration Exercise, Life on the Ganges River

"After the citadel cities disappeared, other people came to India. They were called Aryans. They lived near the Ganges River and the Indus River." OR

"Once the people on earth were thirsty. Shiva told the river goddess Ganga to go down to earth. She didn't want to, so she tried to drown everyone. Shiva stopped her and she turned into the Ganges River."

Review Questions, The Castes of Ancient India

What were the four different castes of ancient India? *Priests, warriors, farmers and traders, servants.*

How did you know what caste you belonged in? *You were born into it* OR *your family belonged to it.*

What was the best caste to be in? *The priests or Brahmins.*

What were the people called who didn't belong to any caste? *Untouchables.*

What kind of work did they do? *Dirty work: burying dead animals, cleaning streets, picking up garbage, working in the fields.*

What story did the Hindus tell to explain castes? *The story of Purusha, the first man.*

Narration Exercise, The Castes of Ancient India

"People in India belonged to four different groups. Some groups were better than others. People who didn't belong to any of the groups were called Untouchables. They had to do dirty work."

Review Questions, Siddhartha

Why did Siddhartha leave his palace and wander through the world? *Because he saw sick, poor, and old people.*

What did Siddhartha teach all men to do? *To live good lives; to be honest, make peace, avoid violence.*

What was Siddhartha's new name? *Buddha*

What were his followers called? *Buddhists.*

Narration Exercise, Siddhartha

"Siddhartha was a prince. He lived in a great palace. Finally he saw that some people were poor and sick. He left the palace. He taught people to be good, and he was called Buddha."

Additional History Reading

The Ganges (Rivers of the World), by David Cummings (Raintree Steck-Vaughn, 1994). An overview of the Ganges River, one of the largest waterways in the world, valued not only for trade and irrigation, but also for its religious importance to Hindus. (RA)

The Ganges, by Michael Pollard (Benchmark Books, 1997). Another simple, illustrated guide to the Ganges River, focusing on its present day uses. (RA)

The Sacred River, by Ted Lewin (Clarion, 1995). This book uses beautiful full-color illustrations to describe Hindu pilgrimage to the Ganges. (RA)

Buddha, by Demi (Henry Holt and Co., 1996). The story of Siddhartha's life and a brief introduction to the teachings of Buddhism. (RA)

Prince Siddhartha: The Story of Buddha, by Jonathan Landaw (Wisdom Publications, 1996). The story of Prince Siddhartha and how he became Buddha. (RA)

My Friend's Beliefs: A Young Readers Guide to World Religions, by Hiley H. Ward (Walker Publishing, 1988). Pages 13-40 discuss Hinduism and Buddhism. (RA)

World Religions, by John Bowker (Dorling Kindersley, 1997). Pages 18-41 cover Hinduism, and pages 54-75 cover Buddhism. (RA)

India (Countries of the World), by Michael S. Dahl (Bridgestone, 1997). Focuses on the modern culture of India, with occasional glances back at the past. (RA)

Corresponding Literature Suggestions

Stories from India, by Vayu Naidu (Raintree/Steck-Vaughn, 2000). Ancient Indian fairytales. (RA)

Savitri: A Tale of Ancient India, by Aaron Shepherd (Whitman, 1992). A brave and resourceful Indian princess saves her husband from death. (RA)

Buddha Stories, by Demi (Henry Holt and Co., 1997). A collection of ten tales told by the Buddha. (RA)

The Wisdom of the Crows and Other Buddhist Tales, by Sherab Chodzin (Tricycle Press, 1998). A nice collection of Buddhist moral tales from India, Burma, Tibet, China, and Japan. (RA)

I Once Was A Monkey: Stories Buddha Told, by Jeanne Lee (Farrar, Straus & Giroux, 1999). This book covers some of the basic teachings of Buddha, through a collection of six classic tales. (RA)

Map Work (Student Page 93)

1. On the blackline map provided, find the Ganges and Indus Rivers and circle their names in red.
2. Use a green crayon to color in the area that made up the Aryan Empire (area inside dashed lines).
3. Use a blue crayon to color in the Bay of Bengal and the Indian Ocean.
4. Did you notice how the Ganges River has a delta just like the Nile River does in Egypt? Use a green crayon to color in the delta.

Coloring Page (Student Page 94)

This is a picture of Siddhartha, who became known as the Buddha.

Projects

Craft Project: Make a Rakhi

One special day in India is called Raksha Bandhan. This celebrates the bond of love between brothers and sisters. During this celebration the sister ties a rakhi (like a bracelet) on her brother's wrist. The brother promises the sister he will look after her.

Materials:

> yarn, ribbon or needlepoint floss
> cardboard or poster board cut into round shapes
> glue
> beads, sequins, glitter, foil, gel pens, and/or anything else to decorate

Directions:

1. Knot the ends of the yarn, ribbon or floss together, and divide the number of strands by three. Braid

as you would braid hair. You want this to be the size of a bracelet.   Attach the ends together but leave the bracelet large enough to slip over your hand.

2. Decorate a small circle of cardboard or poster board with foil, beads, sequins, etc.

3. Sew or glue the decorated circle to the middle of the braided band.

Activity Project: Color Fingernails and Lips

The ancient Indus girls were the first to use lipstick. In ancient Bengal, men painted their fingernails thinking it would attract girls.

Materials:

washable lipstick

non-toxic nail polish OR washable tempera or water colors

Directions

1. Girls: put on your lipstick! Now you look like a girl of ancient India.

2. Boys: time to paint your nails with the polish, tempera, or water colors! Remember, in ancient India, this was a sign of manhood and bravery.

Activity Project: Play Tiger Hunt

In ancient India, royalty hunted tigers for entertainment.

Materials:

yellow construction paper or thin cardboard

markers, paints, glitter

yellow, black, or striped T-shirt

Directions:

1. Make a crown for the "king." Cut a strip of yellow construction paper or thin cardboard with a serrated edge, long enough to fit around child's head. Tape ends together. You can decorate the crown with your paints and art materials if you want to.

2. One child will be the "tiger" and another child the "king." If it's just you and Mom, Mom can be the tiger! The "tiger" should put on the T-shirt. The "king" should wear the crown.

3. Choose a place in the house or yard to serve as "base."

4. Now the "king" should count to ten while the "tiger" hides. Can the king find the tiger and catch him (by tagging him) before the tiger can sneak back to base?

5. If you have additional children, they should serve as the king's "beaters" – they should also try to find the tiger. When they find the tiger, they can't touch him. Only the king can catch the tiger! Instead, they should try to "herd" the tiger back towards the king so that the king can catch him.

CHAPTER THIRTY-ONE
The Mauryan Empire of India

UBWH 83, *UILE* 175
KIHOW 96-97, *KHE* 57

Review Questions, The Empire United

Are cities stronger if they are independent, or if they're united together? *United together*

What was the name of the Indian empire that united the cities of India together? *The Mauryan Empire*

Who was its most famous ruler? *Asoka*

What religion did he follow? *Buddhism*

Can you tell me one of the kind things he did? *He built hospitals, built animal hospitals, made laws against cruelty to animals, gave up violence, planted trees along roads, gave up eating meat.*

Narration Exercise, The Empire United

"Cities are stronger if they're all in one country. The cities of India were all separate. Then the Mauryan Empire made them into one country. Asoka ruled the empire."

Review Questions, The Jakata Tales

Why did the hare offer to roast himself? *So that the priest wouldn't have to kill him*

Was he rewarded for his generosity? *Yes, he lived happily and was rewarded after death.*

Who lived with the hare? *An otter, a monkey, and a jackal*

Were they as generous as the hare? Why or why not? *No, because they stole the food they offered the priest.*

Narration Exercise, The Jakata Tales

Ask the child to draw a picture of the hare and the priest. If he wants to, he can also draw pictures of the otter, the jackal, and the monkey. Ask the child to describe the picture. Write the description on the picture's bottom.

Additional History Reading

Ancient India, by Daud Ali (Lorenz Books, 2001). Illustrations, descriptions, and crafts, all related to ancient India. (RA).

India (Countries of the World), by Michael S. Dahl (Bridgestone, 1997). A very simple introduction to modern India, with some information about India's history. (RA)

India: Festivals of the World, by Falaq Kagda (Gareth Stevens, 1997). Reviews the history and development of major Indian holidays. (RA)

*A Coloring Book of Ancient India (*Bellerophon Books, 1991). Uses images from ancient Indian culture. (RA/activity)

Science in Ancient India (Science of the Past), by Melissa Stewart (Franklin Watts, 1999). Dicusses the scientific achievements of the Indian people; intended for slightly older children, but could be valuable for a child with scientific interests. (RA)

Corresponding Literature Suggestions

I Once Was A Monkey: Stories Buddha Told, by Jeanne Lee (Farrar, Straus & Giroux, 1999). Each animal story has a moral about how we should treat others. (RA)

The Ocean of Story: Fairy Tales from India, by Caroline Ness (Lothrop, Lee and Shepherd, 1995). A collection of 18 classic stories from India. (RA)

The Ringdoves: from the Fables of Bidpai, by Gloria Kamen (Macmillan, 1988). Several animals band together to escape the hunter, in this Indian fable about loyalty and friendship. (RA)

The Monkey and the Crocodile: A Jataka Tale from India, by Paul Galdone (Houghton Mifflin, 1987). A monkey manages to outwit the crocodile who decides to capture him (a retelling of one of the fables relating to the Buddha). (RA)

The Gifts of Wali Dad: a Tale of India and Pakistan, by Aaron Shepard (Atheneum, 1995). An impoverished grass-cutter finds that gifts can be a mixed blessing. (RA)

Map Work (Student Page 95)

1. On the blackline map, outline the Ganges River and the Indus River in blue.
2. Color the Ganges delta gree.
3. Now use a red crayon to color in the area that made up the Mauryan Empire (area inside the dashed lines).

4. Circle the names of the Indian Ocean and the Bay of Bengal in blue.

Coloring Page (Student Page 96)
The Jakata Tale: The Hare, Otter, Jackal, and Monkey

Projects

Cooking Project: Learn How to Make Rice

Rice is a staple food in India, as well as in China and other Asian countries.

Ingredients:

> 2 cups cold water
>
> 1 cup rice

Directions:

1. Explain to your child that you make rice by using twice as much water as rice.
2. Measure the water and rice and pour into a saucepan. Bring to a boil.
3. As soon as the water boils, reduce the heat to simmer. Put a tight-fitting lid on the pot. Don't peek for 12 minutes!

> **Variation: Indian Curried Rice**
>
> Ingredients:
>
> > 3 cups cooked rice
> >
> > 1 chopped onion
> >
> > 1 chopped green pepper
> >
> > 2 Tbs butter
> >
> > 1 tsp curry powder
> >
> > 1 egg yolk
> >
> > 1/4 tsp salt
> >
> > 1/8 to 1/4 tsp black pepper
> >
> > 1/4 tsp cayenne pepper
>
> Directions:
>
> 1. Sauté onion and green pepper in butter until onions and peppers are tender.
> 2. Stir in curry powder, slightly beaten egg, salt, pepper and cayenne.
> 3. Mix into hot rice.

Activity Project: Play a Game from Ancient India [C]

Did you know that cards and the games of Chutes and Ladders both originated in ancient India?

Snakes and Ladders

If you have the game of Chutes and Ladders, get it out and look at it. Ancient Indians played a game like Chutes and Ladders – but they called it Snakes and Ladders! Each one of the slides in the game was a huge, scaly snake! Play the game of Chutes and Ladders, but whenever you slide down a chute, hiss like a snake.

Cards

Get out a pack of cards and look at the card faces. In ancient India, the king card represented the most powerful man in the country – the king of India! The jack card is his general, the man who rules his army. All the number cards are his army followers! Take out the aces and queens from your deck. Now you can play "Indian battle"! This is best played with four players, one for each "army" or suit of cards.

But you can play two-person Indian battle by only using two suits of cards. Whose army will win?

Video Viewing: *The Tiger and the Brahmin* by Rabbit Ears Productions (1991).
This story, told by Ben Kingsley, is a narration of the traditional Indian folktale about a well-meaning Brahmin who makes the mistake of freeing a tiger from its cage. For ages 5 and up. Try your local library; many children's departments make a point of stocking Rabbit Ears videos.

REVIEW CARDS
Chapters Twenty-Eight, Twenty-Nine, Thirty, Thirty-One
(Student Page 97)

CHAPTER THIRTY-TWO
China: Writing and the Qin

UBWH 74-77, UILE 166-167
KIHOW 98-99, KHE 58-59

Review Questions, Calligraphy in China
What was the earliest Chinese writing called – where words looked like the things they named? *Pictograms*
What do we call later Chinese writing? *Calligraphy*
Can you tell me the names of several lines used in Chinese calligraphy? You can look back at the lesson as you answer. *Horizontal line, vertical line, dot, downward stroke, sweeping downward stroke, hook*
What kinds of hair did scribes use for their brushes? *Mouse, rabbit, sheep, wolf*
The Chinese developed a faster way to print books. What did they use? *Ink and blocks of wood*
Had anyone else ever done this? *No, the Chinese were the first.*

Narration Exercise, Calligraphy in China
"The Chinese used to use pictures for writing. Then they wrote characters instead. They didn't look as much like pictures. They used seven different lines." OR
"At first the Chinese wrote by hand. They used special brushes made out of mouse hair, rabbit hair, and wolf hair. It took a long time. Then they figured out how to use wood blocks instead."

Review Questions, Warring States
How many "Warring States" were there in ancient China? *Six*
What Warring State conquered the rest? *Qin (pronounced "Chin")*
Where does China get its name? *From the word "Qin"*
How did Qin Zheng keep control of his new empire? *He made his rivals move into his own city, executed anyone who was planning rebellion, and had books burned.*
Did the Chinese people love their new emperor? *No; many disliked him for his cruelty.*
Qin Zheng, changed his name to Shi Huangdi. What does this name means? *The First Emperor*
What sorts of things did Qin Zheng, or Shi Huangdi, do to keep his people from rebelling? *He melted his enemies' weapons, forced them to move into his capital city, executed anyone planning treason, built roads so his army could move quickly, burnt books.*

Narration Exercise, Warring States
"China used to be six different countries. Then the Qin conquered all the rest. China became one country, but the new emperor was cruel. China is named after the Qin."

Review Questions, The First Emperor and the Great Wall

Why did Shi Huangdi want to build a Wall? *To keep the Mongols out*

What is the full name for the Wall he built? *The Great Wall of China*

How long is the Wall? *Almost 3000 miles, or as long as the United States is wide*

What is the Wall made out of? *Stone in some places, packed dirt in others*

Was it finished during Shi Huangdi's lifetime? *No, it took hundreds of years to finish.*

Can you still see the Wall today? *Yes*

Narration Exercise, The First Emperor and the Great Wall

"The emperor of China wanted to keep the Mongols out. So he built a huge wall. It was made out of stone and out of dirt packed hard. It is called the Great Wall of China."

Review Questions, The First Emperor's Grave

How was the tomb of Shi Huangdi discovered? *Two farmers uncovered clay pieces while digging a well.*

What was found inside the underground city? *Thousands of life-sized clay horses and soldiers*

Can you tell me two things that might be inside the burial mound? *Rivers of mercury, treasure, crossbows, stars, and planets*

Why did Shi Huangdi build such a huge city? *Because he hoped to live forever*

Narration Exercise, The First Emperor's Grave

"Shi Huangdi built an underground city. It had soldiers and horses in it, made out of clay. He is buried in the city, but no one has found his tomb yet."

Additional History Reading

Long is a Dragon: Chinese Writing for Children, by Peggy Goldstein (Pacific View Press, 1992). Explains how Chinese writing developed and demonstrates how to write seventy-five Chinese characters, using detailed instructions and examples. (RA)

The Great Wall of China, by Leonard Everett Fisher (Macmillan, 1986). A brief history of the Great Wall of China, with detailed, large pictures. (RA)

The Great Wall, by Elizabeth Mann (Mikaya Press, 1997). Covers the building of the Great Wall of China and the thousands of years of conflict that preceded it. (RA)

Ancient China (See Through History), Brian Williams (Viking, 1996). Describes daily life in ancient China with 4 see-through scenes. (RA)

Growing up in Ancient China, by Ken Teague (Troll, 1993). Tells the story of life in ancient China from the perspective of a young child. (RA)

The Terracotta Army of the First Emperor of China, by William Lindesay (Odyssey Publications, 1999). Nice pictures of the Terracotta army. (RA)

The Incredible Story of China's Buried Warriors, by Dorothy Hinshaw Patent, (Benchmark, 2000). Covers the archaeological find of thousands of life-sized terra cotta warrior statues discovered in China, and discusses the emperor who had them created and placed in his tomb. (RA)

China (Games People Play), by Kim Dramer (Children's Press, 1997). Discusses the games that Chinese children have played from ancient times to the present, including Chinese checkers, tangrams, pick up sticks, paper making and others. (RA)

Ancient China Treasure Chest: 2000 Years of History to Unlock and Discover, by Chao-Hui Jenny Liu (Running Press, 1996). Text would be a read aloud. Projects include: Chinese Calligraphy (brush, ink and instructions), Chinese fan, I Ching coins, charts, stickers, and a booklet (overview of dynasties, inventions and principles of Taoism). Small children will need help with most of these projects. (RA/activity)

A Coloring Book of Ancient China (Bellerophon Books, 1985). Uses actual images from ancient Chinese art. (RA/activity)

Corresponding Literature Suggestions

The Magic Tapestry: A Chinese Folktale, by Demi (Holt, 1994). The youngest of three sons must overcome frightening obstacles to win back his mother's tapestry. (RA)

Ten Suns: A Chinese Legend, by Eric Kimmel (Holiday House, 1998). A father, Di Jun, looks for a way to stop the destruction after his ten sons walk across the sky together causing the earth to burn from the blazing heat. (RA)

Legend of the Li River:An Ancient Chinese Tale, by Jeanne M. Lee, (Holt, Rinehart and Winston, 1983). A sea princess seeks help to lessen the hardships of the poor laborers employed in building the Great Wall of China. (RA)

The Dragon Prince: A Chinese Beauty and the Beast Tale, by Laurence Yep (HarperCollins Juvenile Books, 1999). A poor farmer's youngest daughter agrees to marry a fierce dragon in order to save her father's life. (RA)

The Ch'I-Lin Purse: A Collection of Ancient Chinese Stories, by Linda Fang (Farrar, Straus and Giroux, 1997). Stories of ancient China, from a number of different traditions. (RA)

Map Work (Student Page 98)

1. On the blackline map provided, use a green crayon to color the Qin Empire (area inside the dashed lines).

2. Find the names of the two important rives in the Qin Empire and circle their names in red. Trace the rivers in blue. What sea is next to China? Color it blue also.

3. Find the Great Wall and color it light brown.

Coloring Page (Student Page 99)
The Great Wall of China

Projects

Art Project: Practice Chinese Calligraphy
Materials:

> several different sizes of watercolor paintbrushes
> black ink or tempera paint (watercolor paint will also work, but not as well)
> white paper

Directions:

1. On one piece of white paper, try making the different lines shown in the chapter. What brushes work best? How do the lines look different if they are made with smaller or larger brushes?

2. Now try combining the lines together into the characters shown in the chapter. Are you able to make similar characters? Don't try to make them small – make them as large as you want.

3. Can you make up your own characters? What do you think the character for "book" should look like? How about the character for "baby," "bread," "sun," or "egg"?

Activity Project: Make a "Great Wall"
Materials:

> popsicle or craft sticks
> superglue
> yarn

garden dirt

Directions:

1. Lay six popsicle sticks side by side on a piece of newspaper. Lay two more sticks horizontally across them (one at the top and one at the bottom) and superglue into place. (Make sure to put a dot of superglue on each stick!). Repeat three more times, so that you have four wooden "walls" made out of popsicle sticks.

2. Stand the "walls" up so that they form a box. Use a drop of superglue at each corner to hold the walls together. Wrap yarn around your wooden box and knot it to keep the walls together.

3. Set the wooden box on a newspaper, baking sheet, or other surface. Pack it full of dirt – as hard as you can! You may want to add stones, grass, or other ingredients to make the "wall" stronger.

4. When the box is full of packed dirt, lift it gently straight up. You should have a section of strong dirt wall that will stand by itself – just like the dirt sections of the Great Wall of China.

5. Experiment. Can you make another section of wall touching the first section? Can you make one on top of it?

Craft Project: Making Paper

The Chinese were among the first ancient people to use paper that is similar to the paper we use today. This project is an extensive one, but it is particularly good if you'd like to include your older children in the study of Chinese culture.

Materials:

> 2 wood picture frames (preferably flattish)
> screen (just like you use in windows)
> large tub (such as a Rubbermaid storage tub)
> blender or food processor
> paper scraps
> liquid starch (optional)
> felt
> newspapers
> scrap board for pressing (optional)

1. Take the glass, backing, and all nails or metal off the picture frames.

2. Staple a piece of screen to the back of one; trim the edges if necessary. These two frames are officially called a mould and deckle. The size of your frame determines the size of your paper.

3. Tear your paper scraps up into small pieces. The smaller, the better.

4. Make paper pulp; construction paper is the very easiest to make into pulp. Fill your food processor or blender about 1/4 full of warm water (2 or 3 cups). Slowly add about 1 cup of paper scraps. The paper turns to pulp easier if you've soaked it overnight. Don't use glossy paper or paper with very much ink on it.

5. After paper is blended with water (you should not see very many individual pieces), pour it into a tub. The tub should be larger than your frame—about 2 inches clearance on all sides minimum.

6. The thicker your pulp mixture, the easier it is to make the paper. The paper project works best if you add one tablespoon of liquid starch to a batch of pulp (a batch being about 6 to 8 cups including water) for sizing. Stir up the water-pulp mixture in the tub between every piece of paper that you make.

7. Put both of your picture frames together, with the screen in the very middle. The frames will be back to back. Slide the frames into the tub from the front. Gently rock the screen back and forth under the water and slowly bring it up to the top of the water. Pull it straight up. It will probably take a few practice runs to get the pulp distributed fairly evenly over the screen. Be careful not to make your first pieces

too thick. You can add handfuls of pulp if the mixture gets too thin. Any mistakes can be recycled right back into the tub (before they dry.)

8. Now, lay down a pile of newspaper (do this outdoors—it's a wet job), and place a piece of felt (bigger than your screen/frame by about an inch) on top of the newspaper. Take the top (empty) picture frame off and carefully turn your frame/screen/paper over on top of the felt.

9. This next part can be tricky. Push your newly made paper down onto the felt, squeezing some of the water out by pressing on the screen. Lift it up, starting at one corner. The new paper should stick to the felt. Unfortunately, it may stick to the screen (this is not good!). Slightly thick paper is easiest for beginners to make. Thin paper is most difficult.

10. Now, place another piece of felt on top of your paper, so that you have a sandwich of newspaper, felt, handmade paper, felt, more newspaper. You can stack several of these sandwiches up (try not to use the slick pages of the paper or you'll have a problem with sliding), place a board on top and stand on the entire stack to squeeze out as much water as possible. Let the stack dry for about an hour. Then carefully dig the paper/felt sandwiches out, peel the felt off. Now you have damp paper.

11. Let the paper dry flat. You can speed up the drying process by ironing the paper between towels.

12. You can add all sorts of fun things to your pulp or sprinkle them onto your paper as you're removing from the tub of water—glitter, confetti, tissue paper, dried flower petals and grasses, etc.

CHAPTER THIRTY-THREE
Confucius

UBWH 76, *UILE* 165
KIHOW 73, *KHE* 39

Review Questions, Confucius

Who was the great teacher of ancient India? *Buddha*

Who was the great teacher of ancient China? *Confucius*

Tell me one thing that Confucius taught. *Obey people in authority; don't do anything to another person that you wouldn't want done to yourself; try to fix your mistakes; giving is more fun than getting; don't be greedy.*

When did Confucius live? *During the Period of Warring States*

Narration Exercise, Confucius

"Confucius lived in China. He taught people to obey their rulers and children to obey their parents. He had many followers."

Additional History Reading

Ancient China: Nature Company Discoveries, by Judith Simpson (Time Life, 1996). Beautiful illustrations
     in this book, which has some information about the religion of ancient China. (RA)

Confucius: Philosopher and Teacher, by Josh Wilker (Franklin Watts, 1999). Intended for slightly older
     children, but you can read sections of it with a young student. (RA)

World Religions, by John Bowker (Dorling Kindersley, 1997). Beautifully illustrated, with a section on
     Chinese beliefs. (RA)

Confucius and Ancient China, by Theodore Rowland-Entwistle (Wayland, 1986). Describes the times of
     Confucius and reviews his teachings. (RA) **Out of print; check your library.**

Corresponding Literature Suggestions

The Empty Pot, by Demi (Henry Holt, 1996). This read-alone book for beginners explains the value of honesty. (IR)

The Greatest Tale, by Demi (Scholastic, 1998). Another ancient Chinese tale that teaches a character quality – in this case, generosity. (RA)

The Chinese Book of Animal Powers, by Chungliang Al Huang (HarperCollins, 1991). Twelve animals, one for each month, illustrated with brush strokes; the character quality related to each animal is explained. (RA)

Map Work (Student Page 98)

1. Look back at the map you used in the last lesson. Use a purple crayon to color in the areas that were not part of the Qin Empire.

2. Now let's make a map puzzle. Spread a thin layer of glue over the entire back side of the map. Place on a thin piece of cardboard and press down firmly. With a black marker, draw "puzzle" shaped lines on the cardboard side. Cut out the pieces. When the cutting is finished, mix up the pieces and see how quickly you can put the Qin Empire back together.

Coloring Page (Student Page 100)
Confucius

Ⓒ Projects

Activity Project: Making Tangrams

Tangrams are an ancient Chinese puzzle. There are seven pieces, and they fit together to form a square. Legend says that a man (either from the T'ang dynasty or named Tan) dropped a tile, and it broke into seven pieces. He tried to fix it by putting it back together again. The Emperor saw him trying to put the seven pieces together, later showed it to all of China, and this became a game the people in China liked to play.

To make your own tangrams you will need a 4 inch square of construction paper or cardboard. First, with a ruler draw 12 squares that are about 1 inch each. Your grid should look like that on page 101 of the Appendix. Next, mark the following lines on the graph. Cut on the bold lines (do not cut the grid lines). If you want to, you can color your pieces. You will now have seven pieces. Try and make a box or animal shapes with the pieces.

Cooking Project: Making Tea

Confucius said, "Let your palate be your guide." What is your palate? It's the part of your mouth that tells you whether something tastes good or not! Read "The Legend of Tea" and then make some simple tea. Does your palate approve?

The Legend of Tea

One afternoon, very long ago, Emperor Shen Nung was enjoying a cup of boiling water. The Emperor felt that drinking very hot water made him feel better. There was a gentle breeze on this afternoon and a few leaves from a nearby tree floated down and landed in his hot water. The Emperor thought the leaves made the water smell nice. He decided to take a sip of the water with leaves and found he enjoyed the taste. He proclaimed the leaves to be sent from heaven. This is believed to be the first cup of green tea.

Ingredients:

fresh or dried mint leaves*

boiling water

tea cup

Directions:

1. Pour boiling water into teacup and have your child add a few mint leaves. Let steep 3-5 minutes then remove mint leaves.

2. Let cool slightly and drink.

*Most children seem to prefer mint herb tea to black or green tea. You can often buy fresh mint in the produce section of a grocery store. Another option is to buy some loose tea. Put it into an infusing basket, add it to the water, and steep. To be very authentic, purchase some Chinese tea.

CHAPTER THIRTY-FOUR
The Rise of Julius Caesar

UBWH 87, UILE 185
KIHOW 115, KHE 63

Review Questions, Caesar is Kidnapped

What city was Julius Caesar from? *Rome*

Who did Julius Caesar's family say they were descended from? *Romulus*

Why did the people of Rome like Caesar? *He was a good speaker; he threw parties for people; he was brave; he defeated the pirates.*

The pirates told Caesar that they wanted a lot of money from his relatives before they would let him go. What did Caesar tell them? *That he was worth more than that*

What did Caesar do when the pirates let him go? *He gathered an army together, hunted down the pirates, and defeated them.*

Narration Exercise, Caesar is Kidnapped

"Julius Caesar was from an important family. He lived in Rome. He was captured by pirates, but when they set him free he punished them. " OR

"Julius Caesar was captured by pirates. Pirates sailed on the sea and stole things. Julius Caesar told the pirates to let him go. Finally they did."

Review Questions, The Consuls of Rome

What did a consul do? *Governed, or ruled, Rome*

What country did Caesar govern, before he became a consul? *Spain*

Why did Caesar weep when he read the story of Alexander the Great? *Because he hadn't accomplished anything great*

Did Caesar become a consul? *Yes*

Once Caesar became consul, how many consuls were there? *Three*

The three consuls were called the "triumvirate." What does "tri" mean? *Three*

Narration Exercise, The Consuls of Rome

"Caesar wanted to be important in Rome. He went to Spain, but he didn't like it there. Finally he got to be a consul in Rome." OR

"Consuls ruled Rome. Caesar wanted to be a consul. Finally he got to be one. There were two other consuls, too."

Review Questions, Caesar and the Senate

What did the Senators think Caesar wanted to be? *King of Rome*

What was Caesar doing that made the Senators angry? *He ignored them and did whatever he wanted.*

What did Cincinnatus do when the people wanted him to be king? *He went back to his fields.*
Do you think Caesar was like Cincinnatus? *No*

Narration Exercise, Caesar and the Senate
"The Senate didn't want Caesar to be king. They thought he should be like Cincinnatus. Cincinnatus didn't want to be king of Rome." OR
"The people of Rome liked Caesar. But the Senate didn't. They were men who ran Rome. They thought Caesar wanted to be king."

Additional History Reading

Julius Caesar, Great Dictator of Rome, by Richard Platt (DK Publishing, 2001). Spectacular illustrations, pull-out sections, and easy-to-read narrative about the rise to power of Julius Caesar. (RA)

Julius Caesar, by Graham Tingay (Cambridge, 1991). A simple, complete, nicely illustrated biography of Caesar, written for younger children. (RA)

Read About Ancient Romans, by David Jay (Millbrook Press, 2000). A young child's guide to ancient Rome. (RA, some sections may be IR for strong readers)

A Pirate's Life for Me, by Julie Thompson and Brownie Macintosh (Charlesbridge Publishing, 1993). A fun, fact filled book about all kinds of pirates. (RA)

Great Pirate Activity Book by Deri Robins (Kingfisher Books, 1995). Instructions for making games, models, and recipes are included along with many pirate facts in this activity book. (RA)

The Legionary (The Roman World Series), by Peter Connolly (Oxford University Press Children's Books, 1998). A detailed, nicely illustrated description of the legionary's duties, equipment, and lifestyle. (RA)

Life of a Roman Soldier, by Don Nardo (Lucent, 2001). Describes the kind of life that Caesar led in his days as a footsoldier. (RA)

Corresponding Literature Suggestions

Famous Men of Rome, by John Haaren and A. B. Poland (Greenleaf Press, 1989). Stories of famous Roman figures, including Cincinnatus and Caesar. (RA)

The Wadjet Eye, by Jill Rubalcaba (Clarion, 2000). The story of Damon, a medical student living in Egypt, who journeys to Spain to locate his father, who is serving in the Roman army led by Julius Caesar. Written for slightly older children; a good read-aloud project over several weeks, particu larly if an older student can read to the younger child. (RA)

Map Work (Student Page 102)

1. On the blackline map provided, color the Mediterranean Sea blue. Color the islands in the sea pink.
2. Find the Tiber River and outline it in blue.
3. Find Rome and circle it in red.
4. The consuls made Julius Caesar a leader of the colony Spain. Locate Spain on the map provided. Using a dotted line, draw a possible route that Caesar and his men might have taken from Rome to Spain.

NOTE: This map is reprinted from Terri Johnson's "Blackline Maps of Ancient History" set, with her kind permission. For a full set of blackline maps, coordinated to *The Story of the World*, visit Knowledge Quest Maps at http://www.knowledgequestmaps.com, or contact Knowledge Quest at 7722 SE 282nd Avenue, Gresham, OR 97080 (503/663-1210). You can also buy these maps from Peace Hill Press at http://www.peacehillpress.com.

Coloring Page (Student Page 103)

This picture is based on a marble statue now in the Vatican Museum in Rome.

Projects

Art Project: Make a Roman Mosaic

A Roman mosaic was made by pressinll pieces of stone into plaster or cement in the shape of a picture. Romans often used mosaics to decorate the floors of their homes, instead of carpets. You can make your mosaic in the pattern of a sun, flower, or cloud, or just make an interesting design.

Materials:

> poster board or heavy construction paper
>
> a variety of dried beans (you can also use squares of colored paper)
>
> glue
>
> pencil, for drawing outline

Directions:

1. Draw the outline of your picture on the poster board or construction paper. Erase and redraw until you have it just right.

2. Squeeze out a line of thin glue onto the pencil lines.

3. Lay beans or colored paper squares along the lines of glue.

4. Now fill in the middle of your picture. You can arrange the beans or colored paper squares into patterns to complete your mosaic!

Activity Project: Play the Ransom Caesar Game

Materials:

> 2 copies of pirate game board (Student Page 104)
>
> 2 pennies
>
> handful of beans

Directions:

1. Each player hides Julius Caesar (the penny) on their game board. Don't let your opponent see your game board!

2. Taking turns, pick a row letter and a column number (i.e., R3). Call the number out to your opponent.

3. If your opponent's penny is on that number, you've found Caesar! But if it isn't, mark that square on your own board with a bean, so that you'll remember not to call it again.

4. The first person to rescue Julius Caesar from the pirate wins.

Craft Project: Make a Crown of Leaves

Roman leaders liked to wear crowns on their heads. This was to show their importance or rank in society. The crowns were made from leaves and formed into the shape of a wreath. Julius Caesar liked to wear wreaths of gold leaves.

Materials:

> ¾ inch wide strip of posterboard, long enough to fit around child's head
>
> leaves (real, fake, or made from construction paper)
>
> glue and scissors

Directions:

1. Form the posterboard into a circle that will fit on child's head. Tape or glue into place.
2. Glue leaves onto crown form and let dry.

CHAPTER THIRTY-FIVE
Caesar the Hero

UBWH 84-85, 87, *UILE* 182-183, 185
KIHOW 112-113, 115, *KHE* 63, 68-69

Review Questions, Caesar Fights the Celts
Why were Caesar's soldiers so loyal to him? *He treated them well, paid them money, and made sure they had plenty of food to eat.*
What country did Caesar want to conquer? *Britain.*
What do we call the people who lived in Britain? *Celts*
Did Caesar ever completely conquer Britain. *No*
What did he tell the people of Rome about his wars with the Celts? *That he was winning*
Do you remember the name of the book Caesar wrote about his wars? *The Gallic Wars*

Narration Exercise, Caesar Fights the Celts
"Caesar wanted to conquer Britain. It was hard because the Celts were very good fighters. He told the Romans that he was winning, but he didn't win all his battles."

Review Questions, Caesar Crosses the Rubicon
Which senator married Caesar's daughter and then became jealous of Caesar? *Pompey*
When Caesar heard that he was going to be arrested, what did he do? *He marched his army towards Rome.*
What river did Caesar cross over with his army? *The Rubicon*
Did Pompey and the Senators fight against Caesar? *No, their soldiers ran away.*
Was Caesar the king yet? *No, but he was very powerful.*
What does "crossing the Rubicon" still mean? *Doing something you can't undo*

Narration Exercise, Caesar Crosses the Rubicon
"The Senators made Pompey jealous of Caesar. Pompey tried to arrest Caesar. But Caesar marched into Rome with his army, and Pompey and the Senators ran away."

Review Questions, Caesar and Cleopatra
What country did Pompey run to? *Egypt*
What queen ruled Egypt? *Cleopatra*
How did Cleopatra and her brother try to make friends with Caesar? *They killed Pompey.*
Why did Cleopatra want Caesar to be on her side? *She wanted to get rid of her brother and rule Egypt all alone.*
Did Caesar help her rule Egypt alone? *Yes, he did.*
What does "Veni, Vidi, Vici" mean? *I came, I saw, I conquered.*
What language is this in? *Latin*

Narration Exercise, Caesar and Cleopatra
"Pompey went to Egypt. Caesar went after him. Cleopatra was the queen of Egypt. She got Caesar to stay and help her in Egypt."

Review Questions, The Death of Caesar
When Caesar became dictator, what could he do? *Anything he wanted*
Can you name one thing that Caesar did when he became dictator? *He took power away from the Senate;*

he could declare war, pass laws, and raise taxes; he made money with his picture on it; he paid for gladiator fighting and chariot racing.

What did Caesar want to be called? *King Caesar*

Who did he want to be king after him? *His nephew Octavian*

Why did the Senate decide to kill Caesar? *They were afraid of his power; they didn't want him to pass his power on to another king.*

Can you remember one strange thing that happened to Caesar on the fifteenth of March? *His horses were crying; a fortune-teller told him to be careful; his wife had a strange dream.*

What did Caesar say when he died? *Et tu, Brute?*

What does this mean? *You, too, Brutus?*

Narration Exercise, The Death of Caesar

"Caesar became a dictator. He could do whatever he wanted. But he wanted to be called "king." So the Senators decided to kill Caesar. They stabbed him to death."

Additional History Reading

The Romans, by Peter Hicks (Thomas Learning, 1995). Illustrates the culture and history of ancient Rome. (RA)

Roman Numerals I to MM, by Arthur Geisert (Houghton Mifflin, 1996). Introduces Roman numerals; by counting pigs in the illustrations, the reader can practice Roman math! (RA)

Cleopatra: The Queen of Kings, by Fiona Macdonald (DK Publishing, 2001). Another in the Dorling Kindersley series "DK Discoveries"; beautiful pictures and interesting narrative. (RA)

Cleopatra, by Diane Stanley (Mulberry Books, 1997). Slightly more detailed account of Cleopatra's life. (RA)

The Celts (See Through History), by Hazel Mary Martell (Viking, 1996). A colorful and interesting guide to ancient Celtic culture. (RA)

Corresponding Literature Suggestions

"Julius Caesar," from *Tales from Shakespeare* by Marcia Williams (Candlewick Press, 1998). Retells Shakespeare's famous play in eye-appealing, comic-book format. (RA, IR for strong readers.

Shakespeare Stories II, by Leon Garfield (Houghton Mifflin, 1995). A read-aloud, story version of Shakespeare's play. (RA)

Cleopatra: The Queen of Dreams, by Haydn Middleton (Oxford University Press Children's Books, 1998). The story of Cleopatra. (RA)

Rome Antics (David Macaulay) - A pigeon carrying an important message takes the reader on a unique tour, which includes both ancient and modern parts of the city of Rome. (RA)

Map Work (Student Page 105)

1. On the blackline map provided (next page), find Britain and color it with a red crayon.

2. Using a blue crayon, trace the Rubicon River.

3. Using a red crayon, circle Egypt. Trace the Nile River in blue.

4. Draw a line from Britain to Rome, to show the route Caesar might have taken when he returned to Rome with his army. Make sure that your line crosses the Rubicon!

5. Now draw another line from Rome down to the Nile delta. What route would Caesar have taken when he went down to Egypt to see Cleopatra?

Projects

Activity Project: Measure Your Height

The Romans were afraid of the Celts because they were so tall. How tall are you?

Materials:

       pen

       paper

       scissors

       measuring tape

Directions:

1. Romans used different measurements than we do. A foot was the actual length of each individual's foot - from heel to toe. On a piece of paper, draw and cut out a model of your foot.

2. Using a measuring tape, see how tall you are.

3. Now, using your foot measurement, see how tall you are.

4. Measure mom or dad's foot. Compare your height using all three measurements. Are they the same?

Craft Project: Make Caesar's Flag

The flag bearer jumped into the water to fight the Celts and immediately the remaining soldiers followed. The flag, also known as a *signum*, was a symbol that reminded the soldiers of their purpose. The flag was not to be destroyed or captured by the enemy. Choose a flag to make:

Flag #1

Materials:

       dowel

       felt

       glue and scissors

       permanent markers

       glitter, sequins, other decorations

Directions:

1. Cut a large rectangle out of the felt.

2. Glue one of the short sides to the dowel. Let dry.

3. Use the permanent markers to draw a symbol on the flag. What will your symbol be?

4. Decorate the flag with glitter and sequins.

Flag #2

Materials:

       wrapping paper tube

       piece of cardboard, 1.5" x 8"

       ribbons, streamers, or yarn

       decorations such as aluminum foil, cardboard or fun foam shapes, fake jewels

Directions:

1. Glue 1"x 8" strip of cardboard toward top of tube. Attach streamers to the edges of the strip.

2. Using your imagination, decorate the rest of the tube anyway you would like. Be sure and leave an empty space in order to hold the flag in your hand.

Art Project: Mint Your Own Coins

Julius Caesar was the first politician to place his likeness on the coins of Rome. Prior to that time, coins were decorated with the pictures of animals, ships, buildings and pictures of the gods. Many coins were minted to commemorate a special event, such a Caesar winning the Gallic Wars. Today you will make coins that will commemorate something special that has happened in your life, such as learning to read or ride a bike.

Materials:

air-drying clay or Sculpey (at a craft store)
rolling pin, sculpting tool, sharpened pencil or toothpick
round plastic lids (hair spray, starch) in assorted sizes
(round biscuit and cookie cutters would also work).
copper, silver and gold metallic paint
paint brush

Directions:

1. Roll out the air-drying clay into a rectangle that is about ¼" – ½" thick. Use the varying sizes of plastic tops or cookie cutters to cut out your coins. It might be easier for the children to work with larger, rather than smaller, circles.

2. Use the sculpting tool, pencil or toothpick to draw a picture on your clay circle. If it is to commemorate the day your learned to ride a two-wheeler, don't forget to add the year you did it in.

3. Place the coins aside and allow them to dry completely.

4. When the coins have dried, take your different colored paints and paint each coin. This will need to be done in a two-step process: paint one side, let dry, paint the other side.

Math Project: Learn the Roman Numerals

Materials:

15 blank index cards
black marker

Directions:

1. On side one, write the Arabic numbers 1, 2, 3, 4, 5, 6, 7, 8, 9, 10, 50, 100, 500, and 1000.

2. On side two, write each corresponding Roman numeral: I, II, III, IIII, V, VI, VII, VIII, IX, X, L, D, C and M respectively.

3. After the cards have finished being made, turn them over Roman numeral face up and see if you can guess the correct value for each card.

4. When you have learned the Roman numerals well, use them to write out the ages of all your family members. Be sure to include grandma and grandpa, since their ages will probably use the L (50) numeral.

REVIEW CARDS
Chapters Thirty-Two, Thirty-Three, Thirty-Four, Thirty-Five
(Student Page 107)

CHAPTER THIRTY-SIX

The First Roman Prince

UBWH 87-89 , UILE 185-191
KIHOW 118-119, KHE 64-67

Review Questions, The First Roman Prince

Who was Octavian's uncle? *Julius Caesar*

How did Octavian make himself popular with the people of Rome? *He threw a big party with Caesar's money; he gave presents and money to the poor families.*

Did Octavian ask to be king? *No, he said that he would quit.*

What title did the Senate give Octavian? *First Citizen, or "princeps"*

What was Octavian's new name? *Augustus Caesar*

Which month is named after Augustus Caesar? *August*

Which month is named after Julius Caesar? *July*

Narration Exercise, The First Roman Prince

"Octavian was Caesar's nephew. The people of Rome liked him because he was generous. He said that he would not be king, but the Senate wanted him to rule. They gave him a title that means 'prince.'"

Additional History Reading

The World of the Roman Emperor, by Peter Chrisp (Peter Bedrick Books, 1999). Describes Rome in the years of Augustus and later. (RA)

Augustus and Imperial Rome, by Miriam Greenblatt (Benchmark, 2000). Covers Augustus Caesar and his role as the first Roman emperor. (RA)

Augustus Caesar's World, by Genevieve Foster (Beautiful Feet Books, 1996). A read-aloud volume covering the personalities and events of the Roman empire; pick and choose what you'll read aloud. (RA)

The Story of Clocks and Calendars: Marking a Millennium, by Giulio Maestro (Lothrop, Lee & Shepard, 1999). Discusses the evolution of the calendar. (RA)

Corresponding Literature Suggestions

Sun-day, Moon-day: How the Week Was Made, by Cherry Gilchrist (Barefoot Books, 1998). Presents the stories behind the names of the days of the week. (RA)

Sun and Moon, by Naomi Mitchison (Thomas Nelson, 1973) Recounts the adventures of Sun and Moon, children of Cleopatra and Mark Antony. (RA) **Out of print; check your library.**

Shakespeare Stories II, by Leon Garfield (Houghton Mifflin, 1995). Tells the play of Antony and Cleopatra in a story format. (RA)

Map Work (Student Page 102)

1. Using the map from Chapter Thirty-Four, use a green pencil to color in the area that made up the Roman Empire when Caesar was killed (the area inside of the dashed lines).
2. Name the sea that was surrounded by the Roman Empire. Find it on the map and color it blue.
3. Locate Cleopatra's home of Egypt on the map and mark it with an X.

Coloring Page (Student Page 108)

This picture of Augustus Caesar is based on a marble statue located in the Vatican Museum in Rome.

Projects

Art Project: Make a Mosaic One-Month Calendar

Materials:

$\boxed{\text{C}}$

      13" x 20" piece of stiff poster board

        old glossy magazines, colored mylar or construction paper

        scissors, glue stick, white glue and paint brush

        8 ½" x 11" monthly planner sheets (available at office supply store) or blank sheet of
            paper.

Directions:

1. Lay your piece of poster board flat on the table. Take one sheet from the monthly planner pad and center it and glue it down 1" from the bottom of the board. (If you can't find the monthly planner sheets, take a piece of blank paper and, using a ruler, draw a grid containing 5 rows and 7 columns.)

2. Write the name of the month and the number of days on your sheet.

3. Now for the fun part. Take old glossy magazines and cut colorful pages in small squares. Use the pieces to make any design that you like in the space above the calendar. You can make a face design, animals or flowers, whatever you like. When you have laid out your design, use the glue stick to glue it all into place.

4. When everything has been glued in place and allowed to dry completely, mix 2 parts white glue to1 part water. This will make a varnish. Use the paint brush to spread the varnish over the entire surface of the mosaic, and let it dry.

5. To hang your calendar, make a small hole in the center at the top of the board and hang on a nail.

Craft Project: Make a Roman Toga

A toga was a very complicated outfit to wear and was usually only worn on very special or important occasions. Traditionally the toga was 2 ½ times as long as the person was tall and about 2 times as wide as the person. Slaves were forbidden from ever wearing a toga, because the toga was considered to be a sign of power and prestige. Only the most important people of the Roman Empire were allowed to use the color purple.

Materials:

      one old white sheet

      3 yards of wide purple ribbon

      double–sided tape

      length of cord

      one of Dad's t-shirts

Directions:

1. Fold the sheet in half lengthwise. Sew, or use the double-sided tape to attach the purple ribbon along one side of the long edge. Trim away any excess ribbon.

2. Put on Dad's t-shirt and use a piece of cord to tie a belt around your waist.

3. Have mom stand behind you, holding the toga by the long straight edge. Have her drape a quarter of the toga over your left shoulder and arm. Push the toga up your arm, so that your hand is free.

4. Bring the rest of the toga around your body, making sure that you go under your right arm. Gather a couple of folds in the toga and tuck them into the waistband securely.

5. Last of all, fold the remaining loose fabric over your left arm. You will need to keep your left arm close to your body to hold it in position. Don't forget to wear the laurel wreath from Chapter 35 and a pair of sandals for the full effect!

CHAPTER THIRTY-SEVEN
The Beginning of Christianity

UBWH 90, UILE 192-193
KIHOW 124-129, KHE 72

Review Questions, The Birth of Jesus

What do we call the time of peace and safety in the Roman empire? *The Pax Romana*

What is the other name for the land of Judea? *Canaan*

According to the story from the Gospel of Luke, where was Jesus born? *In Bethlehem*

What holiday celebrates the birth of Jesus? *Christmas*

Who came running to see Jesus after he was born? *Shepherds*

How did they know he had been born? *Angels told them.*

Narration Exercise, The Birth of Jesus

"Canaan was also called Judea. Rome ruled it. Mary lived in Judea. She had Jesus in Bethlehem."

OR "Jesus was born in Bethlehem. His mother was named Mary. Shepherds came to see him because angels told them to. "

Review Questions, Jesus Crucified and Resurrected

What is Jesus' most famous teaching called? *The Sermon on the Mount*

Do you remember any of the things Jesus taught? *Poor people are blessed; merciful people are blessed; peaceful people are blessed; don't fight back; love your enemies; don't judge other people.*

Why did the Romans get worried about Jesus? *They thought that the Jews would obey Jesus instead of Augustus Caesar.*

What does the Gospel of Luke say happened after Jesus was buried? *He rose from the dead.*

What are followers of Jesus called? *Christians*

What do "B.C." and "B.C.E." mean? *"Before the birth of Jesus" and "Before the Christian era."*

What do "A.D." and "C.E." mean? *"After the birth of Jesus" and "The Christian era."*

Narration Exercise, Jesus Crucified and Resurrected

"Jesus taught people and many followed him. The Romans were afraid that people wouldn't listen to the emperor. They put Jesus to death, but he rose from the dead."

OR "Jesus was put to death because the Romans didn't want him teaching the people any more. The Gospel says that he rose from the dead. People who believe in Jesus are called Christians."

Additional History Reading

DK Read and Listen: First Bible Story Book, by Mary Hoffman (DK Publishing 2000). A simplified Biblical account. (RA)

The Bible, whichever version your family prefers (try the New International Version for up-to-date language). The story of the birth of Jesus is found in Matthew 1:18-2:18 and Luke 2:1-20; the Beatitudes are found in Matthew 5:1-12; and the story of the death and resurrection of Jesus is found in Matthew 26:47-28:20; Mark 14:43-16:20, Luke 22:47-24:53; and John 18:1-21:25

The Jesus Story, by Mary Batchelor (Lion Publishing, 1992). With detailed illustrations, this book presents the Biblical story of Jesus with historical background information. Features include Roman dress, soldiers, architecture, maps and ships. Also highlights Jewish religious practices of that time regarding marriages, farming, the calendar and more. (RA)

Corresponding Literature Suggestions

The Very First Christmas, by Paul Maier (Concordia Publishing House, 1998). Following the
Luke narrative, this beautifully illustrated look at the first Christmas draws readers into
each scene. (RA)

The Parables of Jesus, by Tomie dePaola (Holiday House, 1995). Simple, one-page retellings of
the parables of Jesus. (RA)

The Miracles of Jesus, by Tomie dePaola (Holiday House, 1996). Simple, one-page stories about
the miracles of Jesus. (RA)

The Very First Easter, by Paul Maier (Concordia Publishing House, 2000). Full page illustrations
and a simple story. (RA)

The Tell-me Stories Volume 1, by Ella K. Lindvall (Moody Press, 2000). Short narratives of the
parables Jesus told. (RA)

Jesus is Born, by Claudia Courtney (Concordia Publishing House, 1998). This book and many
others by this author are written for the beginning reader and focus on a certain phonetic
sound. Titles also include *Rise and Shine: The Story of Easter; Little Is Big: Jesus Fed the
5,000; Blow! Jesus Calms the Storm;* and more. (IR)

Map Work (Student Page 109)

1. On the blackline map provided, color the Mediterranean Sea blue.
2. Judea was on the coast of the Mediterranean Sea. Jesus was born in Judea, in Bethlehem. Circle
Bethlehem in yellow.
3. Jesus grew up in Nazareth, in Galilee. Galilee was the northern area of the land where the Jewish
people lived. North is *up* on your map. Find Nazareth and circle it in red.
4. Jesus was crucified in Jerusalem. Find Jerusalem and circle it in green.

**NOTE: This map is adapted from Terri Johnson's "Blackline Maps of Ancient History" set, with
her kind permission. For a full set of blackline maps, coordinated to *The Story of the World*, visit
Knowledge Quest Maps at http://www.knowledgequestmaps.com, or contact Knowledge Quest at
7722 SE 282ⁿᵈ Avenue, Gresham, OR 97080 (503/663-1210). You can also buy these maps from
Peace Hill Press at http://www.peacehillpress.com.**

Coloring Page (Student Page 110)

Color the stained-glass picture of the birth of Jesus.

C Projects

Craft Project: Make a Mosaic Cross
Materials for simple mosaic cross:

cardboard, 9" x 12" for suggested size cross
scissors
glue
small square bits of construction paper or tissue paper

Materials for more complicated mosaic cross:

cardboard, 9" x 12" for suggested size cross
scissors
three ceramic tiles (color or colors of your choice)
paper bag
hammer

caulk (tube)

piping (optional)

Directions:

1. The cross became the symbol of eternal life for the people who followed the teachings of Jesus. Cut the piece of cardboard into the shape of a cross. Suggested size: 11" tall x 8 1/2" wide, cross 2 1/2" thick.

2. Put the tiles into the paper bag and break them into desired sizes with the hammer. Squirt the caulk in small areas on the cardboard and immediately put the broken tiles on the caulk in desired pattern. Continue in this manner, doing small areas at a time until entire cardboard is covered. If you're using the decorative piping, squirt the caulk around the edge of the cross and quickly cover the caulk with the piping to make a finished edge.

OR

Spread glue over the surface of the cross. Arrange your construction or tissue paper squares to cover the glue.

(Special thanks to Sally Keller for project idea and instructions)

Craft Project: Make a Pendant (With a Secret Pocket!)

Materials:

> polymer clay such as Sculpey, light colored
> pencil or pen
> spoon and table knife
> leather necklace cord
> three large beads, your choice of color (optional)
> photocopy of one of the symbols of Jesus and the corresponding verse (following page)
> glass pie plate

1. Symbols are used to remind us of special things we want or need to remember. They can be symbols that keep us safe, like the yellow lines in the road that tell us it is dangerous to pass in that area, or symbols that help us to know where to go, like the symbols for the ladies or men's bathrooms at a restaurant. The people who followed Jesus heard him talk about who he was. Jesus used word pictures that helped the people remember. There are a few of them on page 111 of the Appendix.

2. Preheat your oven to 250 degrees. Decide which symbol and verse you want on your pendant. Copy (or scan) it, cutting around the picture and the verse so they are separated.

3. Knead 1/4 of the rectangle of clay (it comes packaged in a small rectangle). Roll it out a little larger then the symbol is. Using the end of a pencil, make a hole at the top of your pendant or make a loop on the top. Use a table knife to make the edges smooth, if you want.

4. Place the copied (or scanned) symbol on one side of your pendant rectangle, face down. Rub the back of this paper with a spoon. This is to make sure that there are no air bubbles and the copy is completely touching the clay. Slowly flip your pendant over and on to a glass pie plate. Wrap some more clay around a pencil or pen, sliding it off, forming a small sleeve or pocket. On the back side, attach the clay pocket. It will be a tiny hiding place. Roll up a small piece of foil and fit it carefully into the sleeve in the back while you're cooking it. This will help the pocket to keep its shape. After you've cooked your pendant, you can roll up the verse and hide it behind in this secret place. Look under your pendant and check to see if your symbol is still placed correctly.

5. Bake for 20 minutes. Let it cool well before touching. It will not feel completely "cooked" right after you pull it out of the oven. However, if it still feels too soft five minutes later, place back in the oven and cook longer.

6. Hang your leather cord around your neck to determine how long you want it to be, adding 3 inches to

the amount to account for the knots. Cut and then fold the length in half. Slip the folded looped edge through your pendant's hole just a little ways. Make sure you thread it front to back. Then bring the ends through the loop just on through the hole. Tighten it and make sure it is secure. Slip three large beads down the cord to the pendant. Tie a knot after the last one. Then secure the cord at the end by knotting them together.

7. Slip around your neck and slide your verse into its secret place.

Art Project: The Night With a Brilliant Star
Materials

> wipe-off or washable crayons, OR white board or washable markers
> clean window (sliding glass doors work great!)

Directions:

1. The night Jesus was born offered much excitement! Consider all of the characters in the story told by Luke. On a big window, recreate the story in a picture of the night Jesus was born with your crayons or markers. Don't forget the shepherds, angels, sheep, Mary, Joseph, and the baby.

2. The medium will come right off with a damp cloth when ever you are done with it.

Activity Project: Make a Life of Jesus Puzzle
Materials:

> coloring page
> sheet of thin cardboard
> glue
> scissors
> pencil

Directions:

1. After coloring the picture, spread glue over the back of it. Stick it onto the cardboard sheet and let it dry.

2. Turn the cardboard sheet over and draw a pattern of puzzle pieces on the back.

3. Cut out the pieces along the lines. Now try to reassemble your puzzle!

NOTE: If someone in the family has experience with woodworking equipment and owns a jigsaw, you can also make a puzzle by gluing the picture onto a thin sheet of wood and cutting it into pieces with the jigsaw.

CHAPTER THIRTY-EIGHT
The End of the Ancient Jewish Nation

UBWH 90, *UILE* N/A
KIHOW 110-111, *KHE* 61

Review Questions, The End of the Ancient Jewish Nation

What Babylonian king let the Jews go back to their home? *Cyrus*

Who ruled over the Jews then? *The Romans*

Why did the Jews attack the Romans? *They didn't want to pay taxes and obey the Romans.*

What city did the Romans destroy? *Jerusalem*

What did the Romans do the Temple? *They burned it and pulled the stones apart to get the gold and silver inside.*

What happened to the Jewish people then? *They were scattered through all the countries of the world.*

Narration Exercise, The End of the Ancient Jewish Nation

"The Romans made the Jews pay taxes and obey them, so the Jews attacked them. Then the Romans burned Jerusalem and knocked the Temple down. The Jews had to leave their country and didn't come back for a long time."

Additional History Reading

Behold the Trees, by Sue Alexander (Arthur A. Levine, 2001). This beautifully illustrated book tells the story of the trees that grew in Israel, from ancient times until the present – and reviews Jewish history in the process. (RA)

Israel, by Kristen Thoennes (Bridgestone, 1999). A young child's history of Israel. (RA)

First I Say the Shema (Hear, O Israel!), by Molly Cone (Union of Hebrew Congregations, 1998). A simple introduction to Judaism. (RA)

Israel in Pictures (Visual Geography Series), by Steve Feinstein (Lerner, 1992). You won't want to read the text to young children, but this book will give them plenty of chances to look at the scenery of Israel. (RA)

Masada, by Neil Waldman (Morrow, 1998). Tells the story of the Jewish revolt against Romans at the fortress of Masada. This book was designed to be acceptable to younger students, but the story of Masada is a sad and violent one, so be sure to preview it. (RA)

Corresponding Literature Suggestions

Angels, Prophets, Rabbis & Kings from the Stories of the Jewish People, by Jose Patterson (Peter Bedrick Books, 1991). Jewish tales and legends from ancient times. (RA)

Celebrate! Stories of the Jewish Holidays, by Gilda Berger (Scholastic, 1998). Covers the basics of Jewish history through stories of the holidays. (RA)

Festival of Lights: The Story of Hanukah, by Maida Silverman (Aladdin, 1999). An illustrated account of the Maccabean revolt in the first century. (RA)

Jason's Miracle: A Hanukkah Story, by Beryl Lieff Benderly (Whitman & Co., 2000). Twelve-year-old Jason has ambivalent feelings about Hanukkah until he finds himself transported back to the time of the Maccabean revolt in Judea. (RA)

Shabbat, by Miriam Nerlove (Whitman & Co., 1998). Soft-toned watercolors show a happy traditional family observing Shabbat, the Jewish Sabbath. (IR)

Journeys with Elijah: 8 Tales of the Prophet, by Barbara Diamond Goldin (Gulliver Books/Harcourt Brace, 1999). Presents eight stories about the Old Testament prophet Elijah, set in a variety of time periods and in places all over the world where Jews have lived. (RA)

Miriam's Cup: A Passover Story, by Fran Manushkin (Scholastic, 1998). A Jewish mother preparing for Passover tells her young children the story of Miriam. (RA)

Map Work (Student Page 112)

1. On the blackline map provided, use a green pencil show the route Abraham took when he left Haran and went to live in Canaan as God instructed him to do.

2. Find Jerusalem and circle it with a red pencil.

3. Color Judah yellow. Judea occupied much of the same land as ancient Judah.

4. Trace the Tigris and Euphrates in blue.

5. Color the area between the rivers green. Do you remember what this was called? It was called Mesopotamia, because it was "between the rivers."

Coloring Page (Student Page 113)

Today, the Star of David is the most common symbol for the Jewish people. You can color this star any color you want!

The Star of David is on the flag of the modern Jewish nation, Israel. The upper and lower stripes of the flag and the star are all blue.

Projects

Craft Project: Make a Shabbat "Sand Art" Candle Holder

The word Sabbath comes from the Hebrew word "Shabbat", and means to rest. Shabbat is a weekly celebration; it begins at sun down on Friday, with the lighting of the candles and ends at sun down on Saturday. The lighting of the Shabbat candles is a signal that people should set aside their everyday problems and worries and start taking the time to enjoy the company of their family and friends over a good meal. Even though you might not be Jewish, you can still make your family's meals a special celebration; a time to enjoy each other and give thanks. Maybe your family could start the tradition of lighting a candle to signal that "family time" has begun. The directions below are for making sand art candlestick holders for your family's table.

Materials:

      sand, plastic bags, food coloring
      2 baby food jars

Directions:

1. Divide the sand into a different bag for each color. Add several drops of food coloring into each bag, close the plastic bag tightly and knead the color into the sand. Add additional food coloring if you would like to darken the color.

2. Use a spoon to slowly sprinkle the colored sand into the jars, one layer at a time. When you have finished layering the colored sand, carefully push a tapered candle through the sand to the bottom of the jar. The sand will hold the candle firmly.

Craft Project: Make Your Own Dreidel

Hanukkah means "dedication." It is an eight-day holiday that celebrates the victory of Judah Maccabee and his followers over the Syrian King Antiochus. King Antiochus commanded the Jews not to worship God, and dirtied the Temple in Jerusalem. After Judah Maccabee was victorious, his people cleaned the temple and started to rededicate it to God. But, they only found enough pure oil to light the menorah for one day. Then a miracle happened, and the oil burned for eight days instead. This is why Hanukkah is celebrated for an eight-day period, so that the Jewish people will never forget the miracle that happened there. A traditional game played during this holiday is called Dreidel. The Hebrew letters written on each side of the square top stand for the words "A great miracle happened there." There is an old legend as to why this game is played during Hanukkah. Even though King Antiochus forbade the Jews to study their Bible, which is called the Torah, young Jewish boys would gather together and study it anyway. When they heard soldiers approaching, the boys would hide their Bibles, take out their tops and pretend that they were playing games instead.

Materials:

      paper, scissors, glue, markers and pencil, dreidel pattern (Appendix p. 114)

Directions:

1. Cut out the dreidel. If you like, use colored markers to decorate.

2. Fold along each of the solid lines. This will make it easier to glue the tabs down, when you shape the dreidel. Place glue on all of the tabs and form into a four-sided top.

3. Insert a pencil in the middle of the X at the top of the dreidel. Get ready to play!

Game instructions:

1. All players need to start out with 10-15 pieces of candy. Each player puts one piece of candy in the middle (or the pot) to start the game off.

2. Then each player takes a turn spinning the dreidel and does what each letter stands for. The 'N' stands for *nisht* and means nothing. If you land on this you do nothing and pass the dreidel on to the next player. The 'G' stands for *ganz* and means all. If you land on this you get to take everything that is in the pot. The 'H' stands for *halb* and means half. If you land on 'H', you get to take half of the candy out of the pot (take an extra one if there is an odd number of candy in the pot). The 'S' stands for *shtel* and means to put in. When you land on this, you must add a piece of your candy to the pot.

3. When there is only one piece of candy or none left in the pot, each player must add a piece of candy to the pot so the game can continue. The game ends when one person has all the candy.

Cooking Project: Make Hanukkah Latkes

Latkes, or potato pancakes, are another Jewish tradition at Hanukkah. Latkes became part of the tradition, because they are fried in oil, and that helps remind the Jewish people that a little jar of oil burned miraculously for eight days so very long ago.

Ingredients:

> 4 large potatoes, peeled, grated and well drained
> 1 medium onion grated
> 2 beaten eggs
> 1 1/2 tsp of salt
> dash of white pepper
> 2 tbsp all-purpose flour
> vegetable oil

Directions:

1. In a large bowl, combine the potatoes, onions, eggs, salt, pepper and flour.

2. Heat 1" of oil in a 12-inch skillet. When the oil is hot, slowly drop a heaping tablespoon of the potato mixture into the oil. For a crisper latke, gently flatten with the back of a spoon. Fry over medium heat for about 3-4 minutes on each side, or until the pancakes are golden brown and crispy.

3. Drain the cooked latkes on paper towels and set them aside in a warm oven. Finish frying the rest of the batter. You may need to add extra oil between batches.

4. When the cooking is completed, sprinkle the hot latkes with sugar or cinnamon, and serve with applesauce, jam, or sour cream.

CHAPTER THIRTY-NINE
Rome and the Christians

UBWH 90-91, *UILE* 192-193

KIHOW 118-119, 128-129 , *KHE* 72-73

Review Questions, Nero, the Evil Emperor

Where was Nero when Rome burned? *At a party, at a house in the country*

Did he come back to Rome when he heard about the fire? *No, he stayed in the country a little while longer.*

Did Nero help the families who lost their homes? *No*

What did he do instead? *He decided to build a bigger palace where the fire had burned.*

What did the people of Rome think about this? *They were angry with Nero.*

Whom did Nero blame for the fire? *The Christians*

Narration Exercise, Nero, the Evil Emperor

"Nero was a bad emperor. He thought he was a good musician. When Rome burned down, he decided to build a bigger palace. He blamed the Christians for the fire." OR

"A big fire burned down the poor part of Rome. It burned down some of the rich part too. The emperor Nero blamed Christians for starting the fire. He had them arrested."

Review Questions, Christians in the Catacombs

What man were Romans supposed to worship? *The emperor*

Did Christians worship the emperor? *No*

How were Christians punished? *They were put in prison or forced to fight wild animals.*

Where did Christians have their meetings? *Underground, in secret passages*

What were those secret passages called? *Catacombs*

What secret symbol did the Christians use? *The symbol of a fish*

Narration Exercise, Christians in the Catacombs

"Christians were supposed to worship the emperor, but they said that they wouldn't. Some of the emperors had them arrested or made them fight animals. So the Christians met in secret places called catacombs."

Review Questions, The Emperor is a Christian!

What god did Constantine worship at first? *Apollo*

Why did he stop persecuting Christians? *He didn't think people should be put in jail because of the god they worshipped.*

What did he see a vision of? *A cross made out of light*

Do you remember what the words underneath the cross said? *By this sign, you will be victor.*

What battle did Constantine's army win? *The Battle of Milvian Bridge*

What happened to Constantine after the victory? *He became a Christian* OR *He built a new capital city.*

Constantine built a new capital city and named it after himself. Do you remember what it was called? *Constantinople*

Narration Exercise, The Emperor is a Christian!

"Roman emperors persecuted Christians. But Constantine thought that was wrong. He said that Christians should be left alone. Then he had a vision of a cross and became a Christian too."

OR "Constantine and his army were going to a battle. They were very tired and discouraged. Then Constantine saw a cross in the sky. He put the cross on his soldiers' shields, and they won the battle. Then Constantine became a Christian."

Additional History Reading

I Wonder Why Romans Wore Togas? And Other Questions About Ancient Rome, by Fiona Macdonald (Kingfisher, 1997). A good basic review of Roman culture from its beginnings to its final days. (RA)

The Roman Record: Hot News from the Swirling Mists of Time, by Paul Dowswell, (EDC Publications, 1998). A slightly tongue-in-cheek look at Roman history, set up like a tabloid sheet. (RA)

Caves, Graves and Catacombs: Secrets from Beneath the Earth, by Natalie Jane Prior (Allen & Unwin, 1997). Pictures and descriptions of the catacombs beneath Rome. (RA)

What Do We Know About the Romans? by Mike Corbishley (Peter Bedrick Books, 1992).

Beautiful illustrations and a simple survey of Roman history and culture. (RA)

A Coloring Book of Ancient Rome (Bellerophon, 1988). Uses actual images from Roman art and architecture. (RA/activity)

Ancient Rome Treasure Chest: More Than 2,500 Years of History and Adventure to Unlock and Discover, by Lynne Brittney (Running Press, 1998). Activities and information about Rome; first and second graders will need help with most of the contents. (RA/activity)

Corresponding Literature Suggestions

Pompeii... Buried Alive, by Edith Kunhardt (Random House, 1997). A simple retelling of the fateful days in 79 A.D. when Mt. Vesuvius erupted and the people in the ancient town of Pompeii perished. (IR for most readers, RA for beginners)

Heroes, Gods, and Emperors from Roman Mythology, by Kerry Usher (Peter Bedrick Books, 1992). Beautiful illustrations and engaging retellings of legends about gods, mythical figures, and three Roman emperors (including Caligula). (RA)

Roman Myths, Heroes, and Legends, by Dwayne Pickels (Chelsea House, 1999). One-page stories about a selection of Roman gods, goddesses, and heroes. (RA)

Mystery of the Roman Ransom, by Henry Winterfeld (Harcourt, 1990). The purchase of a slave for their teacher leads a group of Roman schoolboys into a dangerous intrigue. A good book, but intended for slightly older readers; this would be a good, long read-aloud project, especially if older children can read to the younger students.

Map Work (Student Page 115)

1. On the blackline map provided, use a green pencil to color in the area that made up the Roman Empire (area inside of the dashed lines).
2. Color the rest of the land with a red pencil.
3. Color the seas and ocean blue.
4. Can you find Italy, Rome, and Britain on the map?

Coloring Page (Student Page 116)
The Catacombs beneath Rome!

Projects

Art Project: Make Nero's New Crown

Nero was the first emperor to wear a crown with points on it. During his reign, he went mad and started believing that he was a living god. He had the crown fashioned to resemble the one worn by Jupiter, king of the Roman gods. This new style was used by most kings thereafter and is still used to this day.

Materials:

      gold colored poster board or construction paper

      measuring tape, ruler, pencil, scissors and tape

      optional: glue, glitter, plastic beads and jewels

Directions:

1. Measure around your head with a measuring tape, then cut a 3" wide strip of poster board the same length.
2. On the inside of the crown, draw a straight line 1" from the bottom. This line will be used as a guide when laying out the saw tooth (/\/\/\) pattern at the top of the crown.

3. With a ruler, draw the lines for your teeth. Start in the middle and work out towards each edge. After the lines have been drawn, have Mom cut the pattern out.

4. If you would like to add more decoration to you crown, this is the time to do it. Otherwise, fold the points down towards the outside. Use the guideline from step 2, to make the folds even. Then the crown ends are joined together with tape, this will give the effect of a sun burst.

Craft Project: Make a Salt Dough Map of Italy

Materials:

> cardboard
> white flour, salt and water
> pencil and paints
> "I" encyclopedia, or globe with geographical features marked on it

Directions:

1. On thin cardboard or posterboard, draw outline of Italy. You can use the map from Chapter 27 as a pattern.

2. Mix two parts flour with two parts salt to approximately one part water. Add the water a little at a time until a thick paste has formed.

3. Spread the dough onto the outline.

4. Consult your encyclopedia or globe. Do you see the mountains of Italy? Make peaks where the mountain ranges belong.

5. Dry thoroughly and then paint. Don't forget to paint in the Rubicon and the Tiber!

Activity Project: Make a Secret Symbol

The Christians in Rome used the fish as their secret symbol. Make a family secret symbol.

Materials:

> paper
> crayons or pencils
> tape, scissors

Directions:

1. Decide what your family symbol will be. It could have to do with your last name, like this:

> Long – a long line
> Rainey - rain drop
> Wise – owl
> Johnson – a man ("John") and his little boy ("son")
> Smith – a hammer (like a blacksmith uses)

It could have to do with where you live, for example:

> trees
> cactus
> seashore (if you live near the ocean)
> mountains or hills

It could be a favorite hobby, for example:

> music - musical note
> baseball – ball

2. Draw your symbol on several pieces of paper.

3. Cut your symbol out and leave it around the house (tape it to the bathroom mirror, or to your father's dresser). In ancient Rome, the Christians drew a fish symbol to let other Christians know that they were present. What happens when your parents find your symbol? Do they know what it means?

Activity Project: Make a Catacomb

Materials:

      sheets

      flashlight

      secret symbol from previous project

      tape

Directions:

1. Make a catacomb (or cave) using sheets draped over tables and chairs.
2. Tape your family symbol signs on the walls of the catacomb.
3. Using your flashlight, pretend you are visiting the Roman catacombs and locate the signs. Optional: Invite extended family and friends over. See if they can identify what the signs mean.

Art Project: Make Your Own Lyre

Materials:

      cardboard egg carton (a half-dozen box can also be used)

      4 ft of pencil-thick dowel

      scissors, paintbrush, paints, pipe cleaners

      rubber bands or fishing line

      hot glue gun.

Directions:

1. Remove and discard the lid from your egg carton, then cut the carton in half. This will leave you with a rectangular six-egg section that will be used as the body of the lyre. Turning the carton bottom side up, use your paints to decorate the lyre body and allow it to dry completely.
2. Place your carton painted side up. Use a pair of scissors to punch a hole on the outside bottom of the top two eggcups. These holes should be made in the middle of each cup. Insert a length of dowelling through these holes, having it extend about a ¼" on either side of carton.
3. To make the lyre's neck, turn the carton painted side down. Take a 12" length of dowelling and attach it to the short dowel at each side of the carton. The dowels should angle out a bit, instead of being straight up and down Do this using a hot glue gun and a length of pipe cleaner. Let this dry completely before continuing.
4. Attach another 12" length of dowelling horizontally across the lyre neck dowels, about 1 ½" from the top. This will make a triangular shape. Again, do this with a hot glue gun and a length of pipe cleaner. Once the glue has dried, the child can decorate the dowels with paint.
5. When the paint has dried, string the lyre, by attaching 7 lengths of fishing line (or rubber bands that have been cut in half) from the top dowel to the smaller dowel secured in the egg carton. The picture on the right gives an example of how your lyre should look.

Craft Project: Make Constantine's Shield

Materials:

      cardboard

      scissors

      glue

      stapler (use brads if cardboard is too thick)

      construction paper

black marker

Directions:

1. Cut out a large rectangle or circle from the cardboard for the shield. Cut a long strip of cardboard to use as a strap to carry the shield.

2. Constantine ordered all of his soldiers to put the monogram for Christ on their shields. The monogram for Christ is Chi Rho, which is our X R. Make an X R on shield.

3. Cut out designs in the construction paper and decorate the rest of the shield. Attach strap to back of shield.   Let dry.

Cooking Project: Make an Edible Shield Cheesecake

Ingredients:

>   1 graham cracker pie crust
>
>   2 8 oz packages cream cheese (do not use low-fat)
>
>   1 14 oz can sweetened condensed milk
>
>   2-3 capfuls of lemon juice concentrate

Directions:

1. Mix cream cheese, condensed milk, and lemon juice together. Pour into crust. Refrigerate at least 2 hours.

2. On top, using cherries, strawberries or some other topping, design the monogram for Christ. Enjoy!

REVIEW CARDS
Chapters Thirty-Six, Thirty-Seven, Thirty-Eight, Thirty-Nine
(Student Page 117)

CHAPTER FORTY
Rome Begins to Weaken

UBWH 90-91, UILE 194

KIHOW 140-141 , KHE 80-81

Review Questions, The British Rebellion

Do you remember the names of two strong, powerful leaders of Rome? *Julius Caesar and Caesar Augustus*

Were the emperors after them strong too? *No, many were weak.*

Who lived in Britain? *The Celts*

Did Rome control all of Britain? *No, only part of it.*

Who was the leader of the rebellious Celts in our story? *Boadicea*

Why were the Romans embarrassed to be beaten by Boadicea? *Because she was a woman*

Do you remember any of the strange things that were supposed to have happened when the Celts were attacking the Romans? *Acceptable answers include: The statue of Victory fell face down, the sea turned red, a ghost town in ruins was seen near Londinium, yells came from an empty theatre.*

Were there more Romans or more Celts? *Celts*

Why did the Romans win? *They obeyed their general and fought together.*

Narration Exercise, The British Rebellion

"The Romans tried to rule Britain. But the people who lived there didn't like the Romans. They were Celts. Their leader was a woman. The Celts fought Rome, but they lost." OR

"The Celts lived in Britain. Their leader was named Boadicea. She led them against Rome. They lost, but Rome had to leave Britain anyway."

Review Questions, Rome Divided in Two

Why couldn't the Roman soldiers defend all the borders of Rome? *It was too big!*

How did the emperor Diocletian try to protect the huge empire of Rome? *He divided it into two pieces.*

What were the two parts of the Roman empire called? *The Western Roman Empire and the Eastern Roman Empire*

What city was the capital of the Western Roman Empire? *Rome*

What city was the capital of the Eastern Roman Empire? You can look on your map as you answer. *Constantinople*

Which city got to be rich and powerful? *Constantinople*

Which city grew poor and shabby? *Rome*

Who invaded the Western Roman Empire? *Barbarians*

Narration Exercise, Rome Divided in Two

"Rome got too big for one emperor. So it was split into two parts. The two parts were the Eastern Roman Empire and the Western Roman Empire. Barbarians invaded the west." OR

"Rome got so big that it split into two parts. Rome was the capital of the west part. Constantinople was the capital of the east part. The east got richer and the west got poorer."

Additional History Reading

Roman Aromas: Smelly Old History of Roman Britain, by Mary Dobson (Oxford, 1998). Interesting text, attractive pictures, poems, and (believe it or not) scratch-and-sniff pages, from Roman perfumed bath oils to Celtic latrines. (RA)

The Celts (See Through History Series), by Hazel Mary Martell (Viking, 1996). Transparent panels peel away so that you can see inside Celtic buildings. (RA)

Step into the Celt World (The Step into Series), by Fiona MacDonald (Lorenz Books, 2000). Celtic culture, including life in Roman Britain. (RA)

Raiders of the North: Discover the Dramatic World of the Celts and Vikings, by Philip Steele (Southwater Publishers, 2001). Focuses on the warlike nature of the Celts. (RA)

Life in Celtic Times, by A. G. Smith, (Dover, 1997). Focuses on the culture of the ancient Celts. (RA)

Ancient Rome (Nature Company Discoveries Library), by Judith Simpson (Time Life, 1997). A good section on Roman Britain and the late, divided Roman empire. (RA)

Corresponding Literature Suggestions

One Hundred and One Celtic Read-Aloud Myths and Legends, by Joan C. Verniero (Black Dog & Leventhal, 2000). Simple stories for young children. (RA)

Celtic Fairy Tales, by Joseph Jacobs (Dover, 1968). A standard collection of wonderful tales. (RA)

Celtic Fairy Tales, by Neil Philip (Viking, 1999). A more recent collection, beautifully illustrated in the style of the Book of Kells, with gold-leaf borders. (RA)

Song for a Dark Queen, by Rosemary Sutcliff (Crowell, 1979). This longer novel, about the life of Boadicea, would be for an older child, or for a read-aloud project. (RA)

Map Work (Student Page 118)

1. On the black line map provided, color the Eastern Roman Empire yellow. East is *right* on your map.
2. Color the Western Roman Empire blue. West is to your *left.*

3. Circle Rome and Constantinople, the two capitals of Rome, in red.
4. Find Britain and color it green.

NOTE: This map is adapted from an original map in Terri Johnson's "Blackline Maps of Ancient History" set. It is reprinted here with her kind permission. For a full set of blackline maps, coordinated to *The Story of the World*, visit Knowledge Quest Maps at http:// www.knowledgequestmaps.com, or contact Knowledge Quest at 7722 SE 282ⁿᵈ Avenue, Gresham, OR 97080 (503/663-1210). You can also buy these maps from Peace Hill Press at http:// www.peacehillpress.com.

Coloring Page (Student Page 119)
Boadicea in her chariot

Projects

Activity Project: North, South, East, West
The Roman Empire was divided into two sections, the Eastern Roman Empire and the Western Roman Empire. Can you find east and west?
Materials:
        chalk
        sunny day
Directions:
1. Outside in an open area, draw a large circle in chalk. Early in the morning, stand in center of circle and face the sun. Mark an E for east on the side of the circle that you are facing.
2. West is behind you. Turn all the way around and face west. Mark a W on that side of the circle.
3. Now turn so that the E is on your right hand, and the W is on your left. You are facing north. Mark an N on the north side of the circle.
4. Now south is behind you. Turn completely around and mark an S on the circle behind you.
(NOTE: this activity will not be precisely accurate, but you can come close!)

Craft Project: Design a Celtic Border
The Celtic people were known for beautiful, intricate patterns, like the pattern around the border of your coloring picture. You can design a border too!
Materials:
        white paper and crayons or markers
        OR
        white cloth and fabric markers
Directions:
1. Practice making one or more of the designs below on a scrap piece of paper.
2. Draw a border around your paper or cloth. Have your parent help you to make this border about 4 inches wide.
3. Draw your design over and over again in a line around your border. You can alternate two or more designs, if you want to. Your Celtic border should look a little bit like the border around the picture of Boadicea in her chariot.

Activity Project: Have a Celtic Feast

The Celtics had great feasts for their warriors to celebrate victories in battles. Borrow some traditional Celtic music from the library, appoint someone to be the "bard" (the person who tells stories or poems about the Celtic heroes) and have them narrate the story of Boadicea or another Celtic tale, and enjoy some simple food. Be sure to eat it with your hands! No silverware allowed!

> Roasted chicken
> Wine (better use grape juice!)
> Berries
> Plain bread with no butter

Activity Project: Play a Roman Ball Game

Some of the Romans who lived in Britain married Celts and stayed. Their children might have played a game very much like this one!

Materials:

> chalk, or something to mark the ground with
> rubber ball
> at least two players

Directions:

1. Draw a circle on the ground. Make it as wide as you are tall. (Lie down on the ground and spread out your arms. Have someone make a mark at your head, feet, and each hand. Then draw the circle by connecting the marks.)

2. Now draw a larger circle around the small circle. There should be about 10 feet between the inner and outer circles. (This should look like a giant doughnut.)

3. The players must stay outside the circles. The first player should throw the ball into the middle circle (the "doughnut hole") so that it bounces out again. The second player has to try to catch the ball as soon as it bounces past the line of the outer circle! If he misses the ball, the first player gets a point.

4. Take turns throwing the ball into the "doughnut hole." The faster you throw, the more your opponent will have to run to catch the ball! But don't miss the "doughnut hole" – if you do, your opponent gets a point.

5. The first player with 10 points wins.

CHAPTER FORTY-ONE
The Attacking Barbarians

UBWH 90-93, UILE 194-195
KIHOW 142-145 , KHE 80-83
Review Questions, Attila the Hun
What do we call the barbarians who came from central Asia? *Huns*
Who was their leader? *Attila*

Who was Honoria? *The sister of the Western Roman Emperor*

Why did she send Attila a letter, offering to marry him? *Because she wanted to get away from the Roman court*

What did Attila do when he got the letter? *He invaded Italy.*

Why did Attila agree to leave Italy? *The Western Roman Emperor paid him to leave.*

Narration Exercise, Attila the Hun

"Attila the Hun was the leader of the Huns. He tried to conquer the Western Roman Empire, but the Emperor paid him to leave. He died of a nosebleed." OR

"The Huns were barbarians. Their leader was Attila. The Emperor's sister wanted to marry him, but she didn't. Attila came all the way to Italy."

Review Questions, Stilicho, Roman and Barbarian

What barbarian tribe invaded the Western Roman Empire? *The Visigoths*

How long did it take them? *Years and years*

Were the Romans able to beat the Visigoths? *No.*

How did they finally convince the Visigoths to go away? *The Romans paid them 4000 pounds of gold.*

Why were people suspicious of Stilicho? *Because his father was a barbarian*

Was he a good Roman, or not? *Yes, he was.*

What happened to him? *He was executed*

Narration Exercise, Stilicho, Roman andBarbarian

"The Visigoths invaded Rome. Stilicho fought against them. He had to pay them to leave. But the Romans had him killed." OR

"Stilicho was part barbarian and part Roman. He fought the Visigoths. But people didn't like him because he was a barbarian. He was executed."

Review Questions, The Coming of the Visigoths

What was the first barbarian tribe to invade Rome? *The Visigoths*

What was the second tribe? *The Vandals*

Which tribe was worse? *The Vandals*

Why didn't the Visigoths burn the churches of Rome? *Because some of them were Christian*

Where was the Emperor when Rome was invaded? *He had gone away to a city in a swamp.*

Why didn't the Eastern Roman Empire send help? *He was afraid of the barbarians invading his own city.*

Narration Exercise, The Coming of the Visigoths

"The Visigoths invaded Rome and took gold. Then the Vandals came and destroyed Rome. They were worse." OR

"Barbarians invaded Rome. The Eastern Roman Emperor wouldn't help. The Western Roman Emperor ran away to a swamp where he was safe."

Additional History Reading

Rotten Romans: Horrible Histories, by Terry Deary (Scholastic, 1997). A simple, amusing guide to Roman history, with a large (and lighthearted) section on the barbarian invasions.

Many of the previously recommended titles also contain sections on the barbarian invasions.

Corresponding Literature Suggestions

Why Are You Calling Me a Barbarian? by Birgitta Petren (J. Paul Getty Museum Publications, 2000). A Roman child makes friends with the child of a barbarian. (RA)

Map Work (Student Page 118)

1. Look back at your map from the last chapter. The Huns attacked from the area north of the Black Sea. (North is *up* on your map.) Write "HUNS" in this area on your map. Draw an arrow from the word HUNS to the border of the Western Roman Empire

2. The Visigoths came from the area we now call Germany. Write "VISIGOTHS" next to the label for Germany on your map. Draw a line from VISIGOTHS down to Rome.

3. The Vandals came from France and north Africa. Write "VANDALS" next to the France and Africa label on your map. Draw lines from the VANDALS to Rome.

Coloring Page (Student Page 120)

Projects

Craft Project: Make Barbarian Bracelets

The barbarians often wore thick, heavy jewelry. These bracelets served as armor as well as decoration – they could stop a sword!

Materials:

> aluminum foil
> posterboard or thin cardboard
> glue or tape, scissors
> measuring tape

Directions:

1. Measure around the upper part of your arm.

2. Cut a length of cardboard or posterboard 3" wide and as long as your arm measurement, plus two extra inches.

3. Cover the cardboard or posterboard strip with aluminum foil. Tape the foil on the inside to secure it.

4. Bend the foil-covered strip into a circle. Overlap it 1" on each end. Tape the ends securely.

5. Push the bracelet onto your upper arm until it stays firmly.

6. Repeat for your arm above the elbow and your forearm. Now you have three bracelets; you look like a barbarian!

Activity Project: Reassemble a Roman Pot

When the barbarians invaded, they destroyed much of Rome – they broke everything they could get their hands on! Centuries later, archaeologists dug in the ruins of Rome to find out more about the invasion. They had to put back together the things that the barbarians broke! Try to be an archaeologist and reassemble a Roman artifact.

Materials:

> pot or dish that your mother will let you break (NOT glass – pottery is best; an old
> > flowerpot works very well. Be sure not to look at it! Ask your mother to choose it
> > herself.)
> glue

Directions:

1. Archaeologists don't know what their artifacts will look like – all they see are the ruined pieces! So don't look at the dish or pot. Ask your mother to take it away and break it. She should be careful to pick out tiny splinters that might hurt you. Ask her to put the pieces into a paper bag.

2. Now it's your turn to figure out how the pot looked before the "barbarian" broke it! Can you reas-

semble the pieces with your glue? Ask your mother whether your reassembled pot or dish looks like the original.

Art Project: Draw a Picture of Attila the Hun

The great historian Edward Gibbon wrote this description of Attila the Hun in his book *The Decline and Fall of the Roman Empire*. Listen: "…a large head, a swarthy complexion, small, deep-seated eyes, a flat nose, a few hairs in the place of a beard, broad shoulders, and a short square body, of a nervous strength, though of a disproportioned form. The haughty step and demeanour of the king of the Huns expressed the consciousness of his superiority above the rest of mankind; and he had a custom of fiercely rolling his eyes, as if he wished to enjoy the terror which he inspired…."

Can you draw a picture of Attila that fits this description?

CHAPTER FORTY-TWO
The End of Rome

UBWH 90-93, UILE 194-195
KIHOW 142-145 , KHE 80-83

Review Questions, The Last Roman Emperor

Why did the Roman people call Romulus Augustus "Little disgrace"? *They didn't want to obey a child who was also a barbarian.*

How old was he when he became Emperor? *Six*

What happened to him, after he was removed from the throne? *He was sent to live in another city.*

Was there another Roman Emperor after him? *No. He was the last Roman emperor.*

What happened to the Western Roman Empire? *It disappeared. Barbarians lived there.*

What happened to the Eastern Roman Empire? *It was called the "Byzantine Empire."*

Narration Exercise, The Last Roman Emperor

"The last Roman emperor was only six years old. After he left his throne, there were no more emperors. That was the end of the Roman empire." OR

"The Western Roman Empire ended and barbarian lived there. The Eastern Roman Empire was called a different name. The last Roman emperor was only six. He was called 'Little Disgrace'."

Review Questions, The Gifts of Rome

Can you tell me three things that we got from the Romans? *Books, swimming pools, coins, names of months, names of planets*

Can you tell me two words that come from Latin? *Flower, P.S., ship, library, family, refrigerator (Names of months and planets are also acceptable.)*

Narration Exercise, The Gifts of Rome

"The Roman Empire is gone, but we still use Roman words. We also use Roman things like books and swimming pools." OR

"The Romans spoke Latin. Some of our English words come from Latin, like flower, navy, and ship."

Additional History Reading

Ancient Rome: History Beneath Your Feet, by Sean Sheehan (Steck Vaughn, 2000). Reviews the history of Rome, with special attention to archaeological discoveries. (RA)

Ancient Rome: See Through History, by Simon James (Viking, 1992). Peel-away sheets reveal the insides of Roman buildings. (RA)

Science in Ancient Rome, by Jacqueline L. Harris (Franklin Watts, 1998). Overview of the scientific advances made during the Roman era. (RA)

Corresponding Literature Suggestions

Cattus Petasatus: The Cat in the Hat in Latin, by Dr. Seuss and Jennifer Morish Tunberg (Bolchazy Carducci, 2000). Just for fun, look through this book together and see if you can spot familiar words that are almost the same in Latin as in English. English borrowed those words from Latin! (RA)

Quomodo Invidiosulus Nomine Grinchus/How the Grinch Stole Christmas, by Terence O. Tunberg (Bolchazy Carducci, 1998). Try the same experiment with this familiar book. (RA)

Map Work (Student Page 121)

1. Let's review what we've learned. On the blackline map provided, can you identify the continents of North America, South America, Europe, Asia, and Africa?
2. Can you find the Mediterranean Sea?
3. Where is Italy?
4. Where is Britain?
5. Where is China?
6. Where is India?
7. Where is the Nile River?
8. Where is Central America?

Coloring Page (Student Page 122)

Projects

Craft Project: Make the Emperor's Scepter
Materials:

length of dowel
tennis ball
spray paint
glue
jewels (or other decorations)

Directions

1. (Parent) Using a sharp knife, cut a small hole in the tennis ball.
2. Slide dowel into tennis ball. Fit should be snug. If too loose, hot glue in place.
3. Take outside and lay on newspaper. Spray paint one side and let dry. Turn over and paint the other side.
4. Decorate with jewels or other decorations.
(Optional) Attach a star or other design instead of a tennis ball.

Craft Project: Make a Gifts of Rome Collage C
Materials:

posterboard
scissors
glue
magazines

crayons or markers

Directions:

Make a collage depicting the gifts of Rome. Use the list in *The Story of the World*. Cut pictures out of magazines, print pictures from clipart or the Internet, or draw pictures.

Activity Project: Have a Roman Feast 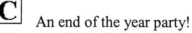 An end of the year party!

You have just completed your year of Ancient History and it is time to celebrate! A great way of doing that would be to have a Roman Feast. Roman parties were very elaborate affairs. Guests would sit on couches and share food that had been set on a table between them. Many different courses were served at these feasts, sometimes as many as 40. How could anyone eat that much food at one time? Romans also loved drinking wine while they ate their meals, but I think we will have grape juice or sparkling cider instead!

Make this a grand affair by gathering all of your saved projects from previous chapters and displaying on a separate table. Be sure to invite some guests.

Directions:

1. Prepare a place for the feast.
2. Plan and make the food.
3. Dress up in your toga (Chapter 38), crown (Chapter 35), and scepter (Chapter 42).

The type of food you might have are breads, salads, a meat dish, fresh fruit and desserts. Try the recipes below for some of your dishes.

Honeyed Dates

Materials:

    chopping board
    frying pan
    food processor or grinder
    pitted dates
    walnuts, pecans and almonds
    ½ cup of honey

Directions:

1. Carefully slit open the side of each date. Be careful not to cut all the way through the date.
2. Use the food processor or grinder to chop the nuts into fine pieces. Stuff a small amount of the nut mixture into each date.
3. Pour some salt on the chopping board and lightly roll each date in it. Make sure that you don't use too much salt.
4. On low heat, melt the honey in the frying pan. Lightly fry the dates for about 5 minutes, turning them with a spoon while they cook.
5. Place the fried dates on a serving dish and sprinkle with more of the chopped nuts.

Roman Four-Bean Salad

Materials:

    large bowl with lid
one can each of green beans, wax beans, kidney beans and garbanzo beans
    1 medium onion, sliced
    1 medium green pepper, sliced

Directions:
1. Drain all of the beans and place in a large mixing bowl.
2. Add 1/3 cup of sugar, ½ cup of vinegar and ½ cup of vegetable oil to the beans.
3. Stir ingredients until well mixed, then refrigerate overnight.

REVIEW CARDS
Chapters Forty, Forty-One, Forty-Two
(Student Page 123)

CONTRIBUTORS

SUSAN WISE BAUER
Susan was home schooled herself and now home schools her own four children. She is the author of *The Story of the World: History for the Classical Child* as well as the co-author of *The Well-Trained Mind: A Guide to Classical Education at Home*. She runs the Well-Trained Mind website at http://www.welltrainedmind.com and serves as editor–in-chief of Peace Hill Press. She enjoys music, reading and writing science fiction, eating chocolate, and jogging (usually done right after eating the chocolate).

JOYCE CRANDELL
Joyce has recently officially embarked upon the adventure of home educating her daughter, Caitlyn Rose in southwestern Ontario, Canada. When not teaching, learning, or having fun with her daughter, Joyce attends university full time in the final year of a Bachelor of Arts degree in Psychology and Geography and works part time as a Captain in the Canadian Forces Military Reserves as the Chief Training Officer of a local air cadet squadron. She also enjoys camping, gardening, and cooking. Together, Joyce and her daughter enjoy visiting zoos, playgrounds, nature trails and museums. They also enjoy baking, reading and being silly. You may contact Joyce at j_crandell@canada.com.

SHEILA GRAVES
Sheila Graves is embarking on her first year of homeschooling. She is teaching her first-grade daughter, also named Sheila and her preschooler Sarah. As a graduate from Park College with a BS degree in Management, Sheila worked many years for a Defense Contractor, supporting the United States Air Force. She now lives with her husband, Todd, and two children in Louisville Kentucky. Sheila's hobbies include genealogy research, sewing and any of the needle arts. The family are all avid readers and are constantly in search of more shelving space. Their new adventure into homeschooling has only exacerbated the problem. If you would like to write to Sheila, her e-mail address is GraveSM@aol.com.

TERRI JOHNSON
Terri is the mother of four children and has been home educating for four years. She studied Linguistics and Speech Pathology at the University of California. Prior to homeschooling, Terri coordinated the mother's group at her local church. She and her husband, Todd, reside in beautiful, but rainy, Gresham, Oregon. She is the owner and creator of Knowledge Quest Maps. Terri's web site can be found at www.knowledgequestmaps.com. In her spare time, she enjoys outings with her family, reading, gardening, cooking and good coffee. Terri can be reached at terrijohnson@knowledgequestmaps.com.

LISA LOGUE

Lisa Logue is a homeschooling mother of two children. She and her family live in southwestern Idaho where they enjoy fishing and camping in the mountains. Lisa's favorite pastime is reading, but she also likes to crochet, garden, and work on scrapbooks. Lisa may be contacted at jleugol@yahoo.com.

TIFFANY MOORE

Tiffany Moore has homeschooled her three children for four years. She studied history, sociology and English at Stephen F. Austin State University in Texas. She earned a graduate degree in intercultural communications at Wheaton College. She served with her family as a missionary in Austria, Albania and England and has lived in the Seattle area for the past five years. Her family has worked hard at making a camper out of her, though her idea of a good time includes a long walk on a beach, a good book, or coffee with a friend. She also volunteers at her local church.

KIMBERLY SHAW

Kimberly Shaw and her husband have home schooled their three daughters in Texas, Hawai'i and California. Being the book-lovers that they are, they met in a bookstore. Their first date was after running a book table at a home school convention in the early 80's. When not teaching or writing, Kimberly spends time researching, evaluating and reviewing educational materials. She moderates several online home schooling groups and enjoys helping families find materials and methods that work for them. You may contact her by e-mail at kimberly@kimberlyslibrary.com.

SHARON WILSON

Sharon is a corporate world dropout who, in 1995, moved to the country in Greenwood, Texas where she continues her life long love affair with nature, raises paint horses, and home schools Adam. Her oldest son Frank is an engineering major at Texas A&M University. Sharon is self-educated and devoted to learning. She enjoys sketching, music, gardening, training horses, camping, trail rides and spending time with her sons.